D0518606

EDUCATION

THE VICTORIAN FAMILY

The Victorian Family

STRUCTURE AND STRESSES

EDITED BY ANTHONY S. WOHL

CROOM HELM LONDON

© 1978 Ch. 1. Anthony S. Wohl
© 1978 Ch. 2. John Hawkins Miller
© 1978 Ch. 3. Theresa McBride
© 1978 Ch. 4. David Roberts
© 1978 Ch. 5. Michael Brooks
© 1978 Ch. 6. Elaine Showalter
© 1978 Ch. 7. Deborah Gorham
© 1978 Ch. 8. Maurianne Adams
© 1978 Ch. 9. R. Burr Litchfield
© 1978 Ch. 10. Anthony S. Wohl

Croom Helm Ltd, 2-10 St John's Road, London SW11

British Library Cataloguing in Publication Data

The Victorian family.
   1. Family − Great Britain − History
   I. Wohl, Anthony Stephen
   301.42'10941   HQ613

ISBN 0−85664−438−2

Printed in Great Britain by Biddles Ltd, Guildford, Surrey

CONTENTS

To my nuclear and extended family —
'A stable for fortified centre.'

1 INTRODUCTION

Anthony S. Wohl

If one had to select for some time capsule just one photograph with
which to evoke both the essential fabric of Victorian society and its
self-image, there could surely be no better choice than a snapshot of
the family. From the regal pose of Victoria, Albert, and progeny, and
the languid grouping of rural, aristocratic family taking tea on the
lawn with servants discreetly gathered in the background, down
through the bourgeois family in the drawing-room, the picture of
somewhat self-conscious probity and solidarity, to the slum family
sullenly peering out at the alien photographer in the dismal court,
it was *en famille* that the Victorians liked to be remembered and were
so often recorded, not in photographs alone, but also in song, print,
and paint. A visit to the Royal Academy at any time in the early
Victorian period, for example, would have afforded views of the
family 'at prayers, at interminable meals, on holiday at the sea, on
picnics in the country, at birthday and wedding celebrations or just
enjoying the domestic hearth.'[1] And, for those evenings around the
hearth, a variety of family journals were available: among them at
mid-century were *The Home Circle, The Home Companion, The
Home Friend, Home Thoughts, The Home Magazine, Family
Economist, Family Record, Family Friend, Family Treasure, Family
Prize Magazine and Household Miscellany, Family Paper* and *Family
Mirror.*[2]

There were few aspects of their society the Victorians regarded
with greater reverence than the home and family life within it. Lord
Shaftesbury was typical in stressing the vital importance of the
family unit to society:

> There can be no security to society, no honour, no prosperity,
> no dignity at home, no nobleness of attitude towards foreign
> nations, unless the strength of the people rests upon the purity
> and firmness of the domestic system. Schools are but auxiliaries.
> At home the principles of subordination are first implanted and
> the man is trained to be a good citizen.

To Shaftesbury the husband's 'authority' and the wife's 'genial

influence, constituted two domestic pillars of society.[3] Even the
normally staid *City Press*, a paper for solid City merchants and bankers,
spoke in softer tones when it wrote of the family: ' "Home" means
comfort, rest, peace, love, holiness. There is sanctity in the word home,
growing out of the sweetness of the affections it cherishes.'[4] The *City
Press*'s use of the word 'sanctity' was not casual, for the Victorians
deified or at least ascribed spiritual properties to the home. Ruskin,
in a famous passage, referred to the ideal home as 'the place of Peace;
the shelter, not only from all injury, but from all terror, doubt, and
division . . . it is a sacred place, a vestal temple, a temple of the hearth
watched over by Household Gods', while to J.A. Froude, adrift in a
world of unbelief, 'It is home . . . Home – yes, home is the one
perfectly pure earthly instinct we have.'[5] Whether valued as a nursery
of civic virtues or as a refuge from the tensions of society, the family
was worshipped throughout the Victorian period; it was more than a
social institution, it was a creed and it was held as a dogma carrying
all the force of tradition that family life distinguished England from
less stable and moral societies. One Edwardian observer noted:

> It is customary to point to the ideal of a united and home-
> loving family as the deepest tradition of English life. The English
> dinner, with its complete circle – the father at the head, the
> mother at the foot of the table, and the youngest saying grace
> – it is a picture frequently compared with the restaurant life of
> the Continent, or the greater independence of boys and girls in
> the United States. So strong is the belief in this family life as the
> key to true English happiness, so intense the desire to retain it
> throughout the land, that it has become usual to test each social
> or economic reform that is advanced by calculating its effect upon
> this national characteristic.[6]

In short, the Victorians regarded it as axiomatic that the home was
the foundation and the family the cornerstone of their civilization and
that within the family were first learned the moral, religious, ethical
and social precepts of good citizenship.

It is, therefore, most surprising that the Victorian family has not yet
been studied with the intensity of breadth of treatment that it merits or
that the wealth of varied sources invites. The important published work
of Peter Laslett, Lawrence Stone, and the Cambridge Group for the
History of Population and Social Structure into the origins and nature
of the modern nuclear family have been in the early modern, not the

Victorian, period. No 'school' of nineteenth-century family historians
has yet appeared, the pages of a specialist journal such as
Victorian Studies are almost completely devoid of articles
specifically concentrating on the family and no historian has yet
attempted to demonstrate how closely reality conformed to
the ideals so piously expressed by Shaftesbury and others.[7]
We thus know far more about the voting habits of the Victorians,
the flow of their investments, the development of their local
and central government agencies or their views on salvation or
the Middle Ages than we do about the relationship, in the various
classes of society, between Victorian parents and children or husband
and wife, or their views on childbirth, the duties of children, or
obligations of parenthood. Despite the present popularity of urban
history, we still know very little about the interaction between the
multifarious processes of urbanization and the composition and function of the family. Some forty years have passed since G. M. Young,
in his *Victorian England. Portrait of an Age*, drew attention, in
remarks all too brief, to the family as one of only two 'vital articles' of
a 'common Victorian faith'.[8] In a brilliant aside, Young suggested
that in the 'incidents and circumstances' of family life might perhaps be
found 'a clue to the Victorian paradox — the rushing swiftness of its
intellectual advance, and the tranquil evolution of its social and moral
ideas. The advance was in all directions outwards, from a stable and
fortified centre.'[9] In the forty years since Young first suggested this
'clue', the Victorian paradox has been studied at length, but its
familial roots, and their supposed stability and strength, have been
practically ignored, and only a handful of serious studies have appeared
which take, as their main theme, various aspects of the Victorian
family.[10] Indeed, it would not be an exaggeration to say that the
attention so far devoted by historians to the Victorian family is in
inverse ratio to the importance and esteem in which the Victorians
themselves held it.

This failure to subject the Victorian family to critical examination
is all the more remarkable in view of the 'new' social history and the
upsurge of interest in labour and urban history. Although over the past
decade there has been a decided shift in historical research away from
the public sector, with its emphasis upon political policies and
administration, to the private, and to a study of heretofore neglected
classes and groups, Victorian historians have apparently been reluctant
to invade the privacy of the home. The door of the Victorian family
has been opened only a crack, and the threshold has been seldom

crossed.

Thus the student of Victorian society still lacks a body of systematic material on the Victorian family and for information on the inner dynamics, stresses, and structure of family life in nineteenth-century England it is still necessary to piece together random material contained in the standard biographies. Many of the biographies are particularly rewarding — the recent works of Blake on Disraeli, Checkland on the Gladstones, Clive on Macaulay, and Mazlich's psycho-historical study of the Mills, father and son, for example — but the biographical approach, traditionally conceived, has several limitations. For obvious reasons it has concentrated mainly on the 'eminent' Victorians — Shaftesbury, Peel, Nightingale, Arnold, Carlyle, Darwin and the like — and quite apart from the problems of typicality and representational value of such distinguished figures, questions of upbringing and family relationships are generally handled only as preludes or background material to the main subject's life of crowded achievement. Only rarely does the intimacy of family life serve as the leitmotif of, rather than just the overture to, the historical orchestration of the life of thought and action.[11]

It was to discuss this unhappy state of affairs — unquestionably the largest area of ignorance about Victorian life — and to encourage historians and literary critics to focus more specifically on the family that the Northeastern Victorian Studies Association held a symposium on the Victorian family in the spring of 1975. *The Victorian Family* represents, in revised and expanded form, the best of the papers presented there. It lays no claim to being comprehensive. The topics discussed are perhaps idiosyncratic in their subject matter, but it is hoped that the breadth of topics and treatments will provoke discussion and point the way to future exploration. It is hoped also that this book will suggest that family history is too broad a subject and involves too many problems to be handled in any one fashion or to be confined to any single methodological orthodoxy. Family history is in its infancy and, as with all new academic disciplines (urban history for example), there is a danger that scholars may become more concerned with finding a 'correct' approach than with encouraging diversity. Seven years ago, with the publication of a seminal symposium on *The Study of Urban History*, urban historians, employing traditional research techniques based upon traditional sources, received a sharp rebuke and challenge, for it was asserted that Clio should embrace genuinely inter-disciplinary techniques and embody quantitative data. 'History', we were told, 'does not of itself provide a sufficient basis on which to rest a real understanding of the town', and 'the urban historian cannot remain an historian *pur sang* for long without running the danger of deserting the problem in front of him.'[12] Students of family history are today faced with a similar challenge and it is a disquieting one, for while few scholars would disagree that the interdisciplinary approach serves to heighten awareness and to sharpen analysis, the claims advanced for the necessity for firm sociological or psychological paradigms threaten as much to contract as expand our approach to and understanding of so manifold and complex a structure as the family.

One can only hope that family history will not fall prey to the often obsessive concern for methodological orthodoxy which has characterised the 'new' urban history. In his inaugural lecture as Professor of Urban History at the University of Leicester, Professor H. J. Dyos stated that it was the occupational hazard of historians to be asked to jump through new hoops: 'But what concerns me about these particular ['new' urban history] hoops is their diameter. They are so narrow.'[13] The new hoops in family history have been sociological (represented in the work of Michael Anderson and Professor Hareven's *The Family in Historical Perspective: An International Newsletter* and her new *Journal of Family History*) and psychological (represented in the *History of Childhood Quarterly*). The disciplinary emphasis may be gauged in the sub-titles of these two latter journals – *Studies in Family, Kinship and Demography*, and *The Journal of Psychohistory*, respectively.[14] These two approaches employ cliometrical and psycho-analytical techniques which are of enormous value to our understanding of the family, but they both contain inherent dangers for while the former may result in family structure being emphasized to the neglect of its heart and mind, the latter may result in family dynamics being divorced from social forces at large. As valuable as both approaches indisputably are, it is to be hoped that the historian *pur sang* and the literary critic will not be frightened away, but will remain in the field to help lift the curtain behind which the Victorian family is still sheltered. The methodological concerns currently so evident in the field of family history are healthy only if they help to promote catholicity of approach and do not drive away younger scholars who are not particularly attracted to either statistical analysis or psycho-history.

It is partly to reassure these scholars and to encourage as diverse an approach as possible and to suggest that the murky back-waters as well as the main streams of family history may be studied with profit that *The Victorian Family* is presented. Although there is no sharp division, the essays in Part One ('Preparation and Possession') deal with birth, child-care, adolescent development, parental control and possessiveness; Part Two ('Kinship and Community') is concerned mainly with the interaction between the family and society. I have not attempted to impose any rigid unity of theme upon the various contributors and they have come to the subject from a variety of backgrounds and incorporate methods and materials as diverse as their subjects. Topics range from changing methods of childbirth in the family to the longing to escape from it. Various classes, from the royalty to slum dwellers are discussed, and economic, psychological, intellectual, artistic, political and sexual aspects of Victorian family life are treated. Despite the variety of classes and themes examined in *The Victorian Family*, a certain cohesiveness does emerge, for all the contributors bring to their discussion an appreciation of the family as a social unit that is both unique in itself and yet is also a microcosm of — or at least indicative of forces in — Victorian society at large. Unifying the separate contributions is a concern with the relationship between the inner dynamics or structure of the family and society. While each essay makes a significant contribution in its own area, they all raise broader questions concerning the nature of the family and its role either as cause or effect in the workings of Victorian society. All the essays in some measure cast light on G. M. Young's concept of the family as the 'stable and fortified centre' of Victorian society. Much of the evidence presented is contradictory, but it has now almost become a truism to talk of Victorian society as an amalgam of contradictory forces, of self-confidence and inner doubts, of dogma and unbelief, of sexual repression and exploitation, of intimacy and alienation, of deference to authority and revolt. *The Victorian Family* may suggest some of the domestic roots of these contradictions and stresses.

The *Art Journal* was no doubt correct when it declared in 1850, with evident smugness, 'We English are unquestionably a domestic people, everything that partakes of home comforts and enjoyments is dear to us', but in fact those two great English institutions, which were so popular in the Victorian period, the club, and, to a lesser extent, its lower-class counterpart the pub, offered attractive alternatives to or indeed escape from family evenings; and the public school, as David Roberts indicates, helped to form the character of the ruling classes outside the home.[15] G. M. Young's theme of stability and strength certainly finds support in Professor Roberts's essay on the paterfamilias, but remoteness, as well as paternalism and benevolence, helped to mould that 'stable and fortified centre'. While Professor

Adams's essay indicates that family intimacy and intellectual bonds could be so intense and emotional that an all-consuming psychological interdependence could arise (one might note in passing that our generation, well-schooled in Freudian themes, but somewhat less familiar with the intensity of sibling love, often mistakenly sees in this intensity incestuous yearnings), Professor Brooks suggests that this intensity of feeling could be at once both creative and destructive, implanting for life bitter-sweet memories of family life and making difficult or impossible a developed life outside the family. The assured contentment, the *making* of a ruling class, seen in Professor Roberts's study, must be balanced against the *unmaking* of an Ernest Pontifex, the sad anti-hero of Samuel Butler's *The Way of All Flesh*, or in the sense of the family as a cell or prison, glimpsed in the essays by Professors Brooks and Showalter. The sensational novels discussed by Professor Showalter, with their theme of escape from the family, or the over-crowded slum-dwellings and their concomitant incest, discussed in my paper, must modify or colour our appreciation of the family as a 'stable and fortified centre' of Victorian society.

The Victorian Family is, above all, concerned with the intensity of family life, with family ties, with patterns of intimacy, neglect, love, duty, the delegation of authority and responsibility, the nurture of ideals and codes of conduct and with the effect of these upon society as a whole. Several of the essays suggest that the family was a self-sufficient unit, an inner world of mutual dependencies that almost precluded contact with outside society. And yet these same families – as Professor Gorham's essay amply demonstrates – regarded their intimacy and protective hot-house atmosphere as an essential preparation for entering and influencing society. Thus the Victorian family emerges as both a refuge and a springboard. Although no political scientist is represented in these pages – and it might be noted in passing that, unlike anthropologists, sociologists, and psychologists, political scientists have been slow to give their work an historical, familial dimension – several essays are suggestive of the interplay between domestic and political or public roles.

The Victorian Family also raises questions about two groups that were largely repressed and exploited in Victorian society – women and children. Both groups have been extensively studied by historians within the context of developing social policy – child labour and infant protection acts, divorce laws, voting rights, and patterns of employment. *The Victorian Family* places both groups within the home and analyzes them in the domestic setting. Professor McBride's

essay casts light (as do those of Professors Gorham and Brooks) upon
maternal and outside influences in child-rearing, and speculates on the
importance of domestic service to the awareness of both employer and
employee of the different values held by the middle and working
classes. Professor Litchfield relates the effect of age-composition
within the family to the family as a unit within the industrial work-
force, and, conversely, the effect of the children's wage-earning power
upon family cohesion and fission. Professor Roberts discusses the
impact of paternalism, remoteness, and surrogate parents upon the
development of the child. Professors Adams and Gorham suggest how
the family could develop among siblings a sense of collective identity
and purpose which they would carry with them outside the family.
My essay indicates how difficult it was for Victorians to face the
realities of domestic life as experienced by many working-class children.
Doctor Miller's essay raises important questions about the attitudes of
women towards childbirth and their control over its techniques in an
age of growing medical professionalism. The essays by Professors
Adams and Showalter indicate why to so many Victorian women the
home constituted a protective but confining cell, a 'cage', in which, as
the former shows, creative energy necessary for survival as a family
could be nurtured, or in which, as Professor Showalter indicates,
thoughts of rebellion developed. The one suggests that for middle-class
women an emotionally satisfying life outside a family (of kinship or
of employment) was difficult, the other reveals how desperately many
women wished it otherwise. Thus as much as it could be a bond of love
and mutual respect, the home could also (and sometimes simultaneously) be an emotional prison where possessiveness could both create
and destroy and where exploitation or frustration characterized
relationships. *The Victorian Family* may help students of Victorian
society understand those strands of affection, ambition, authority and
exploitation which held the family together and the manner in which
the family responded to some of the social and economic challenges
of the day.

Family intimacy and authoritarianism, casual aristocratic
paternalism and evangelical earnestness, warmth and remoteness, the
family as forcing-house for social service and as a unit of employment
and production, the impact of industrialism, urbanization and medical
professionalism upon its inner life and structure, form the themes of
The Victorian Family. Its appearance is timely, for under the impact
of current concerns with feminism (it is perhaps not irrelevant to note
that approximately half the contributors are women) and the future

of the family, perhaps also as a result of the heightened awareness of generational differences which characterized student unrest during the past decade, the study of family history is beginning to enter the academic curriculum.[16] It is clear that many more monographs are needed before we can attempt any general theory about the Victorian family. Rather than an attempt to define the field narrowly what is required at this stage is the broadest possible framework and the most eclectic approach to the subject. As one historian has written in a survey of recent work in family history: 'What historians of the family need at the moment is not brilliant theory but the facts, and modest, tentative interpretations.'[17] It is in this spirit that *The Victorian Family* is offered. It is exploratory and it raises more questions than it can answer, more problems than it can solve. But it also suggests that many of the strengths and weaknesses of Victorian society germinated in the home and that embedded in the family circle are to be found many of the clues to a better understanding of our Victorian heritage.

Thanks are due to my wife, Judy, for helping with the final proof-reading of the manuscript.

Notes

1.   H. Roberts, 'Marriage, Redundancy or Sin: the Painter's View of Women in the First Twenty-Five Years of Victoria's Reign', in M. Vicinus (ed.), *Suffer and Be Still. Women in the Victorian Age* (Bloomington, Indiana, 1972), p. 51.

2.   E. Trudgill, *Madonnas and Magdalens* (London, 1976), p. 42. This is, of course, by no means an exhaustive list for there were many more journals, such as Charles Dickens's *Household Words* designed for reading *en famille*.

3.   Lord Shaftesbury, quoted in C. Potter, 'The First Point of the New Charter, Improved Dwellings for the People', *Contemporary Review*, XVIII (November, 1971), pp. 555-556.

4.   The *City Press*, 12 September, 1857, in a leader 'City Dwellings for the Working Classes', in which it contrasted ideal and reality.

5.   Ruskin, 'Of Queen's Gardens' (1864), quoted in W. Houghton, *The Victorian Frame of Mind* (New Haven, Connecticut, 1957), p. 343, and Froude, *The Nemesis of Faith* (1849), quoted in Trudgill, *Madonnas and Magdalens*, p. 42. Houghton, chap. 13, has an excellent discussion of the Victorian home.

6.   Sir Alexander Patterson, *Across the Bridges of Life by the South London Riverside* (London, 1914), pp. 14-15.

7.   Of the two special issues of *Victorian Studies* devoted to women and children, XIV, No. I (September, 1970) and XVII, No. I (September, 1973), respectively, the former is more useful to family historians. See especially M. Jeanne Peterson's 'The Victorian Governess: Status Incongruence in Family and Society'. For other valuable *Victorian*

Studies articles, see L. Lees, 'Mid-Victorian Migration and the Irish Family Economy', XX, No. 1 (Autumn, 1976), and C.N. Behrman, 'The Annual Blister: A Side Light on Victorian Social and Parliamentary History', XI, No. 4 (June, 1968).

8.   The other was representative institutions – these were two institutions not subject to broad, popular attack. G.M. Young, *Victorian England. Portrait of an Age* (New York, Galaxy edition, 1964), pp. 150-1.

9.   Ibid., p. 153.

10.   Significantly, Professor G. Himmelfarb, in her comprehensive and analytical bibliographical article, 'The Writings of Social History: Recent Studies in Nineteenth Century England', in *Journal of British Studies*, XI, No. 1 (November, 1971), which covers over 200 separate items, confines the family to a handful of titles in a footnote. Among the most useful works for the historian of the Victorian family are the following: M. Anderson, *Family Structure in Nineteenth Century Lancashire* (Cambridge, 1971); and see also his 'Marriage Patterns in Victorian Britain: An Analysis based on Registration District Data for England and Wales, 1861', *Journal of Family History*, I, No. 1 (Autumn, 1976); A. Armstrong, *Stability and Change in an English County Town: A Social Study of York, 1801–1851* (Cambridge, 1974); N. Smelser, *Social Change in the Industrial Revolution* (London, 1959), and his 'Sociological History: The Industrial Revolution and the British Working-Class Family', *Journal of Social History*, I, No. 1 (Fall, 1967); J. Banks, *Prosperity and Parenthood: A Study of Family Planning among the Victorian Middle Classes* (London, 1954), and J. and O. Banks, *Feminism and Family Planning in Victorian England* (London, 1954). It is significant that all these works are by historical sociologists rather than by historians. In addition to the works by Trudgill and Vicinus (see notes 1 and 2, above), see also: L. Lees, 'Patterns of Lower-Class Life: Irish Slum Communities in Nineteenth-Century London', in S. Thernstrom and R. Sennett (eds.), *Nineteenth Century Cities: Essays in the New Urban History* (New Haven, Connecticut, 1969); and M. Young and P. Willnott, *Family and Kinship in East London* (London, 1962). There are of course several studies of housing, diet, women, and children, and other themes relating to the family. Among these are: S. Chapman (ed.), *The History of Working-Class Housing* (Newton Abbot, 1971); A. Sutcliffe (ed.), *Multi-Storey Living: the British Working-Class Experience* (London, 1974); E. Gauldie, *Cruel Habitations: A History of Working-Class Housing, 1790–1918* (London, 1974); and A.S. Wohl, *The Eternal Slum: Housing and Social Policy in Victorian London* (London, 1977); D.J. Oddy and D.S. Miller (eds.), *The Making of the Modern British Diet* (London, 1976), and J. Burnett, *Plenty and Want. A Social History of Diet in England from 1815 to the Present Day* (London, 1966). All these works are useful for an understanding of family budgets and allocation of resources within the family; I. Pinchbeck and M. Hewitt, *Children in English Society*, 2 vols. (London, 1969, 1973); M. Hewitt, *Wives and Mothers in Victorian Industry* (London, 1958); W. Neff, *Victorian Working Women 1832–1850* (New York, 1929); L. Holcombe, *Victorian Ladies at Work: Middle-Class Working Women in England and Wales, 1850–1914* (London, 1973); D. Crow, *The Victorian Woman* (London, 1971); P. Branca, *The Silent Sisterhood: Middle-Class Women in the Victorian Home* (London, 1975); L. Davidoff, *The Best Circles. Women and Society in Victorian England* (London, 1973); O.R. McGregor, *Divorce in England* (London, 1957); for recent work in literary criticism, see J. Calder, *Women and Marriage*

in Victorian Fiction (London, 1977); P. Beer, *Reader, I Married Him* (London, 1975) (a study of Austen, Charlotte Brontë, Gaskell and Eliot and their female characters) and W.S. Johnson, *Sex and Marriage in Victorian Poetry* (Ithaca, New York, 1975); J. Gathorne-Hardy, *The Rise and Fall of the Victorian Nanny* (London, 1972), and T. McBride, *The Domestic Revolution: The Modernization of Household Services in England and France, 1820–1920* (London, 1976), also are pertinent. Many promising titles, such as M. Lochhead's three works, *The First Ten Years: Victorian Childhood* (London, 1956), *Young Victorians* (London, 1959), and *The Victorian Household* (London, 1964), are too narrative or anecdotal to be of great value. It is to be hoped that oral history, so splendidly handled by R. Blythe, *Akenfield, Portrait of an English Village* (London, 1969), and P. Thompson, 'Voices from Within', in H.J. Dyos and M. Wolff (eds.), *The Victorian City*, vol. I (London, 1973), and auto-biographical works, such as R. Roberts, *The Classic Slum* (London, 1973) will encourage others.

11. R. Blake, *Disraeli* (London, 1967); S.G. Checkland, *The Gladstones: A Family Biography, 1764–1851* (Cambridge, 1971); J. Clive, *Macaulay: The Shaping of the Historian* (New York, 1973); B. Mazlich, *James and John Stuart Mill: Father and Son in the Nineteenth Century* (New York, 1975).

12. F. Bédarida, 'The Growth of Urban History in France: Some Methodological Trends', and H.J. Dyos, 'Agenda for Urban Historians', in H.J. Dyos (ed.), *The Study of Urban History* (London, 1968), pp. 48, 7.

13. H.J. Dyos, *Urbanity and Suburbanity* (Leicester, 1973), p. 23.

14. The *Journal of Family History* has set out to be interdisciplinary, with emphasis upon historical demography, sociology, anthropology, psychology, and economic theory. Where this will leave the historian *pur sang*, or the literary critic remains to be seen.

15. The *Art Journal*, XII (1850), p. 235, quoted by Roberts, in M. Vicinus (ed.), *Suffer and Be Still*, p. 50.

16. See T.K. Hareven, 'The History of the Family as an Interdisciplinary Field', in T.K. Rabb and R.I. Rotberg (eds.), *The Family in History. Interdisciplinary Essays* (New York, 1973).

17. B. Harris, 'Recent Work on the History of the Family: A Review Article', *Feminist Studies*, 3, Nos. 3-4 (Spring-Summer, 1976), p. 166.

PART ONE   PREPARATION AND POSSESSION

2 'TEMPLE AND SEWER': CHILDBIRTH, PRUDERY, AND VICTORIA REGINA*

John Hawkins Miller

They ought to invent something to stop that.
Life with hard labor. Twilight sleep idea.
Queen Victoria was given that. Nine she had.
A good layer.

James Joyce, *Ulysses*

I think, dearest Uncle, you cannot *really* wish me to be the
'mamma d'une *nombreuse* famille,' . . . men never think,
at least seldom think, what a hard task it is for us women
to go through *very* often.

Queen Victoria to King Leopold, 5 January 1841

Childbirth regularly punctuated the rhythm of the Victorian family.
It was a rite that had women at its centre and no event in the lives of
Victorian women was more solemnly and even ritualistically observed.
And yet, strangely, even though the Queen herself wrote about childbirth and played an important transitional role in popularizing new
obstetrical procedures, historians have tended to neglect this important
subject. While much is known about the Victorian way of death, little
attention has been given to understanding the rituals and customs of
the lying-in chamber. The Victorian way of birth, however, did have
its peculiar rituals that were transferred, generation after generation,
from mothers to daughters. These customs are important in understanding the life of the Victorian family and to defining the roles that
women and mothers played within it.

The Victorians were often excessively prudish about public
discussion of the physiology of pregnancy and birth, and information
about the emotional and ritualistic aspects of childbearing is not
readily obtainable. Feeling that the subject was indelicate, many
women, including the Queen, disposed of written notes about their
confinements and much other information on the subject was never

* The author would like to thank the Maurice Falk Medical Fund for a grant
  to do research on Victorian attitudes toward childbirth. The present article
  is part of a larger project on this subject.

23

written down but communicated orally and hence lost. However, by examining Victorian novels, diaries, obstetrical texts, lay medical guides and devotional manuals, it is possible to draw together a tentative picture of what Victorian childbirth was like.

During the nineteenth century, before childbirth became a hospital-centred event supervised by men, women usually gave birth at home and were attended primarily by women. In these familiar surroundings, women in labour were often observed by friends and relatives. Far from being hidden, childbirth was frequently a communal event and undoubtedly many women learned about labour and delivery by assisting friends or family members. From an early age, Victorian women learned that childbirth was not only a woman's duty, but also an event that gave her status and position. Observed as she was by friends and family, the woman in childbirth was expected to behave in culturally prescribed ways. As one of the great testing grounds of a woman's life, childbirth was a trial of a woman's strength, her femininity, and her spiritual condition. How a woman prepared for childbirth and how she endured it were matters of great importance to the Victorians, and form, in part, the subject of my enquiry.

On 7 April 1853, Queen Victoria gave birth to her eighth child, Leopold, Duke of Albany. Present in the lying-in room with the Queen were Mrs Lilly (the Queen's monthly nurse),[1] Mrs Innocent, and Dr John Snow. This nominally spiritual and immaculate trinity might well have helped the Queen to overcome her distaste for the 'animal' and 'unecstatic' aspects of childbirth so well-represented in the confinements attended by Mrs Bangham and Sarah Gamp of Victorian fiction. During this confinement, moreover, the Queen did not have to endure the 'sacred pangs' of labour, for, as she wrote later, Dr Snow 'gave me the blessed Chloroform and the effect was soothing, quieting, and delightful beyond measure.'[2] Her personal physician, Sir James Clark, wrote to James Young Simpson, the Edinburgh obstetrician who first used chloroform in midwifery, that the anaesthesia 'was not at any time given so strongly as to render the Queen insensible, and an ounce of chloroform was scarcely consumed during the whole time. Her Majesty was greatly pleased with the effect, and she certainly never has had a better recovery.'[3]

While the Queen testified to the heavenly benison bestowed by the drug in relieving women of the ancient curse upon Eve (that 'in sorrow shall she bring forth'), there were members of the clergy who considered chloroform a 'decoy of Satan, apparently offering itself to bless women; but in the end, it will harden society, and rob God of the deep earnest cries which arise in time of trouble for help.'[4] The more puritanical and abstemious also inveighed against chloroform because of its well-known intoxicating effects: 'To be insensible from whisky, gin, and brandy, and wine, and beer, and ether and chloroform, is to be what in the world is called Dead-drunk,' wrote Dr Meigs, in his *Obstetrics: The Science and the Art*. 'No reasoning – no argumentation is strong enough to point out the 9th part of a hair's discrimination between them.'[5]

This debate was largely resolved by the women themselves – including the Queen, a lady not known for irreligion or drunkenness. It was the Queen, as Head of the Church, who effectively silenced the objections of religious leaders by legitimizing the use of anaesthesia through her own use of it in 1853, and again in 1857 for the birth of her last child. It has even been claimed by Elizabeth Longford that her 'greatest gift to her people was a refusal to accept pain in childbirth as woman's divinely appointed destiny'.[6]

According to a story current at the time, many of the Queen's subjects were eager to learn of Her Majesty's reactions to the use of anaesthesia. John Snow, the anaesthetist, was besieged with requests from his patients for such information. One woman, to whom Snow was administering anaesthesia while she was in labour, refused to inhale any more chloroform until told exactly what the Queen had said when she was breathing it. Snow replied: 'Her Majesty asked no questions until she had breathed very much longer than you have; and if you will only go on in loyal imitation, I will tell you everything.' The woman obeyed, soon becoming oblivious of the Queen. By the time she regained consciousness, Dr Snow had left the hospital.[7]

While we too may be curious about what the Queen said at the time, we do know that she heartily approved of the effects of the anaesthesia, and many of her subjects were persuaded, in loyal imitation, to demand it during their confinements. What was technically called 'intermittent chloroform analgesia', became more commonly known as 'chloroform à la Reine'.

Before the discovery and widespread application of aseptic techniques, preparing for childbirth was in many ways analogous to preparing for death. Cotton Mather, with Puritan grimness, warned the pregnant woman that:

For aught you know, your Death has entered into you, and you
may have conceived that which determines but about nine months
at the most, for you to live in the world. Preparation for death is
that most reasonable and most seasonable thing, to which you must
now apply yourself.[8]

Similarly, nineteenth-century devotional manuals counselled future
mothers to prepare themselves spiritually for the potential dangers
of their lying-in. One such manual advised the woman to examine the
state of her soul before her confinement: 'Let me examine myself,
and try to see what my spiritual state is in the light of God, before my
hour of suffering and danger draws near.'[9]

While such religious attitudes were beginning to disappear in the
nineteenth century, the spectre of death in childbirth and the
expectation of pain for women in labour kept even the secularly
minded aware of the crisis of birth. Victoria would not have become
Queen if Princess Charlotte, the daughter of George IV, had survived
the birth of her stillborn first child. Charlotte's death, after a labour
of more than fifty hours, greatly shocked the public; and though it
happened two years before Victoria was born, it was on everyone's
mind, including Victoria's, when she prepared for her first confinement
in 1840.

Rites of passage, such as childbirth, have always been important
family events and this was particularly true up to and through the
nineteenth century when both birth and death generally occurred at
home. It was not unusual for a woman at her confinement to invite
her mother and a number of her friends, often called 'gossips',[10] and
members of her family to take care of younger children and look after
household chores, as well as to provide her with physical and
emotional support during labour.

Such skill and experience as were needed were generally provided
by midwives. Unlike their Continental sisters, however, English midwives were not legally required to be trained, licensed, or regulated in
any way. While various organizations, such as the College of Surgeons
and the Obstetrical Society of London trained women to become midwives and awarded diplomas and certificates of competence to those
who passed the examinations, these diplomas and certificates had no
standing in law.[11] Consequently, according to an 1870 report of the
Obstetrical Society of London, fifty to ninety per cent of the babies
born to the poor were attended by women who had almost no training apart from the folk traditions passed on to them by other

experienced midwives. The poor training and lack of regulation of midwives undoubtedly contributed to the large number of childbirth related deaths that occurred during the century. The infant mortality rate at the end of Victoria's reign (154 deaths per thousand) was as high as at any time during her reign, and in many areas of the country the infant death rate accounted for almost one half of all deaths.[12] While many midwives were less callous than Dickens's Sarah Gamp — who would go 'to a lying-in or a laying-out with equal zest and relish'[13] — Victorian midwives, like the gossips who assisted them, had their roots in ancient folk tradition and it was not unusual for them to preside over the rituals of both birth and death.

The presence of gossips at a confinement, however, was not encouraged by the emerging medical specialists, the 'man-midwives', or obstetricians; and many Victorian medical guides condemned the practice. One guide advised the pregnant woman not to comply with the request of her female friends to be sent for at the onset of labour, for, the author wrote, 'the patient will find quietness and composure, of far greater service than the noisy rallying round of friends, to awaken and cherish the idea of danger.'[14] Another medical handbook recommended that even the mother of the woman in labour should not be allowed into the room though she could be present in the house,[15] a limitation that Queen Victoria would never have accepted.

During her confinements, Queen Victoria was not attended by ordinary gossips. By law, however, she had to accept the presence of official witnesses to a royal birth. At her first confinement, in 1840, they included various cabinet ministers, the Archbishop of Canterbury, the Bishop of London, and Lord Erroll, Lord Steward of the Household. The Queen insisted upon a certain decorum. The officials were banished from their traditional vantage place in the lying-in chamber to an adjoining room, 'with the door open so that Erroll could see the Queen plainly and hear what she said'. For the record, what she did say when told by Dr Locock, 'Madam, it is a Princess,' was an abrupt 'Never mind, the next will be a Prince.'[16] It was.

In rural areas during the nineteenth century, childbirth remained the communal, family, folk event it had always been. By banishing gossips from the lying-in room, however, and later by moving birth to the maternity hospital, urban society began to deprive women of control over their ancient privileges in supervising the ritual of childbirth. With this control lost, childbirth at its worst could become a Kafka-esque nightmare or an existential 'dark night of the soul' which the

woman in labour, remote from family and friends, would have to face
alone without any comfort or support.

In nineteenth-century towns, lower-class women who were either
very poor or who had become pregnant out of wedlock had their babies
delivered in charity hospitals. Queen Charlotte's Hospital in London
was one of these. There, Esther Waters, the heroine of George Moore's
1894 novel of that name, gave birth to an illegitimate child in one of
the most explicit and horrifying confinement scenes in Victorian
fiction. While ordinary middle-class mothers preferred to have their
babies at home under the gentle ministrations of the midwife and
other female members of the family, Esther Waters, because of her
sin, is made to suffer in childbirth through the indifferent and cold
attitudes of male obstetricians and unsympathetic nurses.

Three weeks before the birth of her baby, Esther, who has been
deserted by her lover, takes up lodgings in a room near the hospital,
where she is cared for by her landlady, Mrs Jones. One afternoon, a
week later, her waters break – 'life seemed to be slipping from her,
and she sat for some minutes quite unable to move.'[17] Esther is
afraid of being left alone and wants Mrs Jones beside her constantly.
After several hours of labour, her landlady walks her to the nearby
hospital and leaves her at the door with kind words of encouragement.
Her sympathetic friend gone, Esther is conducted to the second
floor of the institution by a nurse who admonishes her, 'Come along,
you mustn't loiter.'

Upstairs, a door is thrown open and Esther finds herself in a room
with eight or nine men and women standing about. She is horrified
– 'What! in there? and all those people?' She is informed that they
are the midwives and the students. Against the background of
agonized screams from several women huddled on beds in the room,
Esther is taken behind a screen, undressed, and clothed in an ill-fitting
chemise. Walking to her bed, she notices steel instruments on one of
the tables and basins on the floor.

A young male student approaches her bedside to 'take a pain', as
digital examination of the cervix was called. Esther panics. 'Oh, no, no,
not him! He's too young! Don't let him come near me!' All laugh
loudly at Esther, who hides her head in the pillow in shame and fear.
When the student approaches her a second time, she cries 'Let me go!
take me away! Oh, you are all beasts!' The nurse takes charge. 'Come,
come, no nonsense! You can't have what you like; they are here to
learn.'

Esther is examined; then, left alone for awhile, she falls asleep.

Upon waking, she overhears the nurses talking about a woman who had died in childbirth a week before. While her pains grow worse, the assembled students talk about the progress of her labour. Suddenly, Esther lets out a horrible scream. The doctor comes, examines her, and quickly administers chloroform: 'The sickly odour which she breathed from the cotton wool filled her brain with nausea; it seemed to choke her.' When she regains consciousness later on, she is surrounded by impassive nurses and doctors. She hears her baby crying, and is rather curtly told that it is a boy.

The steel instruments that Esther noticed before being examined no doubt contributed to her fear about what was going to happen. She had reason for concern. While designed to assist the midwife or obstetrician in delivering babies, various mechanical devices — forceps, crochets, dilators, specula — were often used by those who either did not know how to handle them properly or were overly anxious to speed up the progress of a normal labour. The results were often disastrous for both mother and child.

The nineteenth century can be called the great age of 'interventionist' obstetrics. Although the forceps had a long history before this period, the Victorian era saw a boom in the construction and widespread use of a variety of ingenious mechanical devices to extract the child from the uterus. Many of these instruments proved to be invaluable in saving the lives of mothers and infants in cases of difficult labours. Princess Charlotte would probably have survived her prolonged labour had her *accoucheur* been willing to use the obstetrical forceps readily available to him.[18] Given this prodigious obstetrical arsenal, however, many physicians felt compelled to use the new devices to intervene in the natural process of labour, though they were often criticized for it. William Buchan, in his *Advice to Mothers*, counselled non-interference with labour and satirized the methods of the man-midwife: 'The moment an order comes for the man-midwife, he packs up his bag of tools, which may be justly called the instruments of death: he mounts his horse, and gallops away, resolved to hasten the process by all practicable means, that he may be the sooner ready to attend another call.'[19]

By 1866, these 'tools' were so much a part of obstetrical practice that the Obstetrical Society of London organized an exhibition of obstetrical instruments from all over the world to be displayed in the library of the Royal College of Physicians. In the words of a distinguished surgeon, the exhibition was 'one of the most astonishing historical displays of the mechanical appliances of the obstetrical branch of the Art ever collected in one room.'[20]

The president of the Obstetrical Society was also aware of the historic nature of the occasion. In his address, he said, 'An instrument is not less the offspring of a man's mind than is a book; but the security for preserving an instrument so that it shall, even for a brief time, tell truly the working of the mind that produced it, and continue to answer, in the hands of others, the purpose for which it was designed, is very much less than in the case of a book.'[21] Consequently, the society published a catalogue of the instruments in the exhibition so that interested physicians not only could learn about how various devices were made in the past, but also could keep abreast of new instruments. Reflecting the age's fascination with machinery, the editor of the catalogue concludes that 'the permanent utility of such a work will be greatly facilitated if from time to time inventors or modifiers of instruments, and instrument makers, British and Foreign, will send to the Editor for insertion in future editions, descriptions, and, if possible, illustrations, of any novelty they may have introduced.'[22]

These mechanical 'novelties', while they undoubtedly helped to assist women in childbirth when employed by those who knew how to use them, also had the effect of making childbirth a specialized science. Childbirth, once a family event controlled by the womenfolk was slowly becoming a highly specialized medical field. Thus the familial mystique of childbirth was — at least for the middle and upper classes — gradually replaced by the scientific mystique of Victorian professionalism.

'A good layer' was Queen Victoria, though she would have deplored the epithet, and from all accounts she had relatively easy confinements, including seven without the use of anaesthesia. Her attitudes toward childbirth do not appear to reflect any fear of pain but, rather, the age's ambivalence toward human physiological functions. Along with many of her subjects, she would have agreed to the propriety of Kipling's sentiments:

> We asked no social questions — we pumped no
>   hidden shame —
> We never talked obstetrics when the Little
>   Stranger came[23]

If they did talk about it, they preferred to use euphemisms.

In her journal and letters to her eldest daughter, however, the Queen often dwelt on obstetrical details with little inhibition. She called childbirth the 'shadow-side' of marriage, and considered it indelicate and 'dreadful'; but, at the same time, she was fascinated by the drama of birth, proud of her own physical strength in enduring labour, and tireless when extending sympathy and aid to other women in that condition.

In a letter to the Princess Royal, Victoria expressed her distaste for the barnyard aspects of childbirth:

> What you say of the pride of giving birth to an immortal soul is very fine, dear, but I own that I cannot enter into that; I think much more of our being like a cow or a dog at such moments; when our poor nature becomes so very animal and unecstatic.[24]

The Princess Royal was pregnant with her first child when she received this letter in Prussia. The Queen also warned her daughter not to let her feminine modesty be corrupted by life in a foreign court.

> Above all, dear, [she admonished] do remember never to lose the modesty of a young girl towards others (without being a prude); though you are married don't become a matron at once to whom everything can be said, and who minds saying bothing herself — I remained particular to a degree (indeed feel so now) and often feel shocked at the confidences of other married ladies. I feel abroad they are very indelicate about these things.[25]

Twelve years later, the Queen wrote another letter to the Princess Royal, complaining of the indelicacy of new fashions in dress and decorum in elegant English society:

> The animal side of our nature is to me — too dreadful and now — one of the new fashions in our very elegant society, is to go in perfectly light-coloured dresses — quite tight — without a particle of Shawl or Scarf (as I was always accustomed to wear and see others wear), and to dance within a fortnight of the confinement even valsing at 7 months!!!! Where is delicacy of feeling going to![26]

Society was changing, the Queen was not.

The Queen's prudishness extended to the public announcement of a woman being 'in the family way'. When she, herself, became pregnant for the first time, Prince Albert, the proud father-to-be with unblushing Continental directness wanted to announce publicly the Queen's pregnancy, which he referred to as her 'interesting condition'. But Victoria, who even twenty-three years later was to be shocked that Louis of Portugal would 'telegraph such a thing', preferred the fact of her interesting condition to spread without public proclamation. She might have added, as she did many years later in writing to the Princess Royal, that men just do not understand what an affront pregnancy and childbirth are to feminine modesty. In fact, since men are the cause of pregnancy, they really ought to worship women for what they have to endure:

> It is indeed too hard and dreadful what we have to go through and men ought to have an adoration for one, and indeed to do every thing to make up, for what after all they alone are the cause of! I must say it is a bad arrangement, but we must calmly, patiently bear it, and feel that we can't help it and therefore we must forget it, and the more we retain our pure, modest, feelings, the easier it is to get over it all afterwards. I am very much like a girl in all these feelings, but since I have had a grown-up married daughter, and young married relations I have been obliged to hear and talk of things and details which I hate — but which are unavoidable.[27]

Her note of resignation in this letter is reminiscent of the apocryphal story of the English mother who, when asked by her daughter how she should act on her wedding night, advised, 'Lie still and think of the Empire.'

Few Victorian novels directly describe the grim realities of labour and delivery. Instead, by various euphemisms, they tried to transform this indelicate subject into acceptable metaphors.[28] For example, George Eliot, describing the death of a mother in childbirth, uses a botanical metaphor: 'The delicate plant had been too deeply bruised and in the struggle to put forth a blossom it died.'[29] Dora's miscarriage in *David Copperfield* is described through a bird metaphor: 'The spirit fluttered for a moment on the threshold of its little prison, and unconscious of captivity, took wing.'[30] The 'Little Stranger', too, whose physical life Victoria found so unattractive, is often sentimentalized and spiritualized to the extent that one would never believe diapers were necessary.

The trouble with euphemisms, as H.W. Fowler pointed out,[31] is that they soon become as explicit in meaning as the words they were substituted for and must be constantly replaced until we have many names for the same thing. While they may permit the user to feign a girlish innocence about childbirth, for example, their use may in fact reflect considerable knowledge of the anatomical facts involved and how the process was initiated some nine months earlier. What a young, modest girl ought to know, as opposed to what she did know, about such matters, is dramatized in the following scene from a story in an 1828 ladies' magazine.

'I suppose,' said her ladyship, in allusion to Mrs Buckle's condition, 'you expect soon?' 'Hush!' she replied, drawing nearer, 'speak lower, if you please, when Rosa is in the room; she is so innocent, dear girl! She actually believes that all her little brothers and sisters are found under the cherry tree. It is so very delightful to have their minds such perfect white paper . . .'

At the other end of the drawing room, Laura is talking with her friend, Rosa, the supposed innocent:

'So, Rosa, I see Mrs Buckle is in the family way again.' 'Hush, Laura, pray speak lower, for Mama thinks I don't know anything about it. Our old Nurse and Sally always tell me everything, but Mama would be so very angry if she knew.'[32]

Even the medical profession was not exempt from prudery. Medical students were advised to avoid vaginal examinations, but if they did have to perform them they were told to look up at the ceiling while doing so, to avoid offending the woman's delicacy. Doctors often had difficulty delivering babies, for the modest woman was sometimes so excessively draped under sheets that the physician had to grope about blindly for the emerging child. In an 1848 essay, appropriately titled 'Embarrassments in the Practice', Dr Charles Meigs deplored too much knowledge by the public about women's anatomy:

Who wants to know, or ought to know that the ladies have abdomens and wombs but us doctors? When I was young a woman had no legs even, but only feet, and possibly *ankles*; now, forsooth, they have utero-abdominal supporters, not in fact only, but in the very newspapers. They are, surely, not fit subjects for newspaper advertisements, nor would they be advertised but out of our own stupidity or remissness.[33]

Meigs's attitude, while extreme, was widely shared in varying degrees on both sides of the Atlantic. There were others who went even further in condemning the whole practice of 'man-midwifery' as a 'pernicious social and moral influence'. George Gregory, in his *Medical Morals*, advocated the establishment of female medical colleges in America, so that women could be properly trained as midwives and thus eliminate the indelicacy of men being involved in childbirth. The 1853 edition of the book had a notice on the title page that 'The reader is reminded that this work has delicate plates, and is to be opened accordingly.' For those bold enough to go ahead and open it anyway, the pamphlet, in addition to presenting the argument above, had several plates, one of which depicted a fully-dressed standing woman being examined by a gentleman obstetrician who was kneeling in front of her with his right arm inside her voluminous skirts. William Buchan, whose popular *Domestic Medicine* went through several editions in the nineteenth century, felt that there was something improper about men delivering babies. If women would only be adequately trained, he wrote, it 'would prevent the necessity of employing men in this disagreeable branch of medicine, which is, on many accounts, more proper for the other sex.'[34]

The medical profession was only too aware of the truth of St Augustine's observation that we are born *inter faeces et urinam*. This anatomical fact, combined with the religious view of women in childbirth as ritually unclean, partially explains why Victorians viewed childbirth as unseemly and the profession of midwifery as disagreeable, certainly 'not a fit occupation for educated gentlemen.'[35] On the other hand, the state of motherhood — presided over by the image of the Madonna and Child — is pure and undefiled. Buchan, in his *Advice to Mothers*, glorifies the state of motherhood:

The more I reflect on the situation of the mother, the more I am struck with the extent of her powers, and the inestimable values of her services. In the language of love, women are called angels; but this is a weak and silly compliment; they approach nearer to our idea of the Deity: they not only create, but sustain their creation, and hold its future destiny in their hands; every man is what his mother made him, and to her he must be indebted for the greatest blessings in life . . .[36]

These two comments of Buchan, one on the disagreeableness of childbirth and the other on the glory of motherhood, reflect Tertullian's observation about the duality of women — *templum aedificatum super cloacam*, a temple built upon a sewer.

While most Victorians, we have seen, sidestep the cloacal realities of childbirth through euphemism and circumlocution, novelists spare no detail in celebrating and glorifying the Madonna figure of mother and child, and in describing the spiritual transformations that affected women after childbirth. George Moore, after describing the traumatic birth of a child to Esther Waters, goes on to describe the welling-up of mother love in Esther's heart for the little child. She touches the baby and 'her senses swoon with love.' The titular heroine of Mrs Gaskell's novel, *Ruth*, also is overcome by emotion, a 'holy abstraction', in contemplating her baby. When she touches it, 'That baby touch called out her love; the doors of her heart were thrown open wide for the little infant to go in and take possession.'[37] In Mrs Jewsbury's novel, *Zoe*, the heroine, who has just given birth, is bewildered by the pain of labour, but after it is over she meditates on her ability to triumph over what appeared to be certain death. She then weeps for the suffering borne by so many women before her.[38] In *Vanity Fair*, Thackeray discreetly shuts the door of the chamber where Amelia is giving birth to a child. 'Tread silently around the hapless couch of the poor prostrate soul. Shut gently the door of the dark chamber, wherein she suffers, as those kind people did who nursed her through the first months of her pain, and never left her until heaven had sent her consolation.' Consolation comes after an anxious labour when Amelia gives birth to a cherubic boy. The birth over, Thackeray opens the door to the lying-in chamber and describes Amelia with her baby:

> This child was her being. Her existence was a maternal caress. She enveloped the feeble and unconscious creature with love and worship . . . Of nights, and when alone, she had stealthy and intense raptures of motherly love, such as God's marvellous care has awarded to the female instinct — joys how far higher and lower than reason — blind beautiful devotions which only women's hearts know.[39]

In another novel, the heroine, Edith, undergoes a deep religious conversion because of her experience in coming close to death in childbirth.[40] Outside the realm of fiction, Lady Maria Nugent recorded in her journal a similar religious feeling after the birth of her first child:'My misery was great indeed; but the moment my darling boy was born compensated for all past suffering . . . Oh my Heavenly Father, how shall I express my gratitude to thee . . .'[41]

One could go on – the pattern is quite consistent. What this pattern shows is that the Victorians tended to view childbirth as a sacramental event, for it was considered a process that served as an indirect means of grace by producing devotion. Of course, childbirth has always been viewed in this way – the image of the mother forgetting her pain in the joy of holding her baby and her sense of thankfulness to whatever force has saved her and so rewarded her suffering are universal archetypes. The Victorians, however, who well knew the potential of death in 'the great danger of childbirth', were helped through this crisis, not only by making it a communal event but also by emphasizing the spiritual and physical salvation that surviving childbirth meant. Just as the dying were admonished by the Church and by devotional books to prepare for death in accordance with traditional Christian 'rules and exercises of holy dying', so a woman prepared for and behaved in the crisis of childbirth in ways that reflected the joys and potential hazards of what she had to undergo. The dangers of childbirth were well known, but once the woman had endured and survived, the state of motherhood was sentimentalized and glorified. Childbirth was the source of a woman's spiritual redemption on earth, for St Paul said, 'She shall be saved through the birth of a child.' It also ratified the consummation of marriage; and it conjured up the possibility of an earthly immortality by infinite succession.

While Queen Victoria made it clear that she hated talking about certain 'things and details' connected with childbirth and tried to banish them from her mind, she nevertheless lived in an age when births took place in the home and when women were expected to help each other in this unavoidable crisis in a woman's life. The Queen may have preferred to believe that all women should be girlishly innocent, 'their minds such perfect white paper'; but the little Rosas of the world, who always knew more than their mothers thought they did, eventually grew up, married, and found themselves 'in the family way'. When this happened, it was time for the mother, including the Queen, to drop the pretensions of innocence and to speak directly from experience.

When the Princess Royal approached her confinement while living in Prussia, it was impossible for Queen Victoria to be present at the birth of her first grandchild, much as she wished. About a month before the confinement, the tone of the Queen's letters changed abruptly. They no longer emphasized the indelicacies of pregnancy and birth, but got down quickly to the business at hand:

> Mrs Innocent [whom the Queen had sent to Prussia to be with the Princess Royal] has likewise copies of all the notes I put down afterwards of all I did — during my confinements — as I know you will like to know — and this will be a guide. All this I have been particularly anxious about — as my first two confinements — for want of order — and from disputes and squabbles (chiefly owing to my poor old governess who would meddle) were far from comfortable or convenient and the doctors too had not found out quite how to treat me. I am therefore particularly anxious that you should profit by my experience . . . and be spared as much (as possible) all the inconveniences arising from want of experience etc. which are natural in a first confinement. So you see, dear, that though alas far away (which I shall never console myself for) — I watch over you as if I were there.[42]

Victoria's reference to her 'confinement notes' (unfortunately destroyed at her request after her death) is significant not only for the light it sheds on the Queen's deep interest in childbirth, but also as an indication of what may well have been a commonplace practice among many of her female subjects.

A few years later, the Queen was able to attend the confinement of her daughter Princess Alice. In a letter to the Princess Royal, she described the birth:

> Thank God! All goes on most prosperously. Sir C. Locock gave you an account of the labour, and confinement. In fact she was only ill from ¼ past 9 and the child was born at ¼ to 5 as naturally as possible, and during the last hour and a half chloroform was freely given, especially quite at the last. But I thought it the most dreadful thing to witness — possible. Quite awful! I had far rather gone through it myself! It is far more dreadful to be born into this world than into the next! Easter Sunday is a beautiful day for it. Of course I shall take great

interest in our dear little granddaughter, born at poor, sad, old
Windsor in the very bed in which you were born, and poor, dear
Alice had the same night shift on which I had on when you all
were born! I wish you could have worn it too.

As if to counter the sentimental drift of the letter, Victoria went on
to say, 'But I don't admire babies a bit more or think them more
attractive.' She then returned to the sentimental vein in continuing her
description of Alice's confinement, and even suggested that she,
herself, would have liked to have had a tenth child.

She is very calm and quiet, but not as strong as I was. She
reminded me so much during the labour and even now lying in
bed of dearest Papa when he was ill. I was dreadfully shaken and
agitated by it all. I was with her the greater part of the time
and never got to bed till ¼ to 6. To see good Louis, who behaved
beautifully, hold her in his arms was so dreadful! It seemed a
strange dream and as if it must be me and dearest Papa − instead
of Alice and Louis! And then for me to direct every thing which
beloved Papa always did and would have done! I had so wished
for one other and had thought it very likely that Alice and I
would have followed each other very closely! Then to see Mrs
Lilly and Sir C. Locock both there seemed the same thing over
again![43]

Almost lost among the sentimental, wistful, and romantic strands
in this letter is the fact that the Queen assumed a directing role −
almost that of mother-as-midwife − during her daughter's labour and
delivery. Furthermore, Victoria's reference to Alice's wearing the same
night shift in childbirth that the Queen wore during her confinements,
suggests the existence of another tradition − like the keeping of
confinement notes − that was still part of communal, family oriented
childbirth.

Just what role Victoria played in attending family confinements
is indicated in a letter to the Princess Royal in which she describes the
birth of a child to her niece, Marie Leiningen:

Oh! dear child, thank God! darling Marie is safe with her
magnificent baby but it was an awful labour! And at last at two in
the morning of Friday (I was in and out the whole day for it began
at ½ past eight on Thursday morning and only laid down on a

sofa downstairs at 12) after she had three hot hip baths in all her
agony, born without a murmur or more than a little, gentle,
piteous moan and full of love and gratitude to all around her,
that no real progress was made and soon after Dr Farre said she
must not be allowed to go on or she would be exhausted and the
child would die and so instruments must be used!! Poor Ernest
[her husband] was in despair and crying – and so I sat by her
and they put her completely under chloroform and she was like
as if she slept, I stroking her face all the time and while Dr Farre
most skillfully and cleverly delivered her without her knowing
or feeling anything, and only woke when she heard the child cry
and immediately said she wished to have a prayer read to her for
she was so thankful, and wishing only she could give her life for
me and restore beloved Papa to me!! This quite overcame me!
She is an angel of gentleness, resignation and unselfishness and I
love her as a daughter.[44]

Here, the Queen's role included emotional support of the mother,
similar to that provided by traditional gossips, and, like them, she
probably directed members of the household in their work. In
addition, she was an objective observer of the progress of the labour
and of the emotional responses of the mother, whose stoic strength
and Christian charity the Queen greatly admired.

These two letters also show that Victoria regarded childbirth as an
intensely dramatic spiritual and emotional process that held strong
personal associations. Since childbirth was a dangerous and often
painful event, as well as the source of a woman's greatest joy,
a confinement was a real testing place of a woman's physical and
spiritual strength. Those in attendance at this event were also put to
the test, and Victoria, for one, was proud of her endurance in assisting
with a lying-in. Victoria's impulse to keep her own confinement notes,
as well as to record the medical and emotional details of the
confinements of others, suggests how childbirth for many Victorian
women was the most dramatic and memorable rite of passage in their
lives.

Queen Victoria's sentiments about childbirth, while coloured by the
prudish conventions of the age, reflect the universal paradoxes inherent
in the physiological and emotional realities of birth. For an age that
was to produce many advances in science, medicine, and industry
– all of which helped to give man greater mastery over his environment

— the animal and elemental process of birth, and death, must have
been especially viewed as indelicate though unavoidable reminders
of the physical and mortal nature of humanity. Darwin's demonstration
of correspondences and relationships between man and animals,
governed by a dispassionate evolutionary process ages older than any
Genesis account of human origins, flew in the face of prevailing
orthodox views of the uniquely divine nature and origins of human life.
Surely, the process of birth — with its attendant pain and potential
for death — was an unwanted reminder of the physical, barnyard facts
of life from which many middle-class Victorians preferred to look
away as if they were not there.

   And yet they were there. Since birth generally occurred in the
home during the nineteenth century, Victorian prudery can be
understood as an agreement not to talk obstetrics in the open, while
in private, childbirth was frankly accepted as a familiar, frequently
observed event.

   What Victorian fiction, medical literature, and the Queen's own
letters show is how the nineteenth century was a transitional period
between the ancient communal and sacramental childbirth tradition
and emerging twentieth-century medical practice. The Queen's
attitude combined elements of both. As a strong advocate of
anaesthesia in childbirth, she undoubtedly helped to legitimize its use
by silencing those whose fundamentalist religious scruples made them
object to alleviating God's curse on Eve. Also, by barring the
traditional witnesses from being in the same room with her during her
confinements, she helped to give respectability to the trend already
in progress of preventing gossips from hovering about in the lying-in
room. On the other hand, she would have objected strongly to anyone's preventing her from being present at a confinement. Her obvious
interest in the physical and emotional details of birth, and her ability
and willingness to supervise the details of a confinement, ally
Victoria with the slowly disappearing communal tradition of childbirth.

   While Victorian advances in obstetrics helped to reduce maternal
and to a lesser extent infant mortality among the more comfortable
classes, these advances were not effected without causing unforeseen
problems. By insisting on strict asepsis and prudish decorum, the
Victorians got rid of the gossips and, not far behind, the mother of
the woman in labour, then all familiar faces. To relieve the pain
of labour, many women, in royal imitation, demanded intermittent
chloroform analgesia, then came total chloroform anaesthesia, later

'twilight sleep' and scopalamine-induced amnesia with its attendant hallucinations and delirium. Not only did these drugs have the effect of obliterating the woman's consciousness of giving birth, but also they were a potential hazard to the health of the newborn child. Obstetrical instruments were also a mixed blessing. While far from being the 'instruments of death' that some critics held them to be, various mechanical devices tended to make childbirth appear to be more of an engineering feat than a natural biological event that often went best, provided conditions were sanitary, with the least interference.

The prudery surrounding childbirth in the nineteenth century also reveals much about Victorian attitudes toward women. The reluctance to discuss the indelicate subject of pregnancy and labour stems not only from ancient taboos about the ritual uncleanliness of women, but also from the transference to the woman of the dark and 'dirty' sexual drives of the male. Victoria herself said that men alone are the cause of pregnancy, an attitude that placed the woman in the role of being the passive receptacle of male lust. Perversely, however, women became tainted by the male sexual drive, and the only road to redemption was through the uncleanliness of childbirth to the temple of pure and undefiled motherhood. The medical profession also viewed women in this paradoxical way as both temple and sewer. As if contaminated by the uncleanliness of childbirth, the profession of midwifery was viewed as a lower branch of medicine, about which there was something disagreeable and distasteful.

Thus during Victoria's reign, attitudes toward and practices of childbirth were changing. The Queen partly reflected, partly guided these changes and, as her letters show, there was more to the Queen than her concern with delicacy. Her competence in the lying-in room, her ability to endure nine labours and to help others in childbirth with tireless sympathy, and her impulse to record all the interesting events at a birth show Victoria to be a kind of archetypal 'midwife-gossip' figure. Prudish and girlishly modest she wished to appear, but like many of her subjects she was no innocent when it came to childbirth. Like a true monarch, she could maintain a decorous public image of modesty, but when called upon in a time of crisis, she was quite capable of putting aside her decorous protestations to rule authoritatively and sympathetically over all the rituals of childbearing. 'A good layer' she was indeed.

Notes

1.   A 'monthly' nurse was a lying-in nurse, who stayed with the mother approximately one week before and three weeks after the birth of the child.
2.   Elizabeth Longford, *Queen Victoria* (New York, 1964), p. 234.
3.   Harvey Graham, *Eternal Eve* (Garden City, New York, 1951), p. 487.
4.   From a letter quoted in James Young Simpson, *Anaesthesia, or the Employment of Chloroform and Ether in Surgery, Midwifery, Etc.* (Philadelphia, 1849), p. 123.
5.   Charles Meigs, *Obstetrics: The Science and the Art* (Philadelphia, 1849), p. 318.
6.   Longford, *Queen Victoria*, p. 234.
7.   Graham, *Eternal Eve*, p. 488.
8.   *Elizabeth in her Holy Retirement* (Boston, 1710), p. 7.
9.   *Thoughts, Prayers, and Thanksgivings for Mothers* (London, 1882), p. 7.
10.   The word *gossip* has an interesting history. Originally, a *godsib* was one who has contracted a spiritual affinity with another by acting as a sponsor at a baptism. Such a sponsor was usually a familiar acquaintance to the mother of a child, and as a good friend she was often invited to help with the details of a lying-in. The word *gossip* soon came to mean that female friend who was invited to a confinement. The pejorative connotation of the word probably came from the idle chatter and tattling that such a woman might indulge in.
11.   Not until 1902, with the passage of the Midwives Act, and the establishment of the Central Midwives Board in 1903, were legal steps taken to require the training and licensing of midwives. See Thomas R. Forbes, 'The Regulation of English Midwives in the 18th and 19th Centuries', *Medical History*, XV (October, 1971), p. 360.
12.   Forbes, p. 358. For infant mortality figures, I am indebted to A.S. Wohl.
13.   Charles Dickens, *Martin Chuzzlewit* (London, 1844), chap. XIX.
14.   William Buchan, *Advice to Mothers* (Philadelphia, 1804), p. 70. This book went through several editions in the nineteenth century.
15.   Pye H. Chavasse, *Advice to a Wife* (London, 1866).
16.   Cecil Woodham-Smith, *Queen Victoria* (New York, 1972), pp. 216-17.
17.   George Moore, *Esther Waters* (London, 1894), chap. XVI.
18.   Her *accoucheur*, Sir Richard Croft, committed suicide three months after the death of the Princess Charlotte. See Longford, *Queen Victoria*, p. 151.
19.   Buchan, *Advice to Mothers*, p. 68.
20.   From Preface to *Catalogue and Report of Obstetrical and Other Instruments* (London, 1867).
21.   Preface to *Catalogue*.
22.   Ibid.
23.   From R. Kipling, 'The Three Decker', in *The Seven Seas* (1896).
24.   Queen Victoria to Princess Royal, 15 June 1858. In *Dearest Child: Letters between Queen Victoria and the Princess Royal (1858–1861)*, Roger Fulford (ed.) (London, 1964), p. 115.
25.   Ibid.
26.   Queen Victoria to Princess Royal, 17 March 1870. In Longford, *Queen Victoria*, p. 377.
27.   Queen Victoria to Princess Royal, 9 March 1859. In *Dearest Child*, pp. 165-6.
28.   See Madeleine Riley, *Brought to Bed* (New York, 1968), pp. 1-6.
29.   'Mr Gilfil's Love Story', in *Scenes from Clerical Life* (Edinburgh, 1858).

30. Chapter XLVIII.
31. In *A Dictionary of Modern English Usage* (Oxford, 1968), p. 171.
32. Quoted in Cecil W. Cunnington, *Feminine Attitudes in the Nineteenth Century* (New York, 1936), pp. 64-5.
33. *Females: Their Diseases and Remedies* (Philadelphia, 1848), p. 24.
34. *Domestic Medicine* (Exeter, 1828), p. 412.
35. Reportedly said by Sir Henry Halford, President of the Royal College of Physicians. See Walter Radcliffe, *Milestones in Midwifery* (Bristol, 1967), p. 95.
36. Buchan, *Advice to Mothers*, pp. 1-2.
37. *Ruth* (London, 1906), p. 160.
38. Mrs Jewsbury, *Zoe* (London, 1845), Vol. 1, p. 219.
39. William Thackeray, *Vanity Fair* (London, 1853), chap. XXXV.
40. Mrs Emma Jane Worboise, *Married Life* (London, 1872), pp. 66-82.
41. *Lady Nugent's Journal: Jamaica One Hundred Years Ago* (West India Commission, 1834), p. 163.
42. Queen Victoria to Princess Royal, 11 December 1858. In *Dearest Child*, pp. 150-1.
43. Queen Victoria to Princess Royal, 8 April 1863. In *Dearest Mama: Letters between Queen Victoria and the Crown Princess of Prussia*, Roger Fulford (ed.) (New York, 1969), pp. 192-3.
44. Queen Victoria to Princess Royal, 25 July 1863. Fulford, *Dearest Mama*, p. 251.

3 'AS THE TWIG IS BENT': THE VICTORIAN NANNY

Theresa McBride

One of the most pervasive images of Victorian family life includes an army of servants who ran the households and raised the children of middle- and upper-class English families before 1900. Indeed, as a recent study of the Victorian nanny suggests, family life in Victorian England would be inconceivable without the nannies, nurses and governesses who were more important to some English children than their own parents.[1] Yet in spite of the pervasiveness of this image, an understanding of the role of servants in the upbringing of English children is one more missing piece in the very incomplete picture of family life since the Industrial Revolution. Winston Churchill leaves us with no doubts as to the importance to his own life of his beloved Nanny Everest, but how many others of his generation knew their nannies better than their own mothers? What were the responsibilities of Victorian and Edwardian servants in child-rearing and what roles did they assume in English domesticity?

One cannot begin to discuss English domesticity in the nineteenth century without first noting the enormous increase in size and wealth of the middle class in the mid-nineteenth century.[2] For it was this class whose concern for intimacy and domestic comfort produced a wealth of literature in the nineteenth century concerned with three themes: child-rearing, the direction of servants, and household management.[3] The vast proliferation of this literature alone is convincing evidence of the spiralling interest in these interrelated topics, but the literature must be handled carefully when determining the precise nature of the middle-class life style.

The domestic economy literature written to assist the new middle class to adjust to their recently acquired status provides evidence for the commonplace of English social history — that middle-class families employed servants. Servants were a status symbol and to lack such help in the household, argued one historian, was to risk sinking 'from genteel poverty . . . into the darkness of vulgarity.'[4] 'I must not do our household work, or carry my baby out,' insisted the wife of an assistant surgeon in 1859, 'or I should lose caste.'[5] By 1871, the total number of general servants in England and Wales had risen to 780,040 (an increase of 35 per cent over 1851) to stretch almost far enough to cover the estimated 838,000 families whose incomes had risen above £100 per year by 1867.[6] A salary of at least £100 per year is used here to separate the middle class from the ranks of the skilled artisans, even though most clerks and many teachers earned salaries which placed them perilously close to this boundary. This income level probably defines the lowest level of servant-employing households.

It should be obvious that J.A. Banks's portrait of middle-class domesticity as incomplete without three servants does not represent the bulk of the nineteenth-century middle class.[7] That level of middle-class domesticity required a minimum income of £300 per year. Even Mrs Beeton's often-quoted *Book of Household Management* (1861) sets the minimum income level for employment of two servants at £300 per year.[8] At least three-quarters of those who held middle-class occupations in the Victorian period fell below this minimum of £300 per year,[9] and thus employed only one or two servants. The average middle-class family in London at mid-century employed 1.8 servants.[10] It is important to realize that significant elements of the middle class were servantless even at the height of live-in domestic service (1850 to 1880) and that the most typical household included only a single maid-of-all-work, or at most, a cook and a nursemaid-housemaid.

But it is not inconceivable that a middle-class family who could not afford extensive household assistance would use their limited resources to hire a nursemaid or nanny to look after the children. Eliza Warren in her handbook, *How I Managed My House on Two Hundred Pounds a Year* (1864), described how she hired a young country girl to help out with the housework and with caring for the new baby, even though she could afford to pay only a few pounds per year in wages.[11] And Lilian Westall became both a nursemaid and general servant for a London clerk and his wife when she was only fourteen.[12] In fact, Westall's experience as a servant in Edwardian England is highly suggestive of the typical experience of the child-servant relationship. Lilian Westall described her first position as a 'nurse-housemaid' for a London clerk. She cared for three children, one of whom was an infant, and was paid a salary of only two shillings a week.

In the morning I did the housework; in the afternoon I took the children out; in the evening I looked after them and put them to bed. My employers didn't seem to have much money themselves; he was a clerk of some sort, but they liked the idea of having a 'nursemaid' and made me buy a cap, collar, cuffs, and apron. Then the mistress took me to have a photograph taken with the children grouped around me . . . I stayed at this place until I was nearly seventeen, then I left — 'to better myself, mum.'[13]

Westall was much more typical than Churchill's Nanny Everest of the Victorian nurse-nanny, but both cases suggest significant themes of child-rearing and domestic relations in Victorian and Edwardian England.

The character and experiences of the servant herself had important implications for child-rearing in this period. No one was more aware of this fact than the Victorians themselves. The selection and direction of domestics was seen as a central issue in household management and domestic happiness. It is therefore crucial to understand the relationship of the servant to the Victorian family in order to be able to reconstruct other domestic relationships.

The proliferation of domestic economy literature placed a major emphasis on the importance of mothering. In part, this concern reflected the greater opportunities which women of the middle class had to nurture their own children. But the employment of a servant offered two conflicting options: the probability of spending more time in child-rearing (and less in other household tasks) and the possibility of becoming even more estranged from one's children as servants increasingly assumed the daily functions of the parent. Rising standards of health and material comfort produced another paradox. The improvements were accompanied and partly accomplished by the education of the public to the many hazards which threatened their children, and thus served to heighten anxieties about children's health and welfare. 'Thus in a sense,' writes Patricia Branca, 'the Victorian woman was caught in a vicious cycle; she was anxious about her health and the health of her unborn baby, she sought advice, but for the most part all the advice did was to confirm all her anxieties while offering very little in the way of constructive advice.'[14]

A notable example of the way in which this concern about child-care was expressed was in the literature regarding wet nurses. Wet nursing, still widespread on the European continent, was rapidly disappearing from England by the 1860s.[15] Though it is impossible to trace the decline of wet nursing precisely since the census does not distinguish between the types of nurses, the trend is clear.

The practice was strongly disapproved by the British medical profession.[16] But the decline was also undoubtedly due to the growing realization that children's health was at stake, for children entrusted to wet nurses had a much higher mortality rate. Increasingly concerned about their nurturing role, middle-class mothers were more hesitant to use a wet nurse. Their fears were reflected in the almost impossibly high standards of character and health set out for the wet nurse by the domestic economy manuals. Mrs James in *Our Servants: Their Duties to Us and Ours to Them* (1883) described an acceptable wet nurse in this way:

> She should be a well-educated woman — able to read, write and speak grammatically, free from any vulgarism, not too impulsive, firm yet kind, tender, just, sympathetic, large-hearted, with a love of truthfulness, a horror of deceit, and imbued with decided and deep religious feelings.[17]

Since most wet nurses were poor, country women who were trying to supplement their family's meagre income by nursing, these criteria were totally unrealistic. There is probably a deeper, psychological level upon which such descriptions must be understood, for it is clear that the wet nurse and her intimate relationship to the infant was profoundly threatening to the Victorian middle classes. Thus, even in the peak period of domestic service in England, the category of nurses (which included both wet nurses and nannies) encompassed only 39,000 individuals in 1851 and about 75,000 in 1881 in all of England and Wales.[18] This figure representes about four to five per cent of the total number of servants in that period. Wet nursing declined in the last half of the nineteenth century in England, because of the impossibility of finding nurses whose high moral character and impeccable health could assuage middle-class parents' fears for their children.

The trend toward the nursing of infants by their own mothers is an indication of the desire to provide better care for children, but the use of other servants in child-care implies the opposite — for it suggests the second aspect of the paradox. How can one argue that Victorian parents were taking more responsibility for the raising of their children when the number of servants specifically employed in child-care was increasing throughout the Victorian period (nearly doubled between 1851 and 1881)? Some commentators have interpreted the rise in servant-employment to mean that English

parents were less concerned with their children; English mothers were
'unaffectionate' and English fathers 'authoritarian'.[19] On this point,
however, the insight of J.A. Banks is more convincing and the
evidence of the domestic economy literature is unmistakable: 'middle-
class mothers must perforce be provided with domestic assistance,
not that she might indulge in indolence, but that she might be freed
to devote all her energies to the proper upbringing of her children.'[20]
It was not indifference, then, but caring which is exemplified by
this pattern of servant-employment. The lack of evidence of actual
parental behaviour precludes a consensus, but it seems clear that
the so-called indifference or callousness toward children is more typical
of the upper classes, than the middle class.[21] The bulk of middle-
class parents in Victorian England considered their role as parents
important and were concerned about the effects of introducing
servants into the process of child-rearing.

One cannot simply dismiss the charges that Victorian middle-class
parents did not raise their own children, but the charges must be
understood in the context of the whole web of domestic relationships,
involving as they did the employment of a live-in domestic servant.
The enormous increase in the employment of live-in servants of all
kinds in the Victorian period represents the desire of the new middle
class to bolster their new social status, but also suggests the strain of
coping with the hardships of making their new environment
comfortable. In doing so, the middle-class housewife was hampered
by the slow evolution of household technology and of urban services.
For example, lavatories did not come into general middle-class use
until well after 1850,[22] and most London kitchens were dominated
by a huge coal-burning fireplace which required constant
replenishing with coal.[23] The necessity to carry coal, shop daily
for provisions, heat stoves and keep themselves clean without
the benefit of running water was solved by the middle class
at the expense of the servant class. Moreover, the diffusion of household technology at the end of the Victorian period merely resulted
in the changing of women's time-priorities; time saved in tasks such as
cooking was expected to be transferred to other jobs, notably to
child-care.[24]

Although the struggle to maintain certain standards of cleanliness
and comfort among the Victorian middle class may not seem related
to their attitudes toward child-care, the two areas overlap
significantly. Because elements of the middle class had to strain the
family budget to employ a servant, they generally chose a young

woman who could perform a variety of functions and was paid only a low wage. A rather typical combination was that of housemaid and nursemaid, like the young Lilian Westall. A manual on child care, Mrs Pedley's *Infant Nursing and the Management of Young Children* (1866), noted that families who could not afford more than one servant, generally selected one who could care for children but do other work as well. 'The chief object,' wrote Mrs Pedley, 'appears to be the engagement of a person who . . . will not object "to turn her hand to anything". Now a servant of this description seldom does any portion of her work well.'[25] The arrangement was easier on a middle-class budget, but did not always provide the best care for the Victorian child.

The image of the young, and frequently inexperienced nursemaid can be demonstrated to be substantially accurate by a demographic profile of nursemaids in the mid-Victorian period. Most nurses were young: in England and Wales in 1851, 46 per cent of them were under 20; 74 per cent were under 30.[26] In 1871, 51 per cent of English nurses were under 20, and 23 per cent were under 14;[27] thus, new recruits into this group were even younger by 1871. Comparing the average age of the nursemaid to that of a general servant, it becomes clear that nursemaids were most often the youngest servants — about three years younger on the average than the general servant. Cooks, housekeepers, and even housemaids were older than nursemaids.[28]

Mean Ages of Female Servants[29]

	Nursemaids		General servants	
	Mean	Median	Mean	Median
1851	24.1	20.8	27.6	23.5
1861	24.9	19.6	27.0	22.3
1871	25.1	19.9	26.8	22.2

The young age of most nursemaids need not have been a great drawback, for some surely came from large families and had probably had prior experience in caring for siblings.[30] Most nursemaids came from agricultural backgrounds and in the classic cycle of agricultural families the elder children were sent out to work as domestics as soon as they could be spared from home, thus helping to solve the problems of the poor tenant farmer with a too-numerous family.[31]

Most of the nursemaids had left their own families at a very young age; about two-thirds of them by the age of fourteen or fifteen.[32] In other words, Victorian middle-class children were most often cared for by servants who were little more than children themselves.

More important than the simple factor of age was that nursemaids were recruited from among the unskilled, recent urban migrants who were not only new to urban life but generally unschooled. In fact, a position in domestic service was considered a valuable experience for a young woman because it exposed her to the rudiments of education and of domestic training before marriage.[33] Nursemaids were an unskilled group and their low wages and high job turnover underscore their low status. Indeed, they were among the lowest paid domestics, just above the lowly overworked scullery maid.[34] At the end of the Victorian period, the average wage of a nursemaid in London was under £15 — this was the same as a maid-of-all-work, but compared unfavourably to the wages of parlourmaids who earned over £22 and housemaids who earned an average of £17 5s. 0d.[35]

Victorian nursemaids, because they were among the youngest and least experienced of all domestic servants, tended to change jobs frequently. A study done at the end of the nineteenth century found that between one-third and one-half of the nursemaids in London had been in the same household for less than a year.[36] The rate of job turnover implied by the survey is surprisingly high. The average length of service in a single household was fifteen months for four-fifths of the servants. Only one servant in ten stayed with the same family for five years, but those who did averaged nearly eighteen years of service in the same household.[37]

The image of the nurse-nanny which emerges from this general information includes both the Nanny Everests and the Lilian Westalls. About one nanny in ten might fit the stereotype of the matronly family nurse who cared for children throughout their lives. Like Winston Churchill's nurse, these women could be nanny caricatured by H.G. Wells in his *Tono-Bungay* (1909):

> She was that strange product of the old time, a devoted, trusted servant; she had, as it were, banked all her pride and will with the greater, more powerful people who employed her, in return for a life-long security of servitude. She was sexless, her personal pride was all transferred, she mothered another woman's child with a hard, joyless devotion . . .[38]

This old retainer could provide a sense of continuity to family life and be a mother-substitute for children whose own parents' social responsibilities were too extensive to allow them to raise their own children.

Most nurses, however, changed positions too often to acquire long-lasting attachments to particular families. They were continually changing jobs in search of better wages, more comfortable conditions, to escape harrassment, or simply out of boredom. Nursemaids were clearly at the bottom of the servant hierarchy because they were the least skilled. As a servant acquired skills, like Lilian Westall, she was promoted to other jobs within the household or went in search of a better position in a larger, more affluent household. Thus, upper-class families who could afford to support large household staffs had the edge in hiring older, more experienced women as nurses for their children. The bulk of the middle class, however, were frequently confronted with a servant who was young, untrained, sometimes naive and even crude by middle-class standards.[39]

Why then would concerned parents entrust their children to these incompetent individuals who were hired as servants? The answer lies in the hazy, ambiguous area of job-definition and division of functions within the household. The general category into which wet nurses, nannies, and nursemaids were lumped for the sake of the census suggests the nature of the problem. Servants were frequently required to handle a variety of functions; only in the largest households was the division of labour very precise. But in the case of the nursemaid-housemaid combination or in the instance of the general servant, the major responsibilities were undoubtedly the heaviest of household tasks and the least pleasant duties in dealing with children. In the middle-class household in which child-rearing was divided between the mother and a single servant, most of the actual caring for the children was performed by the mother, while the servant would clean up after the children, and feed and help to clothe them. Sunday was the family's day out as it was the servant's day off and on that day the servant might accompany the family to the park, leading the children and watching over them as they played. But this was clearly considered a 'recreational' outing for the servant as for the children, and was not the kind of work which occupied the bulk of a servant's day. This analysis of a servant's responsibilities would also help to explain the divergent connotations of the terms 'nanny' and 'nursemaid', for the first was obviously the manager of the nursery and mother-surrogate in authority and in care, while the second was simply hired help who performed the subsidiary functions. In the majority of households, which employed only a single servant, the division of responsibilities was between the mother and the nursemaid, rather than between the mother and the nanny.

The employment of servants in child-care or simply in general capacities around the house thus had a significant effect upon middle-class domesticity. In some cases, particularly among the upper class, domestics fulfilled their ideal function — to cushion the middle-class family from the discomforts of urban life and to insulate parents from the unpleasantness of dealing with their own children at times. But in other cases, a servant was as troublesome as she was useful, creating tensions in the middle-class household and arousing the fears of middle-class parents for the health and welfare of their children.

Both of these possibilities suggest the most important aspect of the experience which the servant introduced into Victorian middle-class family life. The servant put the middle-class family into intimate contact with a way of life which was at times decidedly different from their own. Middle-class commentators complained endlessly about servants' drinking habits, their sexual promiscuity, their larcenous impulses, and their tendency to use strong language. Children of middle- and upper-class parents frequently acquired their first direct knowledge of drunkenness and petty crime through their contacts with servants. Because of this, the servant, especially the charwoman, acquired the popular image of a gossip and a drunk.[40] Parents were concerned that their children might be exposed to such creatures and thereby learn bad habits. Though middle- and upper-class families were not totally free from such problems themselves, transgressions within the family ranks were more likely to be kept secret from the children.

The youth of the typical nursemaid also seems to have made her the object of the sexual attentions of her employer and perhaps aroused the romantic interest of the older male children. A great hazard for the young female servant in Victorian society was the opportunity to be sexually exploited by her employer, for which the servant's own immorality was frequently blamed. As Henry Mayhew disdainfully commented: 'the servants often give themselves up to the sons, or to the policeman on the beat, or to soldiers in the Parks; or else to shopmen, whom they may meet in the street. Female servants are far from a virtuous class.'[41] Moreover, the sexual initiation of boys by female servants is an important theme in the discussion of the roles of nannies in upper-class families.[42] But it is difficult to sort out the sexual fantasies from actual behaviour, for it is clear that servant girls were often the object of upper-class males' fantasies.[43] Servants as a class also had the highest rate of illegitimate births and had close links with prostitution in the nineteenth century, so that they were often suspected of lascivious intentions when their behaviour does not substantiate the charge.[44] Whether or not sexual initiation by female servants was actually a pattern in the maturing process of upper-class males, children recalled their contacts with servants as providing them with some familiarity with a distinctive culture.[45]

Contacts with servants helped to shape children's attitudes toward class status and behaviour. While servants were learning to be deferential to their employers, children were acquiring either a paternalistic benevolence or disdainful suspicion toward their lower-class employees.[46] The persistence of upper-class paternalism toward the lower classes as well as the pervasiveness of working-class conservatism may be explicable in the context of master-servant relationships.

The other side of this picture was the life of the nursemaid herself. What happened to a young female immigrant who entered the services of a middle-class household at the age of fourteen or fifteen? On the basis of typicality, the experience of the servant was more important than that of the children for whom she cared. One in every three women in Victorian England probably served as a domestic servant at some point in her life, most between the ages of fifteen and twenty-five.[47]

The Victorian nursemaid was generally from an agricultural background, drawn to the city by the promise of a better life than that offered by agricultural work. Domestic service was a traditional occupation for the rural-born, and especially for women. The work was always available, and positions multiplied with the rising affluence of the middle class in the nineteenth century. Positions in service were frequently arranged through family members or neighbours before moving to the city.[48] But domestic service also offered distinct advantages to those willing to profit from the experience. Though badly paid, the young nursemaid did not have to pay for room or board, and thus, unlike the seamstress or factory worker, she could save her wages to provide herself with a dowry for marriage, or with the means to arrange an apprenticeship with a dressmaker or even to set up her own shop. These advantages did not always outweigh the disadvantages, however, of the long hours and almost total lack of freedom required by service. Domestic service, particularly for the young nursemaid, was a transitional occupation and yet was a crucial experience in the life of a young woman.[49]

The life of the Victorian nursemaid was always very difficult and generally lonely. The work was hard and unpleasant. The nursemaid was responsible for dealing with all the unpleasant physical functions of daily life. Middle-class standards of cleanliness were increasingly exacting and were probably necessary for raising general standards of health, but the achievement of that improvement made the lives of many nineteenth-century servants miserable. Since a nursemaid was among the youngest of servants, to her fell the heaviest and least pleasant tasks.

Working alone or with only one other servant in a Victorian home, the nursemaid did not even have the company of other servants. Because her work day commonly extended from six o'clock in the morning until ten or eleven o'clock at night, she was able to form only limited friendships outside the household. Complained the footman William Taylor, 'a servant is shut up like a bird in a cage'.[50] Sundays were her only days off and she would use them to meet men, sometimes soldiers and sailors who could be encountered easily in the parks; for she hoped to find a suitable mate who could free her from a life of servitude. Servant-mates were often in military occupations (the equivalent transitional occupation for men which service represented for women), but some were also artisans and shopkeepers.[51] Since most servants married after an average period of eight to ten years, the experience of servanthood was an important one in their lives. The transition was not always easy, but the attitudes born in service were undoubtedly carried over into the upbringing of their own children. So that whatever the impact of the nanny in educating upper-class children, it should be clear that the experience of service was a highly significant one for the nursemaids themselves.

Though nurses or nannies constituted only a minority of servants (less than five per cent), their experiences were similar to those of other domestics who represented nearly a third of the young women of Victorian England. Women's work experiences were more temporary than men's in the Victorian period, for women did not work consistently after marriage; but domestic service was one occupation which had a significant impact upon women's subsequent marriages. The timing of a woman's marriage, the choice of a spouse and the attitudes which she brought to the marriage were all

affected by the experience of service.[52] Former servants probably had
ambivalent feelings about their experiences; some internalized the
servility and carried with them a deep resentment of their former
employers and perhaps of the whole middle class.[53] Other servants
had undoubtedly learned ambitions for personal advancement which
they passed on to their children. Many servants at least found their
personal horizons widened by the exposure to the very different style
of life of the middle class. Thus, generations of working-class and
artisans' children were brought up by mothers whose attitudes toward
life had been shaped by their experiences in service. Whether or not,
then, contemporary English society owes much to the upbringing of
its children by the Victorian nanny, the impact of domestic service
lingers through the experiences of millions of women who were
nannies or nurses, housemaids and parlourmaids in Victorian England.

Notes

The author wishes to thank the National Endowment for the Humanities for the
summer fellowship which supported this research and to acknowledge her debt to
Patricia Branca and to Gail Mabel Buschmann.

1.   Jonathan Gathorne-Hardy, *The Rise and Fall of the Victorian Nanny*
        (London, 1972).
2.   Geoffrey Best, *Mid-Victorian Britain* (London, 1971), especially p. 85.
3.   Theresa McBride, *The Domestic Revolution: The Modernisation of
        Household Service in England and France, 1820–1920* (London, 1976),
        passim.
4.   Marion Lochhead, *The Victorian Household* (London, 1964), p. 30.
5.   Quoted by Sheila Richardson, 'The Servant Question: A Study of the
        Domestic Labour Market, 1851–1911', unpublished master's thesis,
        University of London, 1971, p. 35.
6.   Patricia Branca, *The Silent Sisterhood: Middle-Class Women in the
        Victorian Home* (London, 1975), p. 45.
7.   J.A. Banks, *Prosperity and Parenthood* (London, 1954), p. 37; the con-
        clusions of this paper are based largely on the manuscript census
        schedules of London for 1851 to 1871, examined in my book, *The
        Domestic Revolution*; all statistical conclusions are drawn from these
        census data unless otherwise noted.
8.   Mrs Beeton, *Book of Household Management* (London, 1861), p. 8;
        see similar estimates in Samuel and Sarah Adams, *The Complete
        Servant* (London, 1825), p. 5; *A New System of Practical Domestic
        Economy* (London, 1823), p. 37; Thomas Webster and Mrs Parkes,
        An Encyclopaedia of Domestic Economy (London, 1884), p. 331;
        Mrs Eliza Warren, *How I Managed My House on Two Hundred Pounds
        a Year* (London, 1864), p. 12.
9.   An excellent discussion of middle-class incomes and material culture
        is contained in Branca, *Silent Sisterhood*, pp. 38-59.

10. My own sampling of the London censuses and the research of David Chaplin, Department of Sociology, Western Michigan, agree that four of five London servant-employing households had only one or two servants.

11. Warren, *How I Managed my House*, p. 12.

12. John Burnett (ed.), *The Annals of Labour: Autobiographies of English Working-Class People, 1820–1920* (Bloomington, Indiana, 1974), p. 216.

13. Ibid.

14. Branca, *Silent Sisterhood*, p. 77.

15. B.L. Hutchins, *Statistics of Women's Life and Employment* (London, 1901), p. 26.

16. *British Medical Journal*, 19 June 1869.

17. Mrs Eliot James, *Our Servants. Their Duties to Us and Ours to Them* (London, 1883), p. 76.

18. Census samples and impressionistic evidence suggest that the number of nursemaids is far greater than that of wet nurses, even though the two groups are lumped together in the same census category.

19. Priscilla Robertson, 'Home as a Nest: Middle Class Childhood in Nineteenth-Century Europe', in Lloyd de Mause (ed.), *The History of Childhood* (New York, 1975), pp. 407-31; see also pp. 423-5.

20. Banks, *Prosperity and Parenthood*, p. 138; see also Sarah Stickney Ellis, *The Women of England* (London, 1839, 2nd edn.), p. 304; Mrs Beeton, *Book of Household Management*, pp. 6-9; Mrs Warren, *How I Managed my House*, preface; Lady A.S. Baker, *Our Responsibilities and Difficulties as Mistresses of Young Servants* (London, 1886), p. 6.

21. Robertson and Gathorne-Hardy rely heavily on upper-class examples when attempting to prove parental authoritarianism or indifference. Note Michael Anderson's conclusions about working-class mothers in nineteenth-century Lancashire: Anderson argues that working-class mothers cared about their children in spite of charges of abuse and neglect. There is even more evidence of middle-class concern about children in M. Anderson, *Family Structure in Nineteenth-Century Lancashire* (Cambridge, 1971), pp. 76-8.

22. Lawrence Wright, *Clean and Decent. The Fascinating History of the Bathroom and the WC* (London, 1960), p. 222.

23. *Domestic Service. By an Old Servant* (London, 1917), p. 37; Lawrence Wright, *Home Fires Burning* (London, 1964), p. 121.

24. Ruth Schwartz Cowan, 'A Case Study of Technological Social Change: The Washing Machine and the Working Wife', Mary S. Hartman and Lois Banner (eds.), *Clio's Consciousness Raised: New Perspectives on the History of Women* (New York, 1974), pp. 245-53, suggests this thesis.

25. Mrs Pedley, *Infant Nursing and the Management of Young Children* (London, 1866), p. 93.

26. Parliamentary Papers, 1852–1853, LXXXVIII, pt. I, cxli: *Census of England and Wales, 1851*.

27. Parliamentary Papers, 1873, LXXI, pt. I, xlvi: *Census of England and Wales, 1871*.

28. Richardson, 'The Servant Question', pp. 258-9.

29. Ibid.

30. Servants' agricultural background is suggested by the census samples, which reveal that three-quarters of London's servants in the mid-Victorian period came from the country or from Ireland.

31. Lutz K. Berkner has described this pattern in 'The Stem Family and the Developmental Cycle of the Peasant Household: An Eighteenth-

Century Austrian Example', *American Historical Review*, LXXVII (April, 1972), pp. 398-418; a similar description is provided by Peter Laslett in *The World We Have Lost* (New York, 1956), and I have analyzed various kinds of evidence which point to the same conclusion in *The Domestic Revolution*.

32. Christina Butler, *Domestic Service: An Inquiry by the Women's Industrial Council* (London, 1916), p. 75; the conclusions are based on the limited returns to an Industrial Council survey.

33. See my article on French domestic servants in this period, 'Social Mobility for the Lower Classes: Domestic Service in Nineteenth-Century France', *Journal of Social History*, VIII, 1 (Fall, 1974).

34. The wage data are drawn from C. Collet, 'Money Wages of In-Door Domestic Servants', Parliamentary Papers, 1899, XCII, tables on p. 13.

35. Ibid., p. 26.

36. Ibid.

37. Ibid.

38. H.G. Wells, *Tono-Bungay* (New York, 1960), p. 38.

39. See a similar conclusion in Genevieve Leslie, 'Domestic Service in Canada, 1880–1920', *Women at Work, Ontario, 1850–1930*, Janice Acton, Penny Goldsmith and Bonnie Shepard (eds.) (Toronto, 1974), pp. 71-125; see page 82: 'Nursemaids and "mother's helps" were usually young, inexperienced, and very poorly paid.'

40. Lochhead, *The Victorian Household*, p. 41; Mrs William Parkes, *Domestic Duties or Instructions to Young Married Ladies on the Management of their Households* (London, 1825), pp. 117-19.

41. Mayhew, *London Labour and the London Poor* (London, 1861; reprinted, New York, 1968), IV, p. 257.

42. James H.S. Bossard, 'Domestic Servants and Child Development', *The Sociology of Child Development* (New York, 1954), pp. 182-98, and especially pp. 190-1.

43. Steven Marcus, *The Other Victorians* (New York, 1964), p. 129.

44. A.M. Royden, et al., *Downward Paths: An Inquiry into the Causes which Contribute to the Making of Prostitution* (London, 1916), p. 15; Butler, *Domestic Service*, p. 96.

45. Gathorne-Hardy, *The Rise and Fall of the Victorian Nanny*, pp. 102-4.

46. Bossard, 'Domestic Servants and Child Development', p. 192.

47. This calculation is based upon the percentage of each age category which was active in domestic service; see the same conclusion in Leonore Davidoff, 'Mastered for Life: Servant and Wife in Victorian and Edwardian England', *Journal of Social History*, VII, 4 (Summer, 1974), pp. 406-28.

48. Michael Anderson, *Family Structure in Nineteenth-Century Lancashire* (Cambridge, 1971), p. 53.

49. Some comment should be made about the interesting but peripheral case of the governess. Even in the peak period of live-in domestic service, there were only a few thousand governesses in all of England and Wales – far too few to be shared among the English upper classes, who numbered at least 50,000 in the 1860s, let alone the ranks of the middle classes. A recent study of the Victorian governess suggested that the social origins of the governess gave rise to her 'status ambiguity' in the middle-class household (M. Jeanne Peterson, 'Status Incongruence in Family and Society', Martha Vicinus (ed.), *Suffer and Be Still* (Bloomington, Indiana, 1974), pp. 3-19). But a more serious crisis afflicted the governess class in the nineteenth century – the influx of poorly educated, lower-class

women. The demographic profile of governesses drawn from the London census sample differs little from that of other female indoor servants — in other words, the governess was generally young, single and rural-born. Although there were obviously some governesses who fit the stereotype of the well-born but impoverished gentlewoman (particularly those employed in country houses, rather than in London), the character of the whole group merely accentuated the ambiguity of their role in the Victorian family.

50.   Burnett (ed.), *The Annals of Labour*, p. 185.
51.   See McBride, *The Domestic Revolution*, chap. 6.
52.   Michael Anderson, 'Marriage Patterns in Victorian Britain', *Journal of Family History*, I, 1 (Autumn, 1976), pp. 55-78, see page 72 on which Anderson discusses the implications for the timing of marriage of domestic servants; for a discussion of some attitudes which were carried over into marriage, see McBride, *The Domestic Revolution*, chap. 6, and Davidoff, *passim*.
53.   Davidoff, 'Mastered for Life', p. 421.

4 THE PATERFAMILIAS OF THE VICTORIAN GOVERNING CLASSES

David Roberts

In early nineteenth-century England the wealthy classes, particularly those wealthy in land, were immensely powerful. Within the families of those wealthy classes the fathers were likewise powerful. They ruled the families that ruled England. It is thus not unimportant to ask what kind of fathers they were.

To answer that question I read the memoirs of 168 Victorians born between 1800 and 1850. They were memoirs found in the biography sections of the Dartmouth College library and in the English history section of the Harvard University library. These memoirs not only tell a great deal about the fathers of these 168 Victorians, but, in the case of 143 of them, who were males and who had children in their turn, they tell us how they performed their paternal duties. The picture of nineteenth-century fatherhood formed by these memoirs is sweeping and complex. It is also a biased picture since these memoirs often tend to the idolatrous. But they still provide a picture from which a wary observer can discern some common characteristics. One can, for example, discern the three features most common to the early Victorian paterfamilias, namely remoteness, sovereignty, and benevolence.

The first of these characteristics, remoteness, was far more common of the paterfamilias of the early nineteenth century than of that of later periods. The reasons for this remoteness were many. Its most irreversible form came with the death of the father. Such was the fate of seventeen persons in this sample of 168, whose fathers died before the end of their fifteenth year; six of them, indeed, had not reached the fourth year before their fathers had died.[1]

For most early Victorians of the governing classes the reason for their father's remoteness was less final. The fathers of sixteen of the 168 served in the army or navy. They were often away, though they did return on occasions. The same was true of imperial proconsuls like the Ninth Earl of Dalhousie and missionaries like Frederic William Farrar. Farrar sent his son home from India at the age of three to be raised by maiden aunts; Dalhousie, on returning from a term as Governor General of Canada, failed to recognize his eighteen-year-old son.[2]

Attendance at Parliament also called Victorian fathers from their homes. Fifty-one of the 168 sat in Parliament, an honour that also fell to forty-one of their fathers. Parliament generally ran from January to July and its sessions ran into the early morning. MPs saw little of their children even when their families were in London. For that reason, many like Henry Chaplin known in the Commons as the 'squire', left their families in the country. MPs were not the only hardworking peripatetic members of the governing classes. Barristers and judges travelled their circuits, prison and factory inspectors visited gaols and mills, and businessmen kept long hours. 'In our childhood,' recollects the daughter of the publisher J.M. Dent, 'my father spent little time with us as business filled nearly all his waking hours.'[3]

Public duty and business were by no means the only reasons for a father's absence. For the more frivolous there were the hunt, the races, the theatre, balls, dinners, endless visits to country houses, and long trips abroad. For both frivolous and serious alike there was of course the club. 'Sir William Hardman,' noted the biographer of this Conservative MP, 'was always about the town . . . clubs, dinner parties.' In early Victorian England, says the social historian, Ralph Nevill, 'clubs multiplied enormously . . . every profession, every pastime, every point of view had its club.' 'Men only' congregated at clubs and 'men only' often took vacations together.[4] The young Gladstone, after telling his wife that his fourteen hour work day would preclude much intercourse with her during the Parliamentary session, then planned an autumn trip to Ireland with two fellow MPs (MPs who would also leave their wives and children behind). The Reverend Edward Miall of Leicester left his large family and betook himself to Scotland for his summer.[5]

Even when at home the father could be remote, if only because of the size of the family. The average number of children in families of the peerage between 1800 and 1850 was 4.5. Of the sixty-four families in the sample of 168 about which there is information of family sizes, twenty-two had more than eight and four had sixteen. One of the fathers of sixteen children, the Reverend Sabine Baring-Gould, found it was all too much for him. At a parish Christmas party he asked a little girl 'And whose little girl are you?' The girl burst into tears and replied, 'I am yours, Daddy.'[6]

If the sixteen children proved confusing to a father, how much more confusing to girls and boys were the large, extended homes crowded with grandparents, aunts and uncles, and endless cousins. Lord and Lady Aberdeen had between them 120 first cousins, and they entertained and visited many of them. Admiral Montagu, whose mother was a Paget, remembers of her home at Uxbridge, 'the numberless uncles and aunts . . . some were half aunts and half uncles . . . and to this goodly array were added more numerous progeny, until to my juvenile mind the world seemed to consist of nothing but Pagets.'[7]

In such large and extended and busy families it was unlikely that sons would become intimate with their father before nine, yet at that age it was likely they would be sent away to school. One hundred and eight of the 156 men in the sample of 168 were sent away to school; the mean age at departure was nine.[8] Most boarding schools in the early nineteenth century had dismal teaching, harsh discipline, bad morals, and wretched quarters. Their half year terms were long and their two vacations short. Most early Victorian fathers knew of these conditions. Why then did they send their young boys to such schools?

The predominant reason, of course, was that it was customary. The father of the First Earl of Cranbrook consoled his departing and tearful six-year-old by telling him that he had, by the age of six, run away from school twice. The eighteenth- and nineteenth-century boy was expected to mature early. Sir Francis Doyle's father was a captain in the army by age eleven. Doyle himself, born in 1813, was sent away early to Eton. He found a home during the holidays, as a rule, 'with my uncle'. Another reason for sending boys to school was the universal desire to be rid of children. 'When nine,' remembers the Fourth Earl of Desart, 'I was sent . . . to school . . . my parents being rather disturbed as to what to do with me when . . . in London.'[9] Such a jaunty and cavalier reason suited a latitudinarian aristocracy, but why did the more serious professional classes send away their young boys. John Duke Coleridge, eminent barrister, literary critic and most certainly of serious mind, gave one answer in a letter to the poet Robert Southey. 'His mightiness,' he wrote in 1827 of his six-year-old son, 'was getting out of hand and evidently required stricter discipline.'[10] A sense of innate sin, shared by both Evangelicals and High Church Anglicans, persuaded many a father to delegate the duty of disciplining errant boys to underpaid but, hopefully, godly curates. Or if not to godly curates of the Anglican faith to stern Quakers. All six of the Quaker fathers in the sample of 168 sent their children at an early age to Quaker schools, there to get that moral and religious training that busy fathers could never give.

The sending of boys to boarding school meant the complete

physical absence of the father, an absence that might actually have been a relief since it provided an escape from the fact that many fathers cared little for their children. For many, children were a bother: they misbehaved, they were noisy, they weren't rational, and they wasted valued time. The Seventh Earl of Shaftesbury said his father's 'natural tendency is to avoid me and all his children.'[11] 'Squire' Chaplin found his children interrupted his social and political life, so, his wife having died, he left them to their Scottish nanny. William Keppel, a landed gentleman of Norfolk, frankly avowed that he disliked small children, a sentiment echoed by the Oxford theologian, William George Ward. For Keppel, 'small children' were bothersome; for Ward, they were not yet rational and until they were, he said, he could have no affection for or intercourse with them. He did, however, add, 'I am always informed when they are born.'[12]

This indifference to children, an inheritance from the eighteenth and earlier centuries, though it lessened considerably in the late nineteenth century, still remained a part of the outlook of some of the more aristocratic fathers. Lord Rosebery, when congratulated in 1882 upon the birth of a son, replied that not only did this 'very common event' not excite him, but it 'may cause a good deal of annoyance to me'.[13] Remoteness, physical and psychological, formed a prominent feature of many a nineteenth-century father.

The remoteness of the paterfamilias to his children also frequently extended to his wife. Isambard Brunel, the great engineer, was so involved with his works that Mrs Brunel's life was compared to that of 'the wife of a sea captain'.[44] The phrase itself is a reminder of how, in a century when Britain had the largest navy, the largest merchant marine, the largest network of trading outposts, and the largest empire, the Seven Seas frequently separated a father from his wife and children.

The early Victorian father, though often remote, did not thereby abdicate sovereignty. Sovereignty is, indeed, the second of the three characteristics of the early Victorian paterfamilias. Sovereign he was and always remained. Like an emperor, he delegated, amply and freely, much of his power, but he could always recall it. 'The governesses and tutor,' said the biographer of the Fourth Duke of Newcastle, 'worked under his absolute rule.'[15] It was a rule based on customs long held, on a social hierarchy never questioned, and on the enjoyment of a healthy portion of England's wealth. With such privileges he often did not have to use violence to manage his many dependants. He could use, instead, his privileges, titles, majesty, and the power of the purse.

The father of Sir Sydney Henry Jones-Parry, for instance, was a large Welsh landowner, a magistrate in three counties, the Deputy Lieutenant of Carnarvonshire and its High Sheriff. He was also an ex-naval captain, one who fought heroically at Camperdown at the age of thirteen. He embodied in himself Max Weber's three forms of power: personal charisma, patriarchal tradition, and bureaucratic authority. 'The raising of the corner of the tablecloth,' said his son, 'meant silence.'[16] The very climate of opinion made the father's recourse to violence infrequent. 'My father,' said the Reverend Thomas Guthrie of Edinburgh, 'seldom used the rod, but none ruled more absolutely ... a look was law, not only to be obeyed, but that promptly, instantly, without any attempt at remonstrance.'[17]

The fathers themselves, if wealthy and titled, expected deference. Sir Thomas Acland sen. of Devonshire, says the biographer of his son, was raised like a prince. He always had his way. He grew into an autocrat who taught his children to worship him.[18] Such teachings were the rule. 'My mother taught us,' said John Duke Coleridge, to think our father's opinions 'always right.' It thus never occurred to Thomas Acland jun. or to John Duke Coleridge to rebel. Acland jun. dearly wished to study law but dutifully accepted his father's prohibition. Lord John Russell just as dearly wished to attend Cambridge, but was equally graceful in accepting his father's prohibition. 'I hope you will do what you think best for me,' wrote Russell to his father, one of the richest dukes in England. He even added obediently, 'without consulting my inclinations.'[19] It was the father's prerogative to choose the son's profession and very few rebelled. To do so would not be financially prudent.

The wives and daughters were even less inclined to question the sovereignty of the paterfamilias. They subordinated themselves totally to the wishes of the master of the household and by doing so won universal praise. J.M. Dent, the publisher who spent so much time at business, praised his wife as an 'entirely self-sacrificing ... a self abnegating and self forgetting creature.' The Reverend John Clifford's wife was equally perfect and docile. 'How wonderfully she looked after him,' exclaims his biographer, 'everything was arranged ... so that he might do the maximum of work.' The wife of Sir Charles Wood also sacrificed herself. 'Though her will was strong,' says her biographer, 'she merged it in his.'[20] The results, according to the above biographers, were perfect marriages — though their praises always sound too mechanical.

The loss of the wife by death was the severest of blows, one made consolable only by a tender, caring, unmarried daughter. Daughters seem a special delight to fathers. When young they were always at home, tender, affectionate, attractive. At least one of them usually remained unmarried, the special servant for the father in his old age. Sarah Ellis, the author of *Daughters of England*, opined that one of the daughter's 'sphere of duty' was in the 'father's chamber'.[21] Everyone in the household in fact had his sphere, not only wives and daughters, but nannies, governesses, valets, and grooms. It was by the firm and clear delegation of duties and powers to various agents that the paterfamilias could resolve the seeming paradox of being both remote and sovereign.

The use of delegation often enhanced the role of the wife and mother. Many were, as heads of large households situated on grand estates, burdened with important business functions. While William Gladstone ran England, his wife Catherine ran Hawarden House in Cheshire and Carlton House in London, each with a large retinue of servants and a large array of sons, daughters, nieces, and nephews. She also managed many charities and was as active an administrator of benevolences as was Lady Adderley in Staffordshire. Lady Adderley, upon marrying Sir Charles Adderley, was told that the visiting and caring for the poor on all their estates was her duty. Many a wife in these wealthy families gained an identity and a dignity from presiding over a hierarchy of servants, relatives, and charities. Even among the less affluent, the wife's sphere was not unimportant:* the wife of William Bennett, a music teacher who gave lessons from nine to nine, managed all his appointments, bill collections, and book-keeping; while the wife of Mr Bradley, headmaster of Marlborough, managed all of his finances.[22]

More important than managing Hawarden or the finances of the headmaster of Marlborough was the raising of children. 'Take care of my boy,' wrote Captain Blackwood from Lord Nelson's *Victory* to his wife on the eve of Trafalgar, 'make him a better man than his father.'[23] That command, 'take care of my boy,' was given by many an early Victorian father, and not only to wives, but to governesses, nannies, grooms, tutors, and school masters. There are far fewer examples in these memoirs of a father's punishing children than of their receiving the blows of nannies, governesses, and school masters. The father much preferred to be remembered for presiding over festive occasions. On such occasions he expressed the third of the three features

---

*   As Professor Gorham's essay in this book indicates. (Editor)

defining the paterfamilias of the Victorian governing class, that of benevolence.

Their reputation for benevolence was in many ways a luxury: it followed from their sovereignty, their latitudinarian outlook, and their great wealth. The landed peerage and gentry, largely Anglican and often easygoing in manner, worried less about spoiling their children than did the evangelical fathers of the mercantile world. The fathers of landed families were often absent at quarter sessions, assizes, Parliament, or the hunt; or else they were just indifferent. But such an absence was no great loss if the groom had the horses ready or if the gamekeeper took the boys fishing. Absent fathers are never smothering, never tyrannical. They also can appear at Christmas or Easter. 'The holidays spent in the country,' wrote the First Earl of Cranbrook of his father, 'were of course the times during which we saw most of him.' The father reserved for himself the delightful task of presenting the son a horse and the daughter a pony. A ride with papa was a serendipitous occasion. 'Had the most delightful ride,' wrote Lucy Littleton, 'with papa.'[24] Among the landed families papas were indeed great fun. They dispensed gifts, took their sons hunting, their daughters to ducal balls, and the whole family to the Alps. They paid their son's debts from university days, bought them army commissions, arranged for seats in Parliament and won them Church livings. Daughters received dowries. Sir William Gregory, sent from Ireland to an English school at ten, confessed that his father's 'great fault was too much kindness to me'.[25] There was a largess about these fathers that was built into the incomes and customs of their estates. William Keppel, the Norfolk landowner who confessed to a dislike of small children, nevertheless presided over a large happy family. He owned 7,000 acres, a pack of beagles, a stable of horses, and a large income. His children, to whom he was remote at first, all later held him in the greatest affection. Lady Dorothy Nevill also loved her father, Lord Walpole, though he was every bit as crusty and sharp-tongued as his Norfolk neighbour Keppel. He not only visited her in the nursery and took her riding, but paid bills for a season in London that included fifty balls, sixty parties, thirty dinners, and twenty-five breakfasts. Lady John Russell remembers her father, the Earl of Minto, as the bearer of the newest books from London, as well as 'the most genial and kindest of fathers'. When he was appointed head of the Admiralty he became 'something of a hero'.[26] Her memories of the great festivities at Minto House in Scotland and the dinners at their town house in London are intertwined with memories of the father who provided them.

When married, with the help of Papa's dowry, many of these aristocratic ladies lived a life far removed from the world that Sara Ellis
describes in her *Letters to the Wives of England.* The memoirs of the
Countess Dowager of Radnor bear no resemblance to Sara Ellis's world
of suffer and be still. The Countess writes: 'I got nine stag that year,
driving or stalking . . . hunted two or three days a week . . . am the
oldest of the Beaufort hunt . . . assisted by a real expert drove the
special train home from the races.'[27] Her memoirs, which include
accounts of her successful public concerts as a singer, show a free,
spirited, buoyant life. Other women, less talented, nevertheless
enjoyed privileges of membership in the wealthier classes. Mary
Ponsonby's letters to her husband, Queen Victoria's secretary, tell of
dinners with the leading politicians and intellectuals of London.
Isolated at Sandringham, Arthur Ponsonby responds, 'You are my eyes
which see the outer world . . . your advice is worth more than anyone's.'[28] Such women were, of course, not numerous except within
the peerage, the gentry, and the richer of the mercantile and professional world. They viewed the paterfamilias as the source of
benevolence rather than tyranny.

So did their sons and daughters. They all belonged to an extended
family household, with a father often absent, but when present, less
concerned with family bible readings than fox-hunts and balls. Even
those gentry families that were evangelical, knew much merriment and
benevolence. Such a home was that of Sir Wilfred Lawson sen., and jun.,
of Cumberland. The family of these two adherents of temperance,
evangelicalism and radical politics was one of the happiest in England.
'Our Father,' said Sir Wilfred Lawson jun., 'provided every imaginable
pleasure for us all . . . pets, gardens, ponies,' and when older 'the best
horses that could be obtained.' Such a home formed a considerable
contrast for Lawson jun. to his days in a grim Yorkshire boarding school,
so much in fact that when he became a father he preserved his sons
from the horrors of boarding school by hiring a tutor. The tutor later
wrote, 'never have I witnessed a happier home'.[29]

Not all homes were as happy as that of the Sir Wilfred Lawsons
nor all fathers as benevolent. Neither were all fathers as sovereign as
Captain Jones-Parry or as remote as W.G. Ward. Benevolence,
sovereignty, and remoteness were the predominant not the universal
traits of the early Victorian fathers. There were always exceptions.

There were in particular many who were not remote as fathers.
Two of these are Stanley Lees Giffard, editor of the *Evening Standard*

and Archibald Alison, Sheriff of Glasgow. Both refused to send their
boys to boarding school. Giffard rose every morning at 4 a.m. and
Alison at 8 a.m. in order to instruct their sons in the classics. Giffard's
son later worked side by side with his father on the *Standard* while
Alison says it was on long evening walks with his son that he tested
out his ideas for his *History of the French Revolution*.[30] Urban fathers
often aped the aristocracy in sending their sons to boarding schools,
but they departed from aristocratic ways in welcoming them back to
the business at age fifteen or sixteen: such was the case at Richard
Cadbury's chocolate firm, Jacob Bright's textile mill, Sir John
Lubbock's bank, Peter Denny's shipyard, Mr Clarke's silver shop, and
Samuel Morley's hosiery firm.[31] In the case of the three brothers
Frederick, Matthew and Rowland Hill, each in his own right a
distinguished Victorian, an intimacy with their genial father expanded
rather than contracted by going to school, since the school they
joined was run by their father – and by the boys too. Not all fathers
were remote.[32]

Neither were all fathers sovereign, though here the exceptions are
far fewer – perhaps not more than ten of the fathers of the sample
of 168 Victorians. Sir Edward Clarke's father, the London silver
merchant, was one of the exceptions. His evangelical wife ran their
household. She forbid her timid and amiable husband from attending
the theatre he so dearly loved. Early Victorian wives could be strong.
Of Mrs Bradley, wife of the headmaster of Marlborough, it was said,
'her influence over her husband was paramount'. But wives were not
the only competitors for power. In the Rathbone household at
Liverpool, the grandmother was 'the central domestic deity of the
family', while in the Paget family the grandfather was 'a veritable
grand seigneur'. Sometimes within the household a governess or nurse
held sway. The Scottish nanny into whose care 'Squire' Chaplin gave
his children, remained 'the family autocrat long after they left the
nursery'.[33]

Fathers were also sometimes anything but benevolent. Here the
exceptions increase. Mr Barnett, an iron manufacturer and father of
Canon Barnett, was malevolent rather than benevolent. When his
daughter-in-law asked his wife why she invariably indulged his
uncompromising selfishness she replied that to cross him caused only
'long days of unbroken sulkiness which hang like a pall over the
house'.[34] The bulk of these memoirs were published before 1914.
They are not only full of uncritical praise but they are also largely
about very successful people. One can thus expect little that is critical

of the marriages of these eminent men and women. But when speaking of other people's marriages some of the memoirs do give hints that not all was felicity. Charles Darwin's father spoke of 'how many miserable wives he had known' while the Unitarian minister, the Reverend Stopford Brooke, brooded, around 1880, over 'the multitude of wives and mothers who . . . are condemned to joyless, loveless lives, exhausted by toil, ill treated by brutal husbands.'[35] Benevolence, like sovereignty and remoteness, though a dominant characteristic of many early Victorian fathers, was by no means a universal trait.

They were also traits that became less dominant as the large, extended, families of the wealthy Anglican landowners gave way before evangelicalism and urbanization, the two transforming forces of the nineteenth century. Each of these forces alone tended to make for a more nuclear family, evangelicalism by centring the family around prayers, bible reading, and serious morality; urbanization by requiring smaller homes and by providing schools near enough so that children could reside at home. But the real transformation came when the home was both evangelical and urban. One has only to think of the Macaulays, the Wilberforces, and the Thorntons of Clapham, or, in its Quaker form, the Cadburys of Birmingham and the Brights of Rochdale, or in its Scottish Presbyterian form, the Reverend Guthrie's household in Edinburgh. These deeply religious urban homes, whether Quaker, Presbyterian, or Church of England, produced a new type of father, one in many ways a contrast to the farmer father of Richard Cobden or the aristocratic father of the Second Earl of Malmesbury: both of whom, having sent their sons to boarding school, never visited them. For three years Malmesbury only saw his father during brief holidays, and for five years Cobden never saw his father at all.[36] The new fathers of the last half of the century would have visited their sons since they now had the railway to whisk them off to Rugby and Eton and a deep conviction that God demanded a closer supervision of their children. These seriously religious fathers were increasingly distrustful of public schools — that is until Thomas Arnold and others reformed them. Raising children became part of one's duty to God. 'God has given us children,' wrote the Reverend William Palmer, father of the Earl of Selborne, Disraeli's Lord Chancellor, 'it is our part to render Him His own, for they are more truly His and we are only the instrument of His will.'[37] Many more fathers became convinced of this duty and in pursuance of it they added two new traits to the pater-familias of the Victorian governing classes: the admonitory and the self-conscious.

The new father felt it his duty to admonish. But since he often sent his son to a boarding school, albeit a reformed and Godly one, he had to do so in letters, a task he performed with energy and self-consciousness. 'Did I lecture you too much,' said the shipbuilder, William Denny, to his son in one of many sententious letters. 'The greater the distance from us,' wrote Richard Cadbury to his eight-year-old son, 'the closer the tie of love.'[38] Both were self-conscious remarks and both were part of a series of letters filled with moral injunctions. The letters of the Congregationalist Samuel Morley, the Presbyterian Reverend Thomas Guthrie, the evangelical Reverend Charles Bridges and the Unitarian Reverend Stopford Brooke were equally admonitory. They are crammed with moral strictures, prudent maxims and religious pieties. They warn against idleness and cheating in school, recommend respectability of dress and politeness in manners, urge the straight way, however others may laugh, but insist that it is still wise to try to please others. They urge an hour of prayer on rising and counsel never to forget the Sovereign Being who is all-seeing. Above all they urge resolution, struggle, and manliness. 'Despise,' said Denny the shipbuilder, 'all effeminate notions.' These letters fill up many pages of the memoirs of these men as they do the memoirs of Macaulay and Wilberforce. They form a distinct contrast to the brief, taciturn letters in the memoirs of Anglican landowners and military men. Indeed, in many of the latter memoirs there are no letters to their sons at all. What letters there are tell of politics, society, war and empire, but very little if anything of their children. In some memoirs they are mentioned only when born. For the urban and devout father the family became a work of art and a duty to God, for the rural and conventionally Anglican father it was an ancient and tried institution. The biographer of the Reverend Stopford Brooke, wrote that 'Brooke's home was to him an end in itself.' The memoir of Richard Cadbury has a chapter entitled 'Home Life', and the memoir of William Denny one entitled 'Paterfamilias'. Denny, said his biographer, 'made conscience habitually of parental duty.' No such chapters occur in the memoirs of naval captains, army colonels, and explorers. The biographer of the explorer, Sir Samuel Baker, writes how Baker, distracted at the death of his wife, journeyed off to Constantinople. He left four small children behind with relatives, a practice he continued as, year after year, he won fame as the explorer of the headwaters of the Nile. His letters neither mentioned his children nor asked about them. Despite this fact, his biographer concludes, 'His home life approximated to that of any other Englishman of his class and station.'[39]

That Samuel Baker's home life was typical may surprise readers of
Edmund Gosse's *Father and Son* or Samuel Butler's *The Way of All
Flesh*. But 'for his class and station', it probably was a typical home life.
Of the 168 Victorians in the sample only twenty-six came from Quaker,
Congregational, Unitarian and evangelical Church of England homes.
Ten more were raised in the Scottish Church. One hundred and five of
the 168 were raised in Anglican homes that were not evangelical and
most of their fathers (and in turn most of the sons when they became
fathers) were not intensely religious. The landlords, politicians, civil
servants, military officers, barristers, headmasters, explorers, and men
of fashion who governed England and its Empire were not the kind of
fathers who smothered poor Edmund Gosse and Ernest Pontifex. The
fathers of the governing classes sent their sons off to school at age nine,
preferred dining at the club to dining with their wives and spent their
days ruling Britain and its Empire and enjoying the wealth it produced.
There were thus throughout the nineteenth century many fathers who
were remote, sovereign and benevolent and very seldom admonitory or
self-conscious.

The great number of such fathers in the early part of the century
and their persistence into the latter part, raise two important questions:
what effect did they have on the formation of the psychological attitudes
of their children and what impact did they have on the social outlook
of these future rulers of England?

The effect on their children's psychological development was
considerable and complex. Of the many ways that they influenced
them three are particularly important: the imposition on the child
of a strong super ego, the delegation of their day-to-day discipline to
the various agents of the patriarchal household, and, in the case of the
boys, the use of boarding schools to reinforce masculine values. Modern
psychologists have found all three of these approaches in some ways
functional. A strong patriarchal father, says Erik Erikson, helps form a
strong super ego. Employing other agents to discipline children, argues
Robert Sears, reduces damaging conflicts with parents. When a father is
absent, says Daniel Brown, other adult males can help boys find a
masculine identity.[40]

In the formation of the child's super ego the early Victorian father
was certainly decisive. The memoirs of the 168 Victorians are full of
recollections of strong fathers. In some cases he is tall, handsome,
exceedingly charming; in others 'a distinct, powerful and commanding
personality'. In the minds of some he was 'the perfect English

gentleman', 'a great sportsman and a good shot', 'Master of the Fox-hounds', or even just 'the President of the tea table'. The portraits are often idealized: 'a remarkable man endowed with many gifts', 'a wonderful charm of manner . . . ready of wit', or simply 'I never knew so good a man'. He was often imperious: 'his will . . . was law', 'he was strict . . . as befits the father of a large family', 'no one could smoke without his permission', 'he destined me for the Church', 'he was sharp of tongue, nervous, a great master at denunciation'. There was some-thing gigantic about father, particularly for Henry Bradshaw who remembered 'standing as a child on the outstretched palm of his father'. Whether charming or stern, dour or merry, the image of the strong father informs most of these memoirs.[41] They could not escape it even when, like Sir Edmund Hornby, they were assigned at a very early age to tutors. Sir Edmund remembered his Scottish tutor as 'a species of Dominie Sampson', and his English one as 'Dear old Trott', but he claims both led him to crooked ways. 'I had,' he thus confesses, 'but one mainstay to keep me straight. I loved my father. To please him I would suffer much; to pain him was my greatest dread.' Most early Victorian fathers in these memoirs were men of pronounced opinions and undoubted authority. They abound in certitudes and were entirely unselfconscious about asserting their prerogatives. They were also often an owner of a great estate and family name and possessor of local or national office, all of which reinforced the children's awe of them. Lady Aberdeen remembers in her childhood 'an abiding terror of bringing the names of my parents and their forebears into disgrace.'[42]

Hornby's dread of paining his father, Lady Aberdeen's terror of disgracing her parents and Bradshaw's memory of 'an outstretched palm' show how formidable was the impact on children of the pre-Victorian and early Victorian father. They may have been often physically absent but they were almost always a mental presence. Psycho-analytical studies of the absent fathers in the families of ancient Athens, black America, or the Germany of the first World War form no analogue to the children of the early Victorian paterfamilias. The Victorian father was often away at London or in the Empire, but he wrote letters, paid bills, gave advice, and at holidays returned in all his glory. He thus established himself firmly in the children's psyche, employing his exalted position and infallible opinions in the fashioning of their system of values. After doing such, he could depart for London. 'Once a patriarchal super ego is firmly established in early childhood,' observes Erik Erikson, 'you can give youth rope.'[43]

Giving Victorian youth rope meant delegating the upbringing of the child to mothers, grandmothers, uncles, aunts, governesses, tutors, grooms, and gamekeepers. Such a delegation began with wet nurses and nannies. Even the mothers, whose first duty was to attend to the pater-familias rather than to the children, were often absent from the nursery. The children were thus left to the discipline, at times lax and at times over severe, of nannies, governesses, and tutors. Jonathan Gathorne-Hardy has shown in *The Rise and Fall of the British Nanny* how at the end of the eighteenth century the nanny became more important than the mother in the raising of the children of the upper classes. Quite a few memoirs corroborate this fact. The Seventh Earl of Shaftesbury owed his religious convictions to his nurse, not his parents, who neglected him, while Sir Arthur Blackwood whose father was off fighting with Nelson at Trafalgar, confessed that 'the most distinct impression that remains to this day is the personality of dear old nurse'.[44] The system of delegation, though perhaps lacking in the warm affection of the nuclear family, was not without its merits. 'Any coercive control from a parent with whom the child identifies,' writes Leonard Benson in *Fatherhood*, 'has a more disturbing impact than a comparable effort from a more neutral or distant parent.'[45] The early Victorian father enjoyed a rather advantageous position: he could delegate severe discipline to others and reserve for himself the presentation of gifts and the delivery of oracular pronouncements.

The delegation within the household of so many responsibilities along with frequent absences did, however, raise problems. It weakened, for the boys, a close identification with their father and so hindered the development of their masculinity — a quality highly prized by early Victorian fathers. The problem was sometimes solved by finding a surrogate father. The Earl of Dalhousie, whose father did not recognize him at eighteen, found such a surrogate father in a tutor 'to whom', he avowed, 'I owe greater obligation than to any man living.' The Earl of Iddesleigh, who was sent to school at eight, praised his tutor for his 'careful and paternal interest'.[46] Gamekeepers and grooms also gained the affection of small boys and the affection lasted a long while. The Earl of Radnor was much saddened by the death of his old game-keeper, 'Robey', while the Earl of Rosebery went out of his way to attend the funeral of the family groom, long 'a great favorite'.[47] Old Robey of course, or Rosebery's groom, could not quite qualify as a surrogate father any more than 'old Benjy' in *Tom Brown's School Days.* Gamekeepers and grooms were not that high in the social hierarchy. But the Robeys and Benjys, along with the countless grooms, tutors, and schoolmasters did represent the world of masculinity that the father was too busy to represent by his day to day presence.

There was in fact usually no one surrogate father in the process of initiation into the masculine world. That initiation, begun by game-keepers, grooms, uncles, and older brothers in the extended household, was a socializing experience, one that was continued at the boarding school — though there the feminine element was quite removed. In that experience there was seldom a single surrogate father. Sometimes schoolmasters loom large, occasionally the headmaster, but more often the dominant influence is the older boys. Their institution of fagging was indeed praised in 1849 by *Fraser's Magazine* because of the need of 'a paternal superintendence' that would teach obedience and duty. The Earl of Granville, who went to Beaconsfield at age eight, remembered years later that 'the present Duke of Northumberland was at the head of the school, was held much in awe . . . but he took me under his protection and inspired lasting feelings of gratitude.' Granville said his friendships at Beaconsfield were far more lasting than those made at Eton, a judgement with which the Marquess of Crewe concurred, saying of preparatory schools, 'Few intimacies, are closer than those made at preparatory schools, fresh from home and not yet making cardinal virtues of reticence and self-reliance.'[48] That intimacy which the father did not give was found in the close friendship of boys. It was an intimacy that was entirely masculine and one which valued manliness, courage, loyalty, honour, even the daring and the mischievous, more than it honoured piety, intellect or sexual fastidiousness.

The easy-going Anglican paterfamilias tolerated in fact many sexual deviations. Collin Brooks, the author of *Mock Turtle; Being the Memoirs of a Victorian Gentleman*, who was born in 1848, later wrote that no boy from a public school was ever 'in ingenuous ignorance of the major facts of life, if I can so phrase the delicate thing'. He then adds, 'The only thing which saved [them] from being corrupted by boarding schools was . . . their having been corrupted by grooms and servant maids . . .'[49] The sexual play only increased the intimacy of schoolboy for schoolboy and lessened it for their father.

The latitudinarian father, by not preaching or censuring such conduct, at least did not become an object of fear and hate. He only became less intimate. But intimacy between father and son embarrassed manly Victorians. The biographers of Archibald Alison, Isambard Brunel, and the radical MP Henry Fawcett, chose to describe the unusual intimacy these fathers and sons had by reference to comradeship or to the relation of brother to brother. 'Our intercourse,' writes

Archibald Alison of his relation with his son, 'was not like father and son, but like an older and younger brother'. The relationship of Henry Fawcett and his father, concludes Leslie Stephen, was that 'of affection-ate comradeship', rather than the 'more ordinary relation, in which affection is coloured by deference and partial reserve'.[50]

Comradeship not fatherhood is the key institution governing the later development of Etonians and Harrovians, Oxonians and Canta-brigians. Has then the awesome paterfamilias faded away before the other-directedness of the peer group? David Riesman, an authority on other-directedness, suggests that fathers do not fade away so easily. 'Adolescents,' he argues, 'may go through a stage of other directedness and identity diffusion in what seems like over dependence upon peers, but then when they reach adulthood . . . parental influences reappear.'[51] The early Victorian father had delegated his functions and duties, not abdicated them. The boarding schools, for centuries the creators of the male governing classes, carried on the father's values of manliness and courage. William Henry Goschen was delighted when his son George, the future Chancellor of the Exchequer, wrote of success in football at Rugby. The Duke of Newcastle gloried in his son's letter that described a fierce fight he had won at Eton.[52]

Being sent to school at nine was a wrenching experience. Tear-stained letters tell of homesickness, particularly during the first weeks at the school. But letters soon come telling of delight in school life. They complain of beatings. bullying, and fagging, yet come to believe in them. Lord Tavistock, eldest son of the Duke of Bedford, argued that fagging made boys 'tyrants and brutes', but added 'it may be a good thing on the whole'. The radical MP, Henry Labouchere, recollects vividly the frequent beatings at his school, to which he went at the age of six, but concludes wistfully that those were 'the days of the bull dog breed, when Britons were men'.[63] The early Victorian father certainly did not spoil his son. Imperious of will, pronounced in opinion, sover-eign in the household, he gave both firm values and a rather unloving (but not ungenerous) upbringing, and then sent his son to schools of harsh regimen and manly ways. The result was the late Victorian imperial governing class, men of reserve and reticence, of honour and loyalty, of comradeship and good fun, and, above all, of autonomous personalities. They were unusually stoical and independent. Buttressed by a strong super ego, a clear sense of class and family identity, and the habit of finding affection in nannies, sisters, brothers, grooms, maids, cousins and schoolmates, they became quite self-contained and, on the surface, well adjusted men. They were good men for imperial posts.

They were also hard and calloused, men who could put down the natives and men who found much of their sexual pleasure outside marriage and much of their intimacy in the comradeship of the club.

The early Victorian father (and the schools he supported) not only bred these psychological traits into many of their sons, but they also bequeathed to them their dominant social outlook, that of paternalism. The paterfamilias was the head of a very large family, one that included a myriad of relatives, servants, and dependents. Charles Adderley, newly married and heir to a very large estate, wrote rather unself-consciously in 1843: 'We at once began home duties to our neighbours in the happiest way.'[54] In the large landed estates home duties extend-ed to neighbours and dependents. Lady St Helier remembers a child-hood when 'our tenants, labourers and servants were friends in every sense of the word and [their] traditional affection was an influence and power . . . impossible to exaggerate.' Such a sentiment would not seem strange to many of the aristocracy. The Earl of Radnor, when his eldest was born, gave a fête for the villagers and took the baby down to the farm 'for the neighbours to see'. Lord Walpole had his daughter 'married in the old English style, the tenantry drawn up at the gate and all the neighbourhood jolly and gay.' Sir Neville Lyttleton remembers playing endless cricket games with the village boys and Catherine Gladstone remembers at Hawarden 'school children, farmers and villagers . . . [at] a great party . . . with high tea in the drawing room and ale in the servants hall'.[55]

Families were not only extended in the sense of the dependents of the great estate but in terms of relatives. Cousins too belonged to the great family, and aunts and uncles and grandparents. The aristocrat even incorporated neighbouring children. Lord Exeter of Ryall, Lincoln-shire, regarded the children of the neighbouring squire 'as belonging. to his own family'. It was a world in which families were not only extended but interchangeable. William Wilberforce seemed to Marian Thorton so entirely of her family that she wrote 'I can not describe my first impression of him any more than of my own father.' Lord Russell describes Holland House as his second home, while Lord Montagu describes his superior officer in the navy as 'almost as much a father to me as an Admiral'.[66] The paternal mode of thought and social organization came out of the extended and interchangeable family of the aristocracy. The Reverend William Palmer was a paternal authority to all the parishioners of Mixbury in Oxfordshire and the Reverend Thomas Guthrie regarded every child in his ragged school as part of his 'large family'. The citizens of Edinburgh called them

'Guthrie's pur bairns'. J.M. Dent had some of the apprentices of his early publishing firm to live in his home. Samuel Morley, Richard Cadbury and William Denny ran their textile, chocolate and shipbuilding businesses along strictly paternalist lines. William Denny told his son that life consisted of three elements, 'work . . . helping others, and home', and he added, 'and from the last springs the force of the other two'.[57]

In the benevolent and authoritarian management of his shipbuilding firm and his many civic charities William Denny showed his son in detail how the 'home' can be the model for work and for helping others, just as Richard Cadbury showed his sons how a chocolate firm and a Sunday school could be like a large family. The paternal authority of such fathers extended beyond the living-room of a nuclear family. It made paternal authority generalized, impersonal, and hierarchical; not intimate, confining or enveloping. It formed a pattern of authority that was repeated in the public schools and universities, in the army and navy, and in the Church and local government. 'A well-conducted college,' said the explorer Samuel Baker to the boys of his old school, 'should be a model of paternal government.'[58] Such a model provided the mid-Victorian governing classes with a paternalist social outlook that not only had deep roots in England's past history and existing institutions, but psychic roots in the very mode whereby the pater-familias directed the raising of children. He taught his children to consider that the deference of those below them formed as much a part of the nature of things as did the power of the landowner, millowner, or JP to discipline and supervise those dependent on them. There was for them no clear line at the local level between the private and the public or between the extended family of cousins and servants and the landed estate or factory. When the eldest son became a JP and MP, he accordingly thought of solving social problems at a local level, within his own sphere and in a paternal manner. It was the extension of the patriarchy of the large extended household to society.

Not all Victorian fathers, of course, had great estates on which to establish extended patriarchal familes — nor even large factories. Victorian fathers, even when limited to those of the governing classes, formed a very diverse group. It is thus difficult to talk of the 'typical' father. English society was too pluralistic and her rulers too often eccentric. There were many kinds of fathers varying from class to class. The focus of this essay has been mainly on the fathers of the wealthy governing classes of the first half of the nineteenth century. And yet even within that smaller world of the governing classes two models are needed in order to bring out their varying characteristics. The first is that of the rural, Anglican, landowning, and latitudinarian father of the large extended family (with cognate branches among the Church of England clergy, the military, and civil and imperial servants). The second model is that of the middle class, urban, earnestly religious father of the nuclear family. Each of these models had its own image of the Victorian paterfamilias, the first of a stout, crusty, cheerful country gentleman, attired in a hunting outfit, gun in hand, waiting at the stable for a last ride with a son about to depart for a boarding school. The second is of a tall solemn gentleman, attired in a black frock coat, standing in the drawing-room, bible in hand, awaiting family prayers. Both kinds of fathers were, if we can believe Victorian memoirists and twentieth-century biographers, usually decent, kindly, and well intentioned.

There were of course differences. The sons from the seriously religious nuclear homes rebelled or fell away from their father's values more often than the sons of the latitudinarian fathers of the extended family. Zachary Macaulay, William Wilberforce, the Reverend Charles Bridges and Thomas Henry Buckle — all of the keenest and most serious Protestant beliefs — produced as sons an agnostic historian, a Catholic priest, a teacher of positivism, and the historian of rationalism. It was not that the fathers of the nuclear families were not benevolent and just, but that earnest religion in urban houses can be smothering.

Far different were the relaxed values of the rural Anglican gentry and peers. The memoirs of forty Victorians (from the sample of 168) were of the sons, daughters, or wives of peers. None of them showed any signs of rebellion, any falling away, indeed any widening at all of the generation gap. Neither do the memoirs of the eighteen military heroes show any departure from paternal values. The fathers of thirteen of these eighteen heroes were military men themselves. Their sons dutifully carried on the traditions of the British officer class just as MPs and lords carried on the traditions of their fathers in Parliament. Fatherhood was a conservative institution in Victorian England, one that prompted continuity more than it did rebellion.

The fathers of the men and women in the sample of 168 were by and large successful fathers. Their children not only loved and esteemed them but in their own careers fulfilled their father's proudest expectations, a fact which points to a second narrowing focus of this essay: it is an essay dealing largely with those fathers whose sons and daughters inherited or won enough fame to deserve an adulatory memoir. There is also a third narrowing factor. Their accomplishments won them memoirs that ended up in the historical, not the literary and artistic sections, of the Harvard and Dartmouth libraries. The above analysis is thus of the fathers of those who succeeded more often in the political rather than (with the exception of historians like Buckle and Macaulay) the literary and artistic world of the governing classes. It is thus largely a portrait of worldly and practical fathers, of wordly and practical sons, sons who mixed well in school, won friends in clubs, gained promotion in army, navy and church, rose to power in Parliament and ended ruling others both as statesmen and as fathers. It is an analysis of those who socialized successfully, held to the dominant values, were self-reliant, could be ruthless, but also gregarious and generous, of the sons of fathers who ran their large households with an imperious sway and did not bother overmuch with the raising of their children. These fathers were confident that their wives, trusted servants, and society's established institutions would see that their children were properly reared. The remoteness, sovereignty, and benevolence of the early Victorian paterfamilias, combined with the sociability of the extended family and the manliness of the boarding school to produce the late Victorian ruling class. These rulers in turn imposed their paternal outlook and their independent temperament on every sphere of English society and on the farthest reaches of the British Empire.

Notes

1.   The six were C.E. Childers, Sir George Grey, Major-General Sir Hugh McCalmont. Lord Norton, Henry Reeve and Lord Rosebery.

2.   Reginald Farrar, *The Life of Frederic Farrar* (New York, 1904), p. 1; Sir W. Lee-Warner, *The Life of the Marquis of Dalhousie* (London, 1904), p. 18.

3.   Edith H. Vane-Tempest-Stewart, Marchioness of Londonderry, *Henry Chaplin, A Memoir* (London, 1926), p. 114. H.R. Dent, *Memoir of J.M. Dent, 1849–1920* (London, 1928), p. 42.

4.   Ralph Nevill, *London Clubs* (London, 1921), p. 143; S.M. Ellis, *A Mid Victorian Pepys* (London, 1930), p. vi.

5.   Georgina Battiscombe, *Mrs Gladstone, the Portrait of a Marriage* (London 1956), p. 59; Arthur Miall, *Life of Edward Miall* (London, 1884), p. 33.

6.   T.H. Hollingsworth, 'British Peerage', *Population Studies* (November, 1964) Supplement II, p. 35; William Purcell, *Onward Christian Soldier, a Life of Sabine Baring-Gould* (London, 1957), p. 2.

7.   Lord and Lady Aberdeen, *We Twa* (London, 1925), p. 163; Victor Montagu, *Reminiscences of Admiral Montagu* (London, 1910), p. 6.

8.   Nine were educated at home until sent to university or into the armed forces. Only seventeen attended a local school alone while residing at home. There is no information on twenty-one of the men. All the women were educated at home.

9.   Alfred E. Gathorne-Hardy (ed.), *First Earl of Cranbrook* (London, 1910),
      p. 13; Sir Francis Doyle, *Reminiscences* (London, 1886), pp. 29, 57,
      379; Lady Sybil Lubbock, *Memoirs of the Earl of Desart* (London, 1956),
      p. 27.
10.   E.H. Coleridge (ed.), *Life and Correspondences of John Duke Lord
      Coleridge* (London, 1904), p. 20.
11.   G.F.A. Best, *Lord Shaftesbury* (New York, 1964), p. 17.
12.   Violet V. Mann, *Life and Times of Sir Henry Keppel* (London, 1967),
      p. 26; Wilfred Ward, *William George Ward and the Oxford Movement*
      (London, 1893), p. 67.
13.   Robert Rhodes James, *Rosebery* (London, 1963), p. 125.
14.   L.T.C. Rolt, *Isambard Kingdom Brunel* (London, 1957), p. 99.
15.   John Martineau, *The Life of the Fifth Duke of Newcastle* (London,
      1908), p. 10.
16.   Sir S.H. Jones-Parry, *An Old Soldier's Memoirs* (London, 1897), p. 6.
17.   D.K. and C.J. Guthrie (eds.), *Autobiography of Thomas Guthrie* (New
      York, 1874), p. 32.
18.   Arthur H.D. Acland, *Memoirs of Sir Thomas Dyke Acland* (London,
      1902), p. 18.
19.   Coleridge (ed.), *Life of Lord Coleridge*, p. 15; Acland, *Memoirs of Sir
      Thomas Dyke Acland*, p. 47; Spencer Walpole, *Life of Lord John Russell*
      (London, 1889), pp. 43, 57; John Prest, *Lord John Russell* (London,
      1972), p. 11.
20.   Dent, *Memoir of J.M. Dent*, pp. 45-46; Sir James Marchant, *Dr John
      Clifford* (London, 1929), p. 171; J.G. Lockhart, *Charles Lindley Viscount
      Halifax* (London, 1935), p. 162.
21.   Sarah Ellis, *Family Secrets* (London, 1842), I, p. 105.
22.   Battiscombe, *Mrs Gladstone*, pp. 48-52, 71, 99, 123; W.S. Childe-
      Pemberton, *Lord Norton* (London, 1909), p. 44; J.R. Sterndale Bennett,
      The Life of W.S. Bennett (Cambridge, 1907), p. 197; Edith N. Lewis
      (Bradley), *As Youth Sees It* (Boston, 1935), p. 28.
23.   Mrs Arthur Blackwood, *Sir Arthur Blackwood* (London, 1896), p. 4.
24.   Gathorne-Hardy (ed.), *First Earl of Cranbrook*, p. 75; John Bailey (ed.),
      The Diary of Lady Frederick Cavendish (London, 1927), I, p. 23.
25.   Sir William Gregory, *An Autobiography* (London, 1894), p. 139.
26.   Vivian Stuart, *The Beloved Little Admiral, the Life and Times of Admiral
      of the Fleet, The Hon. Sir Henry Keppel, 1809–1904* (London, 1967),
      pp. 26-7; Ralph Nevill (ed.), *The Reminiscences of Lady Dorothy
      Nevill* (London, 1906), pp. 2, 52; D. MacCarthy and A. Russell, *Lady John
      Russell* (London, 1911), pp. 2, 6.
27.   Helen Countess Dowager of Radnor, *From a Great Grandmother's Arm-
      chair* (London, 1928), pp. 56, 63.
28.   Arthur Ponsonby, *Henry Ponsonby, Queen Victoria's Private Secretary*
      (London, 1942), p. 372.
29.   G.W.E. Russell (ed.), *Sir Wilfred Lawson* (London, 1809), pp. 5, 6, 8, 283.
30.   Sir Archibald Alison, *Some Account of My Life and Wiritings: An Auto-
      biography* (Edinburgh, 1883), I, p. 355; Alice Wilson-Fox, *The Earl of
      Halsbury* (London, 1929), pp. 8-9, 27.
31.   Helen Alexander, *Richard Cadbury of Birmingham* (London, 1906),
      p. 76; G.M. Trevelyan, *John Bright* (Boston, 1913), p. 15; Horace G.
      Hutchinson, *Life of Sir John Lubbock, Lord Avebury* (London, 1914),
      p. 23; Alexander B. Bruce, *Life of William Denny* (London, 1889), p. 27;
      Sir Edward Clarke, *The Story of My Life* (New York, 1919), p. 25;
      E. Hodder, *Life of Samuel Morley* (London, 1887), p. 20.

32.   Frederick Hill, *An Autobiography of Fifty Years in Times of Reform* (London, 1894), pp. 22, 47. See also the essay by Professor Gorham in this book.

33.   Clarke, *The Story of My Life*, pp. 8-10; Lewis, *As Youth Sees It*, p. 28; Eleanor F. Rathbone, *William Rathbone* (London, 1905), p. 93; Marchionness of Londonderry, *Henry Chaplin*, p. 114; Montagu, *Reminiscences of Admiral Montagu*, p. 2.

34.   Henrietta D. Barnett, *Canon Barnett* (London, 1919), I, pp. 14-15.

35.   Francis Darwin, *Life and Letters of Charles Darwin* (New York, 1888), p. 12; L.P. Jacks, *Life and Letters of Stopford Brooke* (New York, 1917), p. 280.

36.   Earl of Malmesbury, *Memoirs of an Ex-Minister* (London, 1884), pp. 12-13; John Morley, *Richard Cobden* (Boston, 1881), p. 3.

37.   Roundel Palmer, Earl of Selborne, *Memorials* (London, 1896-1898), I, p. 150.

38.   Bruce, *Life of William Denny*, p. 298; Alexander, *Richard Cadbury*, p. 57.

39.   Bruce, *Life of William Denny*, pp. 297, 298; Jacks, *Life and Letters of Stopford Brooke*, p. 413; T.D. Murray and A.S. White, *Sir Samuel Baker* (London, 1895), pp. 35-7, 418.

40.   Erik Erikson, *Childhood and Society* (New York, 1964), pp. 270-93; Robert Sears and Daniel Brown, quoted in Leonard Benson, *Fatherhood* (New York, 1968), pp. 198, 236.

41.   G.W. Rothero, *Henry Bradshaw* (London, 1888), p. 2.

42.   Sir Edmund Hornby, *An Autobiography* (Boston, 1928), pp. 9-10, 16-17; Lord and Lady Aberdeen, *We Twa*, p. 93.

43.   Erikson, *Childhood and Society*, p. 293.

44.   Mrs Arthur Blackwood, *Sir Arthur Blackwood, KCB* (London, 1896), p. 5.

45.   Benson, *Fatherhood*, pp. 198, 214, 236.

46.   Lee-Warner, *The Life of the Marquis of Dalhousie*, p. 8; Andrew Lang, *First Earl of Iddesleigh* (Edinburgh, 1890), p. 9.

47.   Marquis of Crewe, *Lord Rosebery* (London, 1931), p. 162.

48.   *Fraser's Magazine*, September, 1849, p. 295; Lord Edmund Fitzmaurice, *Life of the Second Earl of Granville* (London, 1905), p. 12; Crewe, *Lord Rosebery*, p. 12.

49.   Collin Brooks, *Mock Turtle; Being the Memoirs of a Victorian Gentleman* (New York, 1931), p. 43.

50.   Alison, *Some Account of My Life and Writings*, I, p. 556; Leslie Stephen, *Life of Henry Fawcett* (London, 1885), p. 45.

51.   David Riesman, quoted in Benson, *Fatherhood*, p. 214.

52.   Arthur D. Elliot, *The Life of George Joachim Goschen, First Viscount Goschen, 1831–1907* (London, 1911), I, p. 12; John Martineau, *The Life of Henry Pelham, Fifth Duke of Newcastle, 1811–1864* (London, 1908), p. 15.

53.   Walpole, *Life of Lord John Russell*, p. 9; Hesketh Pearson, *Labby, the Life and Character of Henry Labouchere* (London, 1936), p. 18.

54.   W.S. Childe-Pemberton, *Lord Norton* (London, 1909), p. 50.

55.   Susan M.E. St Helier, *Memories of Fifty Years* (London, 1909), p. 1; Radnor, *From a Great Grandmother's Armchair*, p. 52; Nevill (ed.), *The Reminiscences of Lady Dorothy Nevill*, p. 65; Battiscombe, *Mrs Gladstone*, p. 99.

56.   Marchioness of Londonderry, *Henry Chaplin*, p. 10; E.M. Forster, *Marian Thornton* (New York, 1956), p. 34; Prest, *Lord John Russell*, p. 10; Montagu, *Reminiscences of Admiral Montagu*, p. 43.

57.   Palmer, *Memorials*, I, pp. 57-62; D. and C. Guthrie, *Autobiography of*

Thomas Guthrie, p. 308; Dent, *Memoir of J.M. Dent*, p. 35; Bruce, *Life of William Denny*, p. 287.
58.   Murray and White, *Sir Samuel Baker*, p. 13.

5 LOVE AND POSSESSION IN A VICTORIAN HOUSEHOLD: THE EXAMPLE OF THE RUSKINS

Michael Brooks

> 'Our God is a household God,
> as well as a heavenly one.'
> *The Lamp of Memory*

John Ruskin wrote two of the most important literary documents on the Victorian family and there is a striking disparity between them. The first, *Sesame and Lilies*, contained an idealization of what has come to be regarded as the characteristic Victorian middle-class home with its strict separation of domestic life from work and its equally firm separation of sexual roles. In Ruskin's loving — one might fairly say longing — words, the home is a place of peace and order, separated from the world outside by a metaphorical wall composed of delicate feelings and instinctive withdrawals and by a literal one composed of the bricks which surround a suburban garden. Here the mother rules, and here the father refreshes himself after a day in the coarsening world of commerce. That *Sesame and Lilies* conveyed a satisfying vision to many Victorians, that it achieved something approaching official endorsement, is indicated by the many elegant editions with embossed bindings and wide margins which were presented to young ladies as graduation presents and which can still be found on the shelves of secondhand book shops. Yet the same man who projected this vision in public also wrote privately to Charles Eliot Norton of an 'almost unendurable solitude in my own home, only made more painful to me by parental love which did not and could never help me, and which was cruelly hurtful without knowing it . . .'[1] Near the end of his life, Ruskin wrote an autobiographical volume, *Praeterita*, in which he expressed both gratitude for all that his parents gave and remorse for all that they unwittingly withheld. *Praeterita* gave force to the critical reaction against the Victorian household and many of those who have commented on it have fallen into a kind of word-association game, in which the term disciplined led them on to puritanical and then to grim, cold, severe, harsh, bigoted, repressive and remorseless. Yet when we compare *Praeterita* with such a free-swinging assault on the Victorian family as Samuel Butler's autobiographical novel, *The Way of*

All Flesh, we cannot help seeing that the power of Ruskin's volume grows out of its mixed tone. He describes an austerity which seems heartless and yet insists that he is grateful for it. He describes a family life that has maimed him, yet he seeks to leap back in imagination to the boyhood paradise of his parents' home on Herne Hill. That the same man should have had so many attitudes toward his own family, all of them deeply felt, is surely a puzzle worth explaining.

To some extent, it is a puzzle that we have the means to explain. Of all the factors promoting family cohesiveness in the nineteenth century, few were more important than the letter post. Because the Ruskins wrote often, wrote at length, and saved one another's letters, we know a great deal more about the early years of John Ruskin than we do about those of other literary apologists for the Victorian family such as Coventry Patmore and Charlotte Yonge. Not that this knowledge has always been acted upon. Accounts of Ruskin's childhood have often relied on gossip and one frequently runs across claims — that young John was steadily whipped, for example — which find no support in the family correspondence. Fortunately, the study of Ruskin's life has advanced dramatically in the last two decades. It is fair to say that progress toward a fully adequate understanding of Ruskin's personality began in 1956 with the publication of Helen Gill Viljoen's *Ruskin: The Scottish Heritage*. It was intended as the prelude to a biography, which explains the odd fact that it deals largely with Ruskin's parents and ends with Ruskin's birth. That limits its appeal, and I have never met anyone not a full-time Ruskin scholar who has read it. This is a pity, for it combines empathy and strict scholarship in a way that illuminates early nineteenth-century society as well as the Ruskin family. The biography was still unfinished at the time of Professor Viljoen's death in 1974. Parts of the manuscript exist, however, and it may be that articles drawn from it will soon appear. In the meantime, we can learn a vast amount about Ruskin's early years in Professor Van Akin Burd's two-volume edition of *The Ruskin Family Letters*, which not only gathers together the correspondence but also annotates it with scholarly care. To this collection, which ends in 1843, we may add the 1845 letters from Ruskin to his parents collected in Harold Shapiro's *Ruskin in Italy*, the 1851–2 letters collected in J.L. Bradley's *Letters from Venice* and the extensive correspondence gathered together in Mary Lutyens's volumes *The Ruskins and the Grays, Young Mrs Ruskin in Venice* and *Millais and the Ruskins*. These volumes have the density of social detail that one expects in a Victorian three-decker novel. And there is still more: at the very least, we must add Admiral

Sir William James's *John Ruskin and Effie Gray*, a fascinating but excessively partisan account of Effie's marriage by a member of her family. This is a vast, unwieldy body of materials, but it does have the advantage of taking us inside a Victorian household. There was nothing casual about the ways in which the Ruskins related to one another. They were very deliberate people. They wrote at length about their duties and obligations to one another and when Euphemia Gray joined them they wrote quite explicit accounts of what they expected from a Victorian wife.

The Ruskin story has passed into academic folklore as a tragedy of sex, but Professor Viljoen clearly shows that its origins are to be found in the gritty reality of social caste. John Thomas Ruskin, our Ruskin's grandfather, was a grocer who tried, by success in business and by marriage to a daughter of the landed gentry, to step up from the status of a grocer to that of a merchant. For some years he seemed on the verge of success. John James Ruskin, our Ruskin's father, was raised with expectations. He was sent to the famous Royal High School in Edinburgh so that he might go on to the university and a lawyer's career. He was also given a genteel appreciation of the visual arts: the walls of his home were covered with engravings of such elevating scenes as *The Death of Abercromy* and *Mary Queen of Scots Making Her Escape from Loch Leven*; he was given instruction in drawing and watercolour by Alexander Nasmyth; and, just as if he were a gentleman's son, his portrait was painted by Sir Henry Raeburn. Judging by his adult letters, John James Ruskin was intended by the gods, as well as by his parents, to be a gentleman — a lover of good books, a collector of fine watercolours, a dispenser of hospitality and good conversation. Instead, financial ruin, brought on as much by the father's mental instability as by business conditions, destroyed all of John James's hopes. Instead of a learned profession and a life of culture, he would have to start from the bottom as a drab London clerk.

The family letters that survive this period show considerable emotional suffering. John James's mother kept her son vividly aware of her own distress, while encouraging him toward the success that had eluded his father. Like some bardic poet chanting the exploits of her tribe, she reminded him of his genteel connections — the Lord Dumfries and the General Sir Adolphus Oughton who could be found on distant branches of the family tree, the near relation who became Governor of Gibraltar, the remarkable grandmother who was such a paragon among women that she could, even at the age of seventy, repeat every syllable of Young's *Night Thoughts* from memory. There can have been very little in John James's early career to make him think that he would ever be worthy of such high connections. He learned the sherry trade in a firm partly owned by Sir William Duff Gordon. In 1812, after four years of long hours and patient application without a holiday, financial ruin loomed again. 'The situation of this house is truly disastrous,' he wrote in disgust to his mother, '. . . yet such is [the partners'] infatuation that whilst at this moment one lives in a Gothic Castle on the banks of the Thames, the other is contesting the Worcester Election tho absent in Spain.'[2] Fortunately, John James seized the opportunity to set up as London agent for the wines of Pedro Domecq and after still more years of labour without holidays, he raised his firm's trade from twenty to three thousand butts a year. During all his later success, it remained evident that John James's character — its prudence, its snobbery, its discipline, its quirks — had been formed by the pressure of social climbing, financial distress, and prolonged emotional tension.

His youthful disappointments would have mattered less had he married a woman from a more carefree background. Instead, he chose a wife who had endured the same tensions as he and in the same household.

We do not know exactly why Margaret Cox, the daughter of a Croydon tavern keeper, entered the Ruskin home. Perhaps it is enough to say that it was a common fate of poor female relations to find themselves in a position which was partly that of confidante to the mistress of the house, partly that of domestic servant. It is certain that the young girl must have felt inadequate to the task ahead. In a home keenly aware of caste, her family background, her education and her accent all marked her as inferior. She set out to improve herself and, as the Ruskin troubles grew, to justify her place in the household by creating an area of calm amid the turmoil caused by John Thomas's unruly personality. She was training to become the ideal housewife, the bringer of peace that her son later idealized in *Sesame and Lilies*.

The passage from poor relation to honoured bride would have been a fairy tale had it taken two or three years; in fact, it took sixteen, and its psychic toll was appalling. Margaret was introduced into a home where the warmth of her aunt's affection must have been balanced by the fact that she was totally dependent on the good will of others. Her letters make it clear that even after a considerable campaign of self-improvement she still considered her betrothed far above her:

I pray almost every hour to be made more deserving of your affection when you are from me, for when you are with me, I forget
everything disagreeable in the happiness of having, hearing, and
seeing you, and I reflect upon what you are in abilities person and
age I feel most sensibly the difference between us the fear that
you may become equally sensible of the difference and cease to
love sometimes distresses me greatly. [12 July 1814.]

Such anxieties must have been intensified by the fact that the
marriage had to be postponed until John James had paid his father's
debts. Margaret anticipated a lifetime of bliss if she were wed, but had
no prospects whatever if she were not. As Margaret's mother was later
to write from her deathbed:

Please God to take me there will Be 40 Pound a year for you the
same for your Sister wich gives me Some Comfort as I think itt
will keep you above want and as I think if you outlive your
unkle an Aunt your Prospect will be Verry glomy. [20 September
1817.]

Her happiness was in the balance and there she sat, the real life
counterpart of all those fictional heroines whose fate it was to wait
patiently while men decided their fate. And to add to all this John
Thomas, perhaps bothered by her low origins, perhaps alarmed by some
fear of incest, suddenly announced his opposition to the marriage. Not
surprisingly, Margaret broke. In April 1815, she collapsed and we find
John James writing almost hysterically to his mother:

I cannot survive the sight of Margaret in very bad Health. My
feelings are unfortunately too strong for all I have to struggle with.
I conjure you as you value your Sons Life not to see Margt fall
into Irrecoverable Illness . . . my Father told me this morning She
was in a very bad way besides her affection for me. I cannot exist
under my present anxiety. [13 April 1815.]

Near the end of the same letter he adds: 'She is dying and no one
cares.'
   Margaret survived her illness, survived to spend three years nursing
the man who had provoked it. The complexity of her feelings, and
the strain of containing them, can scarcely be imagined. At last two
events precipitated a happy conclusion to this long engagement.

On 13 October 1817, her beloved Aunt Catherine died. Then seventeen days later, according to a family tradition that may be somewhat dramatized, Margaret looked up from her housework to see John Thomas Ruskin standing in the doorway with a gash in his throat, unable to say a word. Margaret seized a towel, bound up the wound, got the old man into bed and kept the wound closed with her two hands until the doctor arrived. Although she remained cool throughout the ordeal, the impact of John Thomas's suicide was overwhelming. After her marriage, she never entered that house again. When her son was married there, she made excuses to avoid the trip up from London and once, when social convention did require a visit with relatives, she stood chatting in the yard but declined to cross the threshold.

Having survived so many years of pain, and living now in London where they had few acquaintances, it was natural that John James and Margaret should look to one another for all their happiness. But a certain clash of rhetorics in the family letters indicates that they were having some difficulty adjusting their roles. John James, always the lover of Byron, writes with astonishing romantic intensity:

> Oh yes my dearest at this instant my Heart bounds towards you & acknowledges your power. It must be Love & there must be a mighty omnipotence in Love to electrify so dead a mass as I am & thrill every nerve of so nerveless a Being. How is it that you forever hold this amazing sway over me — how can you being a mere mortal wear so unspotted an aspect to me that I can perceive no blemish to bring you parallel with humanity . . . [11 March 1826.]

Such rapt adoration cannot have made Margaret very comfortable; she was far too insecure to stand on the same pedestal as Isolde and Beatrice. Her own letters make it clear that at that stage she felt most comfortable as a proud, but dependent wife:

> I thank God I am united to a man whom I can so esteem and love and even whose chiding would be delightful to me in comparison of the most judicious or well turned praises of every other human being or all human beings put together. [7-8 May 1826.]

Had John James and Margaret been immersed only in one another, there might have been a certain lack of harmony. It was the arrival of young John that made the domestic circle unbreakable. 'Oh! how dull and dreary,' John James wrote from Carlisle, 'is the best society

I fall into compared with the circle of my own Fire Side with my
Love sitting opposite irradiating all around her and my most extraordinary boy filling his nook but making a more important figure
by my chimney side than Gog or Magog, Giants vast in Guild Hall.'
(9 March 1831.)

The family unit was very nearly the sole basis of their happiness.
John James belonged to no club and, though he often travelled on
business, he seems never to have joined any convivial circle of fellow
travellers. Margaret shared the task of alms-giving with the wife of a
nearby coal merchant, but otherwise she had no circle of gossips
among the respectable wives on Herne Hill. Their most important
cultural activities were reading and attending the exhibitions at the
Royal Academy and The Old Water Colour Society and, since they
read aloud and since John took drawing lessons from an early age,
they pursued these interests together. When they attended Camden
Chapel they sat in a family pew. When they left their home to tour
the Lake Country or the picturesque towns of Europe they travelled
as a family group.

Was this a typical Victorian pattern? It seems so, though this may be
only an optical illusion, for descriptions of the Victorian family often
read as though they are based, at least in part, on a reading of *Sesame
and Lilies* and *Praeterita*. No doubt demographers and social
historians will soon sharpen our sense of the alternative family patterns
that could exist among the middle class in early nineteenth-century
England. It is at least true, however, that Ruskin himself thought that
his parents' household was broadly similar to those of the other rising
businessmen who populated the prosperous south London suburb of
Camberwell. He was aware that the villas surrounding his home were
the preferred residences of this class and he must have noted with
amusement that when Dickens wanted to sketch a successful brass
and copper founder in *Martin Chuzzlewit* he gave him, as one of the
essential marks of the tribe, a large and impressive villa in Camberwell.

Since the Ruskins corresponded closely to the popular ideal of the
family that was soon to be widely celebrated in poem and painting,
story and song, it may be well to point out that John James and
Margaret organized their household before most of these cultural props
to domesticity were available. Charles Dickens had not yet written
and Victoria herself, even after she was on the throne, was not thought
to be an inspiring model. When she married her beloved Albert, John
James was frankly dismayed. 'I am surprized to see how wholly
abandoned her Majesty is by all the high families,' he wrote to

Margaret. 'Royalty becomes a shabby affair & if she brings it once into contempt I would not ensure her safety. We are a King & Queen loving people but they must keep up their own dignity & keep the higher classes around them – else we may grow tired of paying for pomp. She the Queen is but a silly child & seems to have no Character.' What most reveals the Ruskin family code, however, is John James's concluding moral: 'We must look to our domestic Circles & our own neighbourhood & let politics alone.' (13 February 1840.)

At the centre of their domestic circle was their only child. What did they expect from this son? First, that he would provide the keystone of their own happiness and, second, that he would enjoy all the culture and social position that John Thomas Ruskin had aimed at, that John James Ruskin had just come in sight of. Their son's life would have been easier had John James and Margaret Ruskin been downright social climbers. But they believed in rank. They scorned new families. They gave thanks every Sunday in Camden Chapel for that station in life to which it had pleased God to call them. So they decided, not consciously of course, to experience the delights of society vicariously through their son. They soon recognized that their boy had remarkable gifts and the planned for him a remarkable career. He was to be not only a famous clergyman, perhaps a bishop, but also a great poet as well – perhaps something like the Reverend George Croly, a pious, romantic versifier whom the Ruskins cultivated as a friend.

Such goals require a first-rate education. Many families would have worked their boy into Eton or Harrow. John James and Margaret decided against this, no doubt alarmed by what Margaret later called 'the depraved tastes, and dissipated habits of the generallity of publick school boys.' (29 November 1828.) Instead, the boy was educated at home by his mother with tutors called in to help with specialized subjects. He experienced only a brief, unsatisfactory experience as a day boy at a nearby school.

Margaret Ruskin's educational programme has never received a sustained examination. This is a pity, for the obsessive concern with a child's education was to become a distinguishing feature of the modern family and in this area, as in many others, the Ruskins were among the pioneers. The only part of Margaret's procedure that is at all well known is her insistence on daily oral Bible reading, with great emphasis on purity of diction. This is cited so often because it fits the popular image of Margaret as an evangelical bigot. But there is another side to her programme, one that puts her in a very different light. This is her use of the children's books associated with the circle of Maria

Edgeworth.

Best known today for her novels, Miss Edgeworth was one of the first writers to give serious attention to early childhood education. She was led to this by her father, Richard Lovell Edgeworth, who had more than twenty children and kept careful notes on their development. The union of the father's theories and Maria's literary gifts produced a remarkable series of books. The first of these, the only one to give a full theoretical and practical guide, was Richard Lovell's *Practical Education*. I have no evidence whatever that Margaret read it though I admit that I would very much like to believe that she did. If she had, certain odd features of Ruskin's childhood might be explained. There is a famous incident related in *Praeterita*, in which a bright Punch and Judy show is presented on young John's birthday by gay Aunt Bridget, then hidden away in a closet by dour Margaret. This is regularly mentioned as one of the horrors of Ruskin's childhood. Perhaps, but it also sounds like a reflection of Edgeworth's view that children should be protected from useless gilded toys and given instead what we now call 'creative playthings'. Certainly young John had no shortage of the recommended balls, bricks and drawing materials. It is, in any event, certain that Margaret did employ a number of other books from the Edgeworth circle. One of these was Anna Laetitia Barbauld's *Evenings at Home*, a series of conversations for children between three and five years. This was followed by Maria Edgeworth's *Frank*, in which, among many other things, the young hero learned to draw a house to scale. Ruskin's copy, which survives, contains a crude elevation and floor plan of his Herne Hill home and an early attempt to represent a winding staircase. *Frank* was to be followed by *Harry and Lucy*, and for older children there was *Sandford and Merton* by Thomas Day, which came into the Ruskin household when John was fourteen. These were supplemented by such volumes of stories as *The Parent's Assistant* and *Popular Tales*. Of course other books, not associated with the Edgeworths, were used as well, among them *Aesop's Fables, Mother Bunch's Fairy Tales, Dame Wiggens of Lee* and *Grimms' Fairy Tales*. These last, incidentally, had only just been translated into English and they were not at all the household classics that they have since become. But although John was given a variety of books, it was the products of the Edgeworth circle that formed the basis of the curriculum. In one sense this is surprising, for the Edgeworths made no effort to provide religious training for young minds and they were sometimes attacked for this omission by evangelical critics. Margaret no doubt felt that she could handle that end herself, and welcomed the assistance provided by a well written, carefully graded series of texts.

One striking assumption of the Edgeworths, which excited some surprised comment at the time, is that parents should demonstrate a constant, painstaking concern for the education of their children. They should always be willing to explain to them, to read to them, to reason with them. This was surely congenial to Margaret and her husband, for they had few adult friends who shared their intellectual interests. Margaret found in her son a companion for her reading of the Bible and of such classics as *Robinson Crusoe*. John James could please himself as well as his son by discussing the art of watercolour and by reading aloud from Pope's *Iliad*, Byron's *Don Juan* and Scott's poems and novels.

Another assumption of the Edgeworths was that children should be taught how to think, should know not simply principles, but also how they are arrived at. Harry and Lucy not only reach conclusions, but also discuss at great length the means by which they reach them. This desire to make children self-conscious about their thought processes provides the only explanation I can think of for Margaret Ruskin's decision to favour her ten-year-old son and his cousin Mary with short daily readings from so dry a work as Adam Smith's *Theory of Moral Sentiments*. 'The children may not at present understand much of them,' she wrote to her husband, 'but it may be the means of making them even now observe something of the working of their own minds and this may lead in time to more and more knowledge of themselves.' (4 March 1829.)

Of all the Edgeworths' books, it was undoubtedly Maria's *Harry and Lucy* which had the greatest influence. It was as important for Ruskin's childhood as his first sight of Turner's paintings or his 1845 journey to Italy was to be for his later career. The book consists of dialogues between a young, slightly literary girl and her older, scientific brother. Each lesson consists of something that they actually do and a scientific principle that they discover together. They construct a thermometer, a hydrometer, a hygrometer. They visit an industrial centre to see how cotton is spun and Digby Castle to learn the principles of Gothic architecture. The adventures are very exciting and it is only natural that young John should have been inspired to imitate them. His early attempt to invent a machine that would measure the blue of the sky was a Harry and Lucy adventure. So were his efforts at bridge building and his wish to build a canal in the back garden at Herne Hill. He said himself that when he

collected minerals during his father's visits to Bristol he was inspired
by memories of Harry and Lucy's visit to Matlock and he admitted
that some of his boyhood poems had their origin in the same book.
And his own first 'book' — carefully drawn so as to resemble real
type with printed illustrations — was a continuation of the Harry and
Lucy stories.

Yet there is a radical difference between the tone of Ruskin's mind
and that of the Edgeworth books. The tales are precise, rational and
dry. Young John's disposition was imaginative and passionate. His
emotions could have found little outlet in Margaret Ruskin's household.
Peace and order were her gifts, not variety and excitement. She permitted no disruption of the domestic order that she had laboured so long
to create. Even servants, who provided some other middle-class children
with an existing alternative society, were carefully integrated into the
bland background of Margaret's domestic routine. Had his mother alone
been in charge of young John's education, he might have grown up as
John Stuart Mill did, with his intellect precociously developed and his
passions scarcely stirred. Fortunately, Ruskin's father brought another
kind of influence to bear. It was John James who encouraged the boy
to become one of the most romantic, though also one of the most
derivative, of poets. It was also John James who brought into the
household the early nineteenth-century passion for the picturesque and
the sublime. At an astonishingly early age, in his ninth and tenth years,
the boy became expert in beetling cliffs and looming crags. Mountain
worship and poetry gave a necessary outlet to his passionate emotions.

I hope I am giving the impression that the influence of Ruskin's
parents was creative, that his spirit was moulded in boyhood, not
broken. His letters provide an index of his mind. Here is an extract
from one written when John James was away on a business trip:

> Papa I do believe that the last year of my life was the happiest and
> shall I tell you why because I have had more to do than I could do
> without all possible cramming and ramming and wishing days were
> longer and sheets of paper broader, though that is a wish which has
> nothing to do with time I do think indeed am sure that in common
> things it is having too much to do which constitutes happiness and
> too little unhappiness. [10 May 1829.]

Naturally the boy tells his father what the father will have pleasure in
hearing, but there is nothing forced or formal about this. The boy's
pleasure in the English language seems a convincing accompaniment

to his mood and the equation of pleasure and industry, while no doubt a conventional piety, is also an authentic expression of Ruskin's temperament.

There is no doubt, of course, that John James and Margaret deliberately set out to raise a prodigy. *Harry and Lucy* was written for children of ten to fourteen. Ruskin had it at seven. But this was not force-feeding. The boy really was as much a literary prodigy as Mozart had been a musical one. At the age of four he was writing his father letters, at the age of eight he was writing them in blank verse. At nine he was sending epistles in the style of *Childe Harold* and turning Scott's novel, *The Monastery,* into verse. *The Iteriad,* a topographical poem of more than 4,000 lines, was written when he was ten. Lucky indeed is the child who can please his parents by indulging his own natural gifts.

Yet at a certain point all this happiness began to slip away and become part of a golden past. Ruskin only discussed the change obliquely and never discussed it very well. All Victorians had learned from Wordsworth that the child was father to the man and they had a vocabulary adequate to discuss the relation between the two. The intermediate concept of adolescence, by contrast, was not fully evolved until the American psychologist, G. Stanley Hall, published his two volumes on the subject in the early twentieth century. Clearly, we need to remember that a nineteenth-century Englishman does not always visualize a clearly defined stage of life in which a boy adjusts to his sexuality and forges an identity which, however much it may owe to its parents, is still his own. Of course some writers did describe this, or some of it. The notable examples are John Stuart Mill and Edmund Gosse. Their struggles for independence succeeded and they wrote about them at length. Ruskin's struggle did not succeed and was never concluded. A thorough discussion of it would have been unendurably painful and would have required a more direct confrontation with his own sexuality than Ruskin ever accomplished. The odd mixture of loving gratitude and aching regret in *Praeterita* can only be explained by the fact that Ruskin is looking back on a happy childhood across the gulf of a miserable adolescence.

Even had the Ruskins thought of encouraging independence in their son, their way of life would have made it difficult; the extraordinary self-sufficiency of the Ruskin domestic circle ensured that young John would have no patterns to follow except those provided by his parents. His own talents made it difficult to strike up friendships with more modestly-endowed young men, but the real limiting

factor was his parents' social ambition. Friendships between boys in
Ruskin's time and place depended to a much larger extent than now on
the relations between their parents. Children did not wander at will
through a series of suburban front gardens, making whatever friends
they pleased; visits were arranged by parents, and John James and
Margaret were not at all skilful at such things. Like many rising middle-
class families, they were eager to disassociate themselves from those
below, not certain how to approach those above, and unsure as to who
might be an equal. Ruskin recalled in *Praeterita* that his parents preferred to entertain county gentlemen rather than the thriving grocers,
haberdashers, or tallow-chandlers who lived near them, yet their friendships with county gentlemen could only be formal. Social insecurity
also limited the blessings of the extended family. Margaret had a large,
joyous brood of relatives living in Croydon, but they were neither
prosperous nor polished. When John was only seven, Margaret explained her reluctance to visit her Croydon sister by saying that young
John 'observes so closely and left were he any time there together the
ways and manners might affect him'. (25 May 1826.)

It was, of course, when their son entered Oxford that the parents
should have finally relaxed their hold. Instead, as all the world knows,
Margaret took lodgings in the High Street and required a visit each
afternoon. The ostensible reason was that John's tubercular condition
was likely to recur, and this piece of self-justification should not be
cast aside with entire contempt. The only son on whom these middle-
aged parents had staked their happiness was born in a time of high
infant mortality and once the diseases of childhood were past the
menace of consumption lay ahead. In this situation, reasons of health
were easily stretched to cover a multitude of sins.

Margaret's presence was no doubt a disaster for John, but it has the
advantage of providing a series of letters to John James that give a
detailed picture of his son's life at Oxford. John was not a recluse and,
though he visited his mother every afternoon, he was not tied to her
apron strings. But although a success at Oxford, John was not the kind
of success that his parents had anticipated. They had enrolled him as
a gentleman commoner, expecting that since he wore a purple gown
and dined at a special table, he would make friends among the young
aristocrats. They had not anticipated that he would be drawn to the
young men who sketched old churches and hammered away at geolog-
ical formations. On 15 February 1838, Margaret had to reassure her
worried husband:

> I think I must leave him to remove your fears about his losing
> ground with the higher class — he does not now as formerly when it
> was a rarity mention when he is with any of this class because it
> is now so common so much a thing of course but from what I hear
> in the course of ordinary detail I think he is quite as much with
> them as formerly and on a more intimate footing . . .

After some chit-chat, in the course of which she manages to mention
John's intimacy with 'Lords Ward, Carew, Kildare, and the whole of
that set', Margaret goes on to defend the guest list that her son had
compiled for an evening during which, it appears, a little too much wine
had been consumed:

> I entirely agree with you that literary men are almost without excep-
> tion unpleasant guests in a sober family. They should have public
> nights in apartments provided to show themselves where those who
> wished to cultivate their acquaintance or gratify their curiosity
> might have opportunities of doing so, and coming away when they
> were tired, but I really cannot see that the objection holds with
> regard to John cultivating the regard of his college tutors. I believe
> they drink very little generally . . .

It is hard to believe that the gentlemen commoners drank much less.
Margaret assumes that members of the higher classes are sober and
virtuous. This is not an assumption that all evangelicals had made,
but it must have been very dear to the Ruskins. It was part of their
constant habit of deference. In one of his abortive bids for independence, their son was to astonish them with the news that Lords March
and Ward had kept their drawers filled with pictures of naked bawds.

The next occasion on which Ruskin should have achieved his independence was his marriage, but once again we find the parents living
vicariously and avidly through their son. A letter sent by John James
to Effie's father on 31 August 1848 is symptomatic. John James is
attempting to explain politely and at length, but very firmly, why
Effie's brother, who was coming down to London to pursue a mercantile career, was unlikely to see much of his distinguished relations.
He reviews the progress of his son's education, outlines his personal
traits, and concludes:

> I deem this long History due to George, that he may comprehend
> my hinting the probability of a divided society. It is not George

alone but Mrs. Ruskin and myself are equally excluded. John has
brought Lords to our table but we are very marked in regarding
them as Johns Visitors and when Sir Wr and Lady James last break-
fasted here John and Effie presided and neither Mrs R nor I ever
appeared. I have got them their House in Park St. to be among
their own Set — when they like to put up with Wine Merchts or
Colonial Brokers they may dine here now and then . . .[3]

No doubt John James thought he was writing with modesty, but the
tone of self-satisfaction is far more evident. Lords were being entertained in his own home, his son was mingling with 'the High Classes',
and yet no one could accuse him of social climbing.

This last letter brings us to the years of Ruskin's marriage, a subject
on which Mary Lutyens has said all that can justifiably be said. It can
be looked at from two points of view: the psychological, with attention
to individual pathology, and the sociological, with attention to typical
family patterns. It must be said that the first point of view is very
difficult to maintain. Clearly, some tangle of individual pathology
produced Ruskin's impotence and his fascination with young girls,
but an attempt to explain it involves a long series of speculations. A
sociological perspective, however, is more rewarding. Whatever individual pathology was created in the Ruskin household, it was created
within the framework of a representative middle-class family. The
ambiguity of this situation is very well captured in two letters of
Effie's. The first was written when she was visiting the Ruskin household as a guest at a time when John James and Margaret were trying
to promote a match between their son and Charlotte Lockhart, the
grand-daughter of Sir Walter Scott and the daughter of the editor of
the *Quarterly Review*. Effie thought John would go along not out of
love but out of duty and she knew that such an extreme interpretation
of a child's obligation of obedience was preposterous. 'Did you ever see
such a philosophy,' she asked one of her friends. 'I think Mr. and Mrs.
R. are doing wrong — at least they are wishing for their son's happiness
and going the wrong way to work. He adores them and will sacrifice for
them, as I see, too easily.'[4] Here she saw the pathology, but once it
was a question of her own marriage she could see only the typical
family pattern. 'You who are so kind as a son,' she wrote to her fiancé,
'will be a perfect lover as a husband.'[5]

In the actual breakdown of the Ruskin marriage, it is possible to
discern many instances in which the typical family pattern effectively
masks unhealthy emotions. Neither the parents nor Effie doubted that

the struggle was over who was to command John's loyalty. A wide
variety of local skirmishes took place within this overall campaign.
There was an opening struggle over whether John should marry Effie at
all; significantly, John James and Margaret were able to console themselves with the thought that they would have lost their son had he
married into a sphere too far above them. Then there was a conflict
over whether Effie's conduct was properly feminine. Before the engagement Margaret wrote her son a long letter listing the characteristics of
a good wife, which ranged from beauty and kindly social feeling to an
eagerness to do what John thought proper and avoid what he thought
improper. Effie was by no means a rebel against conventional notions
of womanhood, but she could scarcely avoid an occasional lapse. When
she took a turn rowing a gondola in Venice, for example, John James
wrote twice to express his dismay: it might be justified, he thought, in a
passage to the Lido, but 'in the Grand Canal I cannot reconcile the
notion at all to what is beautiful'.[6] All of these things were minor,
however, compared to the parent's suggestion that Effie might be
hindering John's climb up the social ladder. 'Their going into the highest
society,' John James wrote in 1852, 'could all have happened in a more
prudent manner . . . . had Phemy dressed more quietly, they would
have been at parties higher than they ever reached, but the old and high
families repel any new people attempting to be on an exact equality
or trying to dress up to them or I would say beyond them for they are
distinguished for quietness of Demeanour.'[7] Actually, it was Effie rather
than John who enjoyed society and cared about meeting the best
people. Had not the parents' intense need to maintain control over their
son triumphed over their common sense they would have noticed that
she was their natural ally. Had John been able to achieve sexual
potency with Effie or had he found her fully entering into his concerns
with painting and architecture, he might have established at least an
area of neutral ground between parents and wife and so achieved a
measure of independence. Instead, obedience to parents offered safety
from the challenge of his marriage. It even offered a measure of
emotional satisfaction.

With his marriage, his impotence and his inability to adjust his
loyalties between wife and parents, the Ruskin tragedy was well under
way. After the marriage was annulled, Ruskin continued to feel the
conflict between a need for independence and a wish to be obedient.
He opposed his parents by writing social criticism, yet conceived an
ideal society that was only an enlarged version of the Ruskin household.
He rejected his mother's religion, yet fell in love with the very evan-

gelical Rose La Touche, and, in 'Of Queen's Gardens', asked that young lady to become the bringer of peace to the adult Ruskin that Margaret had been to the child. Bursts of rebellion alternated with gestures of obedience. The most dramatic bid for freedom came when Ruskin determined to live alone in Switzerland. Though he knew the pain that this decision would cause this parents, he still told them stoutly: 'I am an incomparably nobler and worthier person now, when you disapprove of nearly all I say and do, than I was when I was everything you and my mother desired me.'[8] This gesture of independence, however, had an ironic complication; John Ruskin could only defy his father if John James first provided the necessary funds. No doubt John James would have done so, but the very act of defiance would have contained a reminder of the son's dependence. The house in Switzerland, in any event, never materialized, and the death of John James in 1864 left his son with a permanent legacy of guilt. During the remaining seven years of his mother's life, Ruskin very carefully played the dutiful son: he was submissive when she rebuked his nonsense about political economy, he read to her from the evangelical tracts that he despised, and he carefully refrained from interfering with Margaret's elaborate management of household affairs.

As the years passed Ruskin's mingled impulses of obedience and revolt became merged in an overwhelming nostalgia, one that is all the more affecting because it is tinged by bitterness. He was sure that childhood, at least, had been paradise and he was determined that other children should enjoy the peace and harmony that he had known. 'When do you suppose the education of a child begins?' he asked the readers of *Fors Clavigera*.

At six months old it can answer smile with smile, and impatience with impatience. Do you suppose it makes no difference to it that the order of the house is perfect and quiet, the faces of its father and mother full of peace, their soft voices familiar to its ear, and even those of strangers loving; or that it is tossed from arm to arm among hard, or reckless, or evil-minded persons in the gloom of a vicious household, or the confusion of a gay one.

Recalling how his mother had carefully withdrawn all foolishly gilded toys, Ruskin counsels parents that 'quiet, and the withdrawal of objects likely to distract, by amusing, the child, so as to let it fix its attention undisturbed on every visible least thing in its domain, is essential to the formation of some of the best powers of thought.'[9] Especially in his directions to the tenants on the land of the St George's Guild is Ruskin eager to recreate the circumstances of his own childhood. Obedience was to be their first lesson as it had been his. The books that he wanted children to read were those that he had enjoyed. He lent *Harry and Lucy* to young friends, he persuaded a publisher to reissue *Grimms' Fairy Tales* with the original illustrations by Cruickshank and he himself prepared a new edition of *Dame Wiggens of Lee.* In only one respect was the childhood of a late Victorian boy or girl to differ from his own: the parents on the St George's estate are carefully warned against becoming obsessed by the idea that their children might rise to a higher station.

What do the Ruskins show? What Victorian trends does this family reveal? We must not look for dramatic new developments; structural similarities between the generations are more striking than any discontinuities. Both John Thomas and John James, for example, focused their ambitions on the next generation: the father would succeed in trade so that the son might enjoy dignity and culture. In all three generations, the extended family provided an important arena for social life: even though John James and Margaret had reason to keep their relatives at arm's length, their son married a cousin as indeed his father had done before him, and Margaret when she was old and in need of a companion called upon a distant niece just as Catherine Ruskin had called upon her so many decades before. Evidences of change, suggestions that some features of the Ruskin household may be labelled Victorian, are not dramatic. But they are present. It is striking that while Catherine Ruskin's letters show her to be very aware of her distant relatives, John James and Margaret are very aware of one another and of their darling son. They respected their obligations to relatives, but they did not take pride in the extended family as Catherine had done. They found their most intense life at their own hearth. There are two important consequences of this turning inward. One is that Margaret Ruskin was just as important as John James throughout her son's life; there was no time when John passed from being a toddler watched over by women to being a youth in the company of men. For all the pride she took in deferring to her husband, Margaret's letters from the birth of her child on reveal a woman who was at last confident of her own importance. In so far as the family was held together by emotional intimacy, the mother had sources of power that could provide a counterweight to the patriarchal bias of church and state. The other result of the Ruskins' absorption in one another is that for both parents there was a blurring of the distinction

between themselves and their son. There is nothing Victorian in the fact
that they projected their ambitions on to the son; that is a very old
story indeed. But there may be something especially Victorian in the
fact that they expected him to complete the frustrated aspects of their
own sensibilities. It is a commonplace that the modern family — that is,
the Victorian family slightly modified — expends an amazing amount
of its resources on the education of its children. The Ruskins were an
early and extreme example. They cared not simply about the contents
of their son's mind but about its very tenor. His mind, after all, was to
be their joint mind brought to perfection. He was to be as deeply
religious as Margaret and as romatically poetic as John James. When he
became himself — when he gave up poetry for prose, when he showed
an interest in the wrong Church Fathers, and especially when he turned
toward social criticism — they felt wounded and abandoned. It is very
difficult to read the Ruskin letters without being appalled by the
extraordinary possessiveness that lurked beneath the surface of their
love. The real tragedy of the Ruskins is that John James and Margaret
never realized that their son's mind had evolved into something quite
different from theirs and that he never found a way to tell them. It
is his failure to consider that the loving wish to live for the child is also
a selfish wish to live through him that makes *Sesame and Lilies* seem
so sentimental and it is the realization that possession is the underside
of love that makes *Praeterita* so complex and so dismaying.

Notes

1. *Letters of John Ruskin to C.E. Norton* (Boston, 1904), I, p. 106.
2. *The Ruskin Family Letters, 1801–1843*, Van Akin Burd (ed.) (Ithaca,
    1973), I, p. 54. Unless otherwise noted, all further references to corre-
    spondence are to this edition and are identified by dates in the text.
    Professor Burd reproduces the original letters as nearly as possible and
    does not correct spelling, add punctuation, or otherwise normalize the text.
3. Quoted in Mary Lutyens, *The Ruskins and the Grays* (London, 1972),
    pp. 143-4.
4. Lutyens, *The Ruskins and the Grays*, p. 37.
5. Ibid., p. 89.
6. Quoted in Mary Lutyens, *Young Mrs. Ruskin in Venice* (New York, 1965),
    pp. 76-7.
7. Quoted in Mary Lutyens, *Millais and the Ruskins* (London, 1967), p. 6.
8. *Works*, XXXVI, pp. 418-9.
9. Ibid., p. 611.

6 FAMILY SECRETS AND DOMESTIC SUBVERSION: REBELLION IN THE NOVELS OF THE 1860s

Elaine Showalter

On 14 December 1861, Prince Albert died of typhoid fever at Windsor Castle. 'The Prince is *dead*! It is quite, quite true!' wrote a young female subject in her diary. 'The poor Queen; how will she bear it? It is dreadful to think of. I cannot, without tears. She loved him so fondly, so devotedly – it will, it must break her heart. God grant it will not upset her reason.'[1] Yet even as provincial maidens like the Hall sisters were participating in the national mourning for Victoria's domestic idyll, other young women were lining up at Mudie's Select Circulating Library to demand quite another sort of family chronicle. In the sensational bestsellers of the 1860s, such as the Bigamy Novels of Mary E. Braddon, Mrs Henry Wood's *East Lynne,* and Rhoda Broughton's *Cometh Up as a Flower,* readers enjoyed fantasies which countered the official mythology of the Albert Memorial. In these novels, the death of a husband comes as a welcome release and wives who lack the friendly agency of typhoid seek desperate remedies in flight, adultery, divorce and ultimately murder. As a critic reviewing sensation fiction for the *Westminster Review* in 1864 noted, with characteristic cautious reserve, 'The institution of marriage might almost seem to be . . . just now upon its trial.'[2]

Sensation fiction appearing in the first decade after the Matrimonial Causes Act (1857) certainly seems to be recording a new kind of family pattern. It portrays an unhappy marriage as a cage rather than a spiritual opportunity. Wives running away from husbands who are boring rather than brutal create new expectations for marital success. Marriages and elopements which cut across class lines as in Braddon's *Aurora Floyd* and Collins's *No Name* challenge the matrimonial market. Novels in which the heroine 'expresses her hatred for one parent and contempt for the other'[3] and 'brothers and sisters are the deadliest enemies of brothers and sisters'[4] cast doubt, to say the least, upon the realities of domestic contentment. Stories of domestic murder struck a note of uncomfortable psychological authenticity, one assumes from critical reactions, clerical panic, rumours, jokes, and legal action centring on the possibility of widespread female homicide. In *Six to Sixteen,* Juliana Ewing satirized the exaggerated journalism of the 1860s which

101

led one 'student of human nature' to the conclusion that 'every girl of
fifteen was a murderess at heart'.[8] E.E. Kellet recalls being told by a
physician that 'he did not believe there was a single medical practi-
tioner in London, of twenty years standing, who had not serious
reason to believe that wives in his practice had poisoned their husbands
and husbands their wives.'[6] While the actual number of women
executed for murder in England between 1830 and 1874 was not very
great, forty per cent of them had indeed killed their husbands.[7] By
1868, public concern over availability of the preferred female weapon,
arsenic, led to its control in the Sale of Poisons Bill.

To some degree, these anxieties and precautions reflect a primordial
fear of women as 'the dangerous sex', a fear which also surfaces in
medical pronouncements of the mid-century about female hysteria
and insanity; and a tacit acknowledgement of the wretchedness of
many middle-class wives. But it can be argued that some women were
indeed driven to murder as an escape from the family. The
Victorians were fascinated and perplexed by the enthusiasm with which
respectable women followed the trials of Madeleine Smith for poison-
ing her lover (with arsenic in his cocoa) in 1857, and of sixteen-year-old
Constance Kent, accused of stabbing her four-year-old brother in
1860.[8] Officially, criminal behaviour in 'proper' women was
considered to be impossible, just as impossible as sexual behaviour.
As one criminologist wrote, female offenders 'inverted the qualities
which distinguish the normal woman, namely reserve, docility, and
sexual apathy'. In *Victorian Murderesses*, however, Mary S. Hartman
argues that homicidal women 'may have been among a group which
was especially sensitive to certain problems and tensions which were
endemic in various middle-class settings'. She sees the relationship
between the female spectators and the accused as psychologically
meaningful:

> The trials to be sure gave everybody an obvious occasion to indulge
> in the morbid thrills of exotic tales, but more importantly, as their
> behavior demonstrates, the women found in them an opportunity
> for release of frustrations and for vicarious fulfilment of
> inarticulated desires. The accused murderesses, it appears, had acted
> out what many of these women, in their most secret thoughts, had
> hardly dared to imagine.[9]

In short, the murderess, like the sensation heroine whose exploits were
often copied from current criminal cases, acted out a collective anger

and rebellion.

The delight with which audiences responded to the morbid thrills of sensationalism is recorded by sales and circulation figures in the hundred thousands, by widespread imitations, parodies, and adaptations both in England and America, and by literary influences on novelists from Charlotte Yonge to Thomas Hardy and George Eliot. Wilkie Collins, Mary Braddon, Charles Reade, Mrs Henry Wood and Rhoda Broughton vied for the best-seller lists.[10] Their success was vividly apparent. In 1860, ladies who wished to 'give themselves an air of mystery and to prove they know what is in fashion' wore white bonnets, shawls or gowns, in honour of Collins's *The Woman in White*.[11] *Lady Audley's Secret*, which went through eight English editions in its first year of publication, was also the most widely-read book in the United States in 1862.[12] By 1863, dramatic versions of *Lady Audley* and another Braddon novel, *Aurora Floyd*, were playing at eight London theatres and Braddon's publisher William Tinsley bought himself a villa in Barnes which he gratefully named Audley Hall. Mrs Henry Wood's *East Lynne* became one of the greatest publishing successes of all time, translated into 'every known tongue from Parsee . . . to Welsh'.[13] English critics, however offended they might be by the commercialism, vulgarity and depravity of sensational narrative, had to concede that the appetite for this strong meat had overwhelmed more refined palates: 'There is no accounting for tastes,' lamented the *Westminster Review* in 1866; 'blubber for the Esquimaux, half-hatched eggs for the Chinese, and sensational novels for the English.'[14]

Twentieth-century criticism has not gone much beyond the *Westminster* in attempting to account for this mysterious and distasteful craving. Yet the vogue of sensationalism in the 1860s is clearly a sociological as well as a literary phenomenon. As John Goode has noted, it is 'a mode which is responsive to a new situation', the other side of the tensions which give the decade its reputation for prudery and Podsnappery.[15] Such celebrations of submissive womanhood as Ruskin's 'Of Queen's Gardens' (1864) can be seen as a kind of desperate propaganda, an effort to defuse and contain female rebellion. Even Podsnappery could be a sign of guilty obsession, as Coventry Patmore recognized when he commented in 1865: 'The more I know of English chastity, the more it reminds me of that of a saint of whom I was reading . . . in Butler's *Lives*, that he was so chaste that he could never remain in a room alone with his mother.'[16] Sensation novelists seem to have grasped the principle of the bestseller, a popular art-form which, as Henry Peyre and Leslie Fiedler have argued, embodies the communal unconscious, 'fulfils a secret expectation in the public and unleashes latent emotions and reactions in readers . . .'[17]

The 'purest type of sensation novel', according to Kathleen Tillotson, 'is the novel-with-a-secret'.[18] These secrets almost always concern such crimes as forgery, blackmail, bigamy and murder, and such family secrets as alcoholism, drug addiction, adultery, illegitimacy and insanity. The power of Victorian sensationalism derives, however, from its exposure of secrecy as the fundamental and enabling condition of middle-class life, rather than from its revelation of particular scandals. The essential unknowability of each individual and society's collaboration in the maintenance of a facade behind which lurked innumerable mysteries were themes which preoccupied many mid-century novelists, and which greatly alarmed those readers professionally or emotionally committed to the preservation of the facade. In a crusading sermon, the Archbishop of York accurately perceived that the novels could be subversive: 'They want to persuade people that in almost every one of the well-ordered houses of their neighbours there was a skeleton shut up in some cupboard; that their comfortable and easy-looking neighbour had in his breast a secret story which he was always going about trying to conceal.'[19]

Without directly confronting the hidden world or explicitly attacking the conventions which protected it from view, sensationalism nonetheless drew attention to the artifice of the facade. And for some readers, this self-consciousness was too much; the social contract was easily ruptured. Once one admitted the existence of unlawful passions and forbidden drives, people regarded each other with a wild surmise; and thus sensational novels, according to the *London Quarterly Review*, shook 'that mutual confidence by which societies, and above all, families, are held together'.[20] The innermost secrets of the novels often concerned the ultimate secret life of sexuality; their characters, especially their heroines, are the Other Victorians, for whom (as another clergyman protested) 'all breaches of the Seventh Commandment are provided with apologetic excuses; antenuptial connections are treated of as inevitable; adultery is a social necessity'.[21] No wonder that critics disowned sensationalism as a 'plant of foreign growth' imported from France or Italy or traced its moral tone to the working classes.[22]

Portraits of women in the novels were so unlike the prevailing stereotypes of the docile, apathetic and sickly Victorian Lady that they were often regarded as bizarre and inartistic inventions, quite removed from reality. In the novels of Collins, Braddon, Broughton, Ouida, Florence Marryat, and others, readers found heroines who 'throb with sexual energy';[23] irresistible seductresses, 'barbarous, intoxicating, dangerous, and maddening',[24] with luxuriant pre-Raphaelite hair and a 'tigerish tingling'[25] in their blood. Women writers of an older generation were scandalized by the passionate girl of the period represented in the new fiction. 'What is held up to us as the story of the feminine soul as it really exists underneath its conventional coverings,' wrote a shocked Mrs Oliphant, 'is a very fleshly and unlovely record. Women driven wild with love . . . women who marry their grooms in fits of sensual passion; women who pray their lovers to carry them off from husbands and homes they hate; women, at the very least of it, who give and receive burning kisses and frantic embraces . . .'[26]

Female sensation novelists always denied that they were writing about sexuality. 'I defy any critic,' Mary Braddon wrote to Bulwer-Lytton, 'to point to one page or one paragraph in that book [*The Doctor's Wife*] . . . which contains the lurking poison of sensuality.'[27] Even sensation heroines found it necessary to exonerate themselves: 'I was not, I think, one of those fiery females,' Rhoda Broughton's Nell L'Estrange (in *Cometh Up as a Flower*) insists. 'And really I don't think that English women are given to flaming, and burning, and melting, and being generally combustible on ordinary occasions, as we are led by one or two novelists to suppose.'[28] Mrs Henry Wood takes pains to eliminate sexual attraction as a motive for Lady Isabel's elopement with Francis Levison in *East Lynne*.

These disclaimers are the necessary concessions to Victorian propriety, and to the circulating libraries; there was hypocrisy on both sides, as Henry James drily observed when he wrote that Miss Braddon 'knows much that ladies are not accustomed to know but that they are apparently very glad to learn.'[29] But it was also true that the escape from sexual bonds and family networks rather than sexual gratification or frustration was the real subject of female sensationalism. In the angry, rebellious, and outspoken heroines of the novels, women readers found sisters under the skin whose protests against the confining roles of daughter, wife and mother were both welcome and cathartic.

Other kinds of evidence suggest that the surfacing of this protest in popular fiction in the 1860s was part of a broader female discontent with the institutions of family life. In 1852, Florence Nightingale had raged against the tyranny of the middle-class family in 'Cassandra': 'The family uses people, not for what they are, nor what they are intended to be, but for what it wants them for — for its own uses . . .

If it wants someone to sit in the drawing-room, *that* someone is supplied
by the family.' The chief appeal of reading novels, she bitterly pro-
claimed, was that 'the heroine has *generally* no family ties (almost
invariably no mother), or, if she has, these do not interfere with her
entire independence.'[30] In the novels, the daughter sitting sullenly
in the family drawing-room — from Maggie Tulliver wishing that like
her brother she had some active part to play in the world to the
Braddon heroine meditating arson — is a figure with whom the
novelists transparently identify. 'It must be confessed,' wrote one
woman novelist in 1861,

> that the so-called happy homes of England belie their name
> miserably. A family of grown-up daughters . . . debarred from
> freedom of action and freedom of opinion, with miserable little
> occupations which fritter away, but do not occupy time — often
> prohibited the healthy exercise which is as necessary to the mind as
> the body, and systematically leaving the intellect, the heart, the
> blood, in total stagnation — is it surprising that such women grow
> old as sickly invalids or confirmed hypochondriacs?[31]

Sensation novelists never tired of reminding their readers that home,
at best, was deadly dull. In Wilkie Collins's *Armadale* (1866), for
example, the glamorous murderess Lydia Gwilt is hiding out in a
lunatic asylum run by her confederate, Doctor Downward. He has
sent out invitations to an Open House at his sanitarium, invitations
accepted, to his delight, by all the women of the neighbourhood.
'Short as the notice had been, cheerless as the Sanitarium looked to
spectators from without,' Collins writes, 'in the miserable
monotony of the lives led by a large section of the middle classes
of England, anything is welcome to the women which offers them
any sort of harmless refuge from the established tyranny of the
principle that all human happiness begins and ends at home.' When
the visiting women discover that in the sanitarium there is music,
even on Sunday; a large library of novels; and no housework for
inmates, they are enchanted, and have to be forced to leave. The
company of the amusing and fortunate lunatics is far better than
what they get at home.

The Matrimonial Causes Act of 1857 still limited women's rights
to obtain a divorce, making it possible for a husband to petition on
the grounds of adultery, while the wife had also to prove desertion,
cruelty, incest, rape, sodomy, or bestiality. But at least the Act

recognized that the Victorian home so rapturously celebrated in theory could, in reality, be a prison or a madhouse. The Divorce Act, according to Margaret Maison, 'caused a minor social revolution in England'; and in part it is the revolution of rising expectations. Fantasies of extramarital love, involving adultery, divorce, or bigamy, become the thematic obsessions of the novelists of the 1860s. Novelists wrote ostensibly to condemn all three: divorce was castigated as 'adultery made easy', 'legalized bigamy', or 'unwiving unlimited'.[32] Defending *Griffith Gaunt* (1865) against the attacks of 'prurient prudes', Charles Reade insisted that his purpose in making his hero a bigamist was moral and artistic: '. . . Instead of shedding a mild lustre over Bigamy, I fill my readers with a horror of Bigamy, and a wholesome indignation against my principal male character.'[33] Adulterers, divorcés, and bigamists in the novels usually do come to a bad end; if the novelists had not initially conformed to moral formulas, they made changes in accordance with the criteria of stern readers for Bentley or Macmillan. Nonetheless, a clever novelist like Mary Braddon could easily manipulate the plot in such a way that the erring wife escaped her punishment through some technicality; and, as Maison points out, 'Many authors gave their sinners such a good run for their money before subjecting them to the pangs of remorse, and making the grave close over the "polluted creatures", that they could hardly be said to be serving the true interests of morality.'[34]

By 1863, when Dean Henry Mansel, an Oxford don and clergyman, reviewed twenty-four sensation novels for the *Quarterly Review*, eight were about bigamy. 'So popular has the crime become, as to give rise to an entire sub-class in this branch of literature,' Mansel observed.[35] At the very least, the Divorce Novel and the Bigamy Novel imply a criticism of monogamy, even if these were fantasies very far from actualization. Such themes were to become familiar later in the century from the pens of Gissing, Meredith, Moore, and Hardy; and as Mansel shrewdly predicted, a society more accustomed to divorce would find the Bigamy Novel tame and unnecessary. In the 1860s, however, and from women novelists, the shock value of extramarital passion was intense. When Florence Marryat, in *Love's Conflict* (1865), speculates whether modern young wives would be as true to elderly husbands as the heroines of sentimental fiction, and when Rhoda Broughton's heroine in *Cometh Up as a Flower* openly admits that she adores her lover even more 'regretfully, passionately, longingly' after her marriage to someone else, the most sacred precepts about womanly fidelity, about woman's very nature, were being violated.

Parodies of the Bigamy Novel, such as *Quintilia the Quadrigamist*, and *Laura the Lone One; or the Wife of Seven Husbands*, suggest that it was the spectre of female sexual insatiability which horrified and stimulated readers. Commenting on Mary Braddon's connection with the Bigamy Novel in 1866, the *Westminster Review* used a metaphor which plainly referred to the sexual titillation of the theme:

> When Richardson, the showman, went about with his menagerie, he had a big black baboon, whose habits were so filthy and whose behaviour was so disgusting, that respectable people constantly remonstrated with him for exhibiting such an animal. Richardson's answer invariably was, 'Bless you, if it wasn't for that big black baboon I should be ruined; it attracts all the young girls in the country.' Now Bigamy has been Miss Braddon's big black baboon, with which she has attracted all the young girls in the country.[36]

By the end of the 1860s, the middle-class birth rate had begun to decline, and the press began to analyze the emancipated woman's 'flight from maternity'. One representative journalist saw signs of the atrophy of the maternal instinct:

> No one who studies the present temper of women can shut his eyes to the fact that there is a decided diminution among them in reverence for parents, trust in men, and desire for children . . . It is rare to find a woman, boasting herself of advanced culture, who confesses to an instinctive love for little children, or who would condescend to any of that healthy animal delight in their possession which has always been one of the most beautiful and valuable constituents of feminine nature.[37]

In sensation fiction, the cult of motherhood comes under strong, if indirect, attack. Both Lady Audley and Mrs Wood's Lady Isabel desert their children. In other novels, accounts of childbirth become a metaphor for sexual incompatibility: 'I fear I bore it badly, Archibald,' Lady Isabel tells her husband, 'but let us be thankful it is over.'[38]

Both the sexual frustration of young women married to old men and what Dr William Acton, in 1875, called the 'spirit of insubordination' in wives refusing to fulfil their conjugal duties, become subjects for the sensationalists. The nineteen-year-old bride in *Cometh Up as a Flower* finds her husband 'horribly, needlessly, irksomely loving' and knows herself to be 'his chattel as much as his pet lean-headed bay mare'. She does her best to hide her 'disrelish' for her spouse, and to 'receive his blandishments' with good grace. Acton reported that, judging from husbands' complaints, other wives were less tractable, an unhealthy state of affairs he blamed on John Stuart Mill's *The Subjection of Women* (1869).[39]

In *East Lynne* and *Lady Audley's Secret*, two great best-sellers of the 1860s too long neglected or scorned, we find the most complete accounts of the spirit of female insubordination. Each novel is a fantasy of escape, revenge and retribution, but Braddon's Lady Audley is a heroine in control of her mind and body, while Mrs Henry Wood's Lady Isabel is the oppressed and pathetic Perfect Lady of Victorian domestic romance. Both novelists wrote rapidly and easily; unlike the painfully-constructed three-deckers of Charles Reade, their volumes seem to have flowed irresistibly from their own female psyches, from their own experiences, feelings and grievances. Like their sister sensationalists, Braddon and Wood possessed indefatigable industry, iron nerves, and a total inability to write an uncommercial book. Their intuitive sense of the market, so distressing to such male competitors as Reade, Wilkie Collins, and, later, Gissing, Hardy, and James, suggests their close attunement to the typical Mudie's customer, a leisured middle-class wife or daughter like themselves.

Braddon's life was in fact rather sensational; she went on the stage, lived with a married man whose wife was in a mental asylum, bore him five children and finally married him. Wood's life was placid, boring, and routine until she began to write novels in her forties. Both, however, presented themselves as domestic, motherly, retiring souls. Each had an adoring son who grew up to memorialize her. 'No home duty was ever put aside for literary labours,' Charles Wood declared.[40] Similarly, William Maxwell, the novelist son of Mary Braddon and John Maxwell, recalled that his mother, who died at her desk at the age of seventy-eight, leaving the unfinished manuscript of her eighty-eighth novel, 'got through her immense amount of work as if by magic. She never seemed to be given any time in which to do it. She had no stated hours, no part of the day to be held secure from disturbance and intrusions. She was never inaccessible.'[41] There is something so intimidating, even today, in the account of these formidably disciplined women, that one cannot wonder at the ambivalence of other novelists toward the female sensationalists.

As Jeanne B. Elliott observes in her recent essay on *East Lynne*,

'Lady Isabel seems extraordinarily passive and lacking in ego strength in comparison with the heroine of almost any novel by George Eliot, Anthony Trollope, or the Brontë sisters.'[42] Yet there are few heroines in the works of these novelists who approximate Lady Isabel's experience of seduction and betrayal; we must look at minor women characters, such as Hetty Sorrel and Lydia Glasher, to supply the parallels. Giving in to the insinuations of her first love, Sir Francis Levison, Lady Isabel impulsively abandons her husband Archibald Carlyle and her three children, and elopes to Normandy. Levison has convinced her that her husband is involved in an affair with a neighbourhood woman, Barbara Hare, but he is mistaken. Disgraced and heartbroken, Lady Isabel learns that her husband has obtained a divorce; but Levison, arguing that a man in his position cannot marry a divorced woman, deserts her and her illegitimate child. Worse misfortunes follow; attempting to return to England, Lady Isabel is involved in a terrible train crash; her baby is killed; she herself is reported dead, but actually sustains injuries which leave her unrecognizably disfigured. Stripped of her position, her beauty, and her identity, she goes back to East Lynne as governess to her own children. No one knows her. Her husband has married Barbara Hare. Even at the deathbed of her eldest son, she cannot reveal herself.

It is an appalling and relentless melodrama, but for all its contrivance, it expresses the sense of hopeless dependency, the lack of alternatives, in the lives of Victorian gentlewomen. Detail by detail, Mrs Wood builds up her case study of women's position in a patriarchal society. It is appropriate that Isabel ends without a name, without a past, with only initials carved on her tombstone; for the novel tells us repeatedly that a woman is a void, a cipher. Isabel's father, Earl Mount Severn, regrets all her life that she is not a boy; he gambles away his own fortune so thoroughly that upon his death she is left a pauper, without so much as a shilling to buy herself a ribbon. She is fortunate that the first man who proposes to her is decent; love cannot be in question, since marriage is her only means of survival. When her daughter is born, her husband is so sure the child must be male that he tries to name her William. Mrs Wood condemns her heroine's weakness and folly, but she also gives the reader a sympathetic documentary of Lady Isabel's empty hours, her loneliness, isolation and hopelessness: 'As the days went on, a miserable feeling of apathy stole over her: a feeling as if all whom she had loved in the world had died, leaving her living and alone. It was a painful depression, this vacuum in her heart which was making itself felt in its keen intensity.'[43]

Mrs Wood herself had suffered from a prolonged depressive illness, cured not by adultery but by authorship. The symptoms must have been familiar to her readers as well. Indeed, the punishments for Lady Isabel's flight, severe as they are, seem commensurate with the magnitude of the temptation. In a famous passage, Mrs Wood warns her readers not to risk their security, even at the cost of heroic self-discipline:

> Lady — wife — mother! Should you ever be tempted to abandon your home, so will you awaken! Whatever trials may be the lot of your married life, though they may magnify themselves to your crushed spirit as beyond the endurance of woman to bear, *resolve* to bear them; fall down on your knees and pray to be enabled to bear them.[44]

Ill-equipped as she has been to cope with the roles of daughter, wife and mother, Lady Isabel finds a heroic capacity to suffer and endure in her role as Madame Vine, the governess. In exile and dispossession she finds a kind of strength which qualifies her, in Elizabeth Hardwick's beautiful distinction, as a betrayed heroine rather than a merely betrayed woman. It is because she chooses to return to East Lynne, to subject herself to the vision of all she has lost, that Lady Isabel is so poignant a figure. She accepts the full consequences of her one rebellion; and thus, despite her passivity, her apparent weakness, she is finally the most interesting character in the novel, and morally much more compelling than her respectable husband. As Hardwick explains this phenomenon,

> When love goes wrong, the survival of the spirit appears to stand upon endurance, independence, tolerance, solitary grief. These are tremendously moving qualities, and when they are called upon it is usual for the heroine to overshadow the man who is the origin of her torment. She is under the command of necessity, consequence, natural order, and a bending to these commands is the mark of a superior being.[45]

Mary Braddon's Lady Audley is a heroine because she dominates her environment, not because she endures its punishments with stoic fortitude. She is a determined and resourceful woman with many secrets who set out to liberate herself from economic and emotional bondage. The force of the novel may best be appreciated by those readers familiar with the conventions of Victorian domestic fiction and with the work of Dickens and Wilkie Collins; for Braddon satirizes and subverts many of the orthodox literary views of women. Her major innovation was to make her murderous heroine the frail and pretty angel of the house, rather than the brooding rebel or intellectual. One may expect trouble from a Miss Wade, but not from a Pet Meagles. Both Lady Audley and her creator manipulate the sentimental expectations of their audience. Braddon's tone is sometimes palpably mocking ('Wherever she went she seemed to take joy and brightness with her. In the cottages of the poor her fair face shone like a sunbeam.') and sometimes more delicately ironic ('Better the pretty influence of the tea cups and saucers gracefully wielded in a woman's hand than all the inappropriate power snatched away from the unwilling stern sex.').[46]

Like Lady Isabel, Lady Audley is seduced and betrayed. Her first husband persuades her to marry him, although his family disowns him for choosing a bride from outside the ranks of aristocracy. He goes off to seek his fortune in the Australian goldfields, leaving her with their infant son. Believing herself completely deserted (her husband neither tells her he is leaving nor writes to her from Australia), she leaves the child with her father, takes another name and goes out as a governess. In marrying Sir Michael Audley, she does not mean to commit bigamy, but to free herself from drudgery and dependence. The first husband's return precipitates her career as a criminal.

Readers were astonished, as Braddon intended they should be, to find the adorable and childlike heroine, 'as girlish as if she had just left the nursery',[47] carrying out murder and arson, with the 'nerves of a Lady Macbeth'.[48] Lady Audley's fragility masks physical as well as mental strength. She can walk three miles without tiring; when her first husband confronts her, she manages to push him down a narrow well, although he is 'tall and powerfully built', an ex-cavalry officer.[49] In every crisis, she saves herself by activating plots which, in other people's novels, operate *against* women. She creates a new identity for herself by switching places with a consumptive girl and then faking her own death (the plot which Count Fosco and Percival Glyde use against Laura Fairlie in *The Woman in White*). She conspires to have the detective who is on her trail committed to a private lunatic asylum. To the very end, when she herself is forced to accept a life sentence in a *maison de santé* in Belgium, she is totally self-possessed.

While Lady Audley has many secrets, her essential mystery is psychological rather than factual. Towards the end of the novel the question of her insanity is raised. The Victorians believed that women were more vulnerable to hereditary insanity; and insanity is the term which generally is used to describe a variety of sexual and assertive behaviours by 'respectable' women. In Lady Audley's case, we are obviously not intended to take it very seriously. The doctor called in to examine her cannot at first find any

> . . . evidence of madness in anything she has done. She ran away from her home, because her home was not a pleasant one, and she left in the hope of finding a better. There is no madness in that. She committed the crime of bigamy, because by that crime she obtained fortune and position. There is no madness there. When she found herself in a desperate position, she did not grow desperate. She employed intelligent means, and she carried out a conspiracy which required coolness and deliberation in its execution. There is no madness in that.

Eventually he is persuaded that she has 'the hereditary taint in her blood', latent insanity, which might appear under 'extreme mental pressure'. Lady Audley is not mad, but she is dangerous.[50]

The danger, as Braddon has indicated from the start, lies in the duplicitous lives, the secret lives, of women. Like Audley Hall, of which the author gives us a number of descriptions, Lady Audley's personality is a labyrinth of mysteries, 'a house in which no room had any sympathy with another', a house full of secret chambers'.[51] She is devious and perfidious not because she is a criminal and mad, but because she is a lady and sane.

The effects of divorce court proceedings and of sensation fiction in undermining the sense of decorum, propriety and family secrecy, were considerable. The Reverend Francis Paget thought that by 1868 'incalculable mischief has been done among the upper and middle classes, through their insatiable perusal, for years past, of all this pernicious nonsense.'[52] The Queen herself was in despair at seeing the names of 'Highborn beings' appear in the divorce courts, and vainly urged that divorce proceedings should not be reported in the press.[53] In 1870, not even a decade after the death of his saintly papa, the Prince of Wales himself was summoned in a divorce court suit brought by Sir Charles Mordaunt against his wife and twelve of the Prince's letters to Lady Mordaunt were read in court. Lady Mordaunt herself did not appear in the case — she had been committed to a lunatic asylum.

We may argue that Lady Audley and Lady Mordaunt made little progress in moving out of the doll's house and into the madhouse. But their careers and the careers of their sisters in fiction, adultery and crime make strong statements about the way women confined to the home would take out their frustrations upon the family itself. The women who wrote the novels and the women who read them may not have been aware of their own motives. As Leslie Fiedler explains,

. . . the authors and audience of Popular Art, and the market place mechanism which is their nexus, are typically unconscious of the Unconscious — which is to say, they operate on levels beneath the perception and control of anyone, even of the authors themselves. The novel is subversive because it speaks *from* and *for* the most deeply buried, the most profoundly ambivalent levels of the psyche of the ruling classes.[54]

Behind the polite rhetoric of the petitions for women's suffrage which begin to appear at the end of the decade, was a more urgent demand made manifest in the quiet sound of pages turning — the threat of new fantasies, new expectations, and even female insurrection.

Notes

1.   A.R. Mills, *Two Victorian Ladies* (London, 1969), pp. 66-7.
2.   Justin McCarthy, 'Novels with a Purpose', *Westminster Review*, LXXXII (1864), quoted in Richard Stang, *The Theory of the Novel in England* (New York, 1959), p. 209.
3.   Charlotte Jackson, reader's report for Bentley, British Library Add. Ms. 46661.
4.   Joseph Hatton, *The Tallants of Barton* (1867), p. 59, in Myron Brightfield, *Victorian England in its Novels* (Los Angeles, 1968), Vol. IV, p. 334.
5.   Juliana Ewing, *Six to Sixteen* (Boston, n.d.), p. 126.
6.   E.E. Kellet, *As I Remember* (London, 1936), pp. 232-3.
7.   See the Introduction to Mary S. Hartman, *Victorian Murderesses* (New York, 1977), pp. 5-6.
8.   For accounts of these cases, see Mary S. Hartman, 'Murder for Respectability: The Case of Madeleine Smith', *Victorian Studies*, XVI (June 1973), pp. 381-400; and 'Child Abuse and Self Abuse: Two Victorian Cases', *History of Childhood Quarterly*, II (Fall 1974), pp. 221-48.
9.   Caesar Lombroso and William Ferrero, *The Female Offender* (New York, 1895), p. 297. I am indebted to Mary Hartman for allowing me to quote from the manuscript version of *Victorian Murderesses*. The published text (p. 269) is slightly different.
10.   For an excellent survey of sensation fiction in the 1860s, see Kathleen Tillotson, 'The Lighter Reading of the Eighteen-Sixties', Introduction to

The Woman in White (Boston, 1969). Among the most popular books of the decade are Wilkie Collins, *The Woman in White* (1860), *No Name* (1862), *Armadale* (1866), and *The Moonstone* (1868); Mary Braddon, *Lady Audley's Secret* (1862), *Aurora Floyd* (1863), and *The Doctor's Wife* (1864); Rhoda Broughton, *Not Wisely But Too Well* (1867) and *Cometh Up as a Flower* (1867); Charles Reade, *Hard Cash* (1863), *Griffith Gaunt* (1867), and *Foul Play* (1868); and Mrs Henry Wood, *East Lynne* (1862).

11.   Nuel Pharr Davis, *The Life of Wilkie Collins* (Urbana, Illinois, 1956), p. 216.

12.   James Hart, *The Popular Book* (New York, 1950).

13.   Adeline Sergeant, 'Mrs Henry Wood', in *Women Novelists of Queen Victoria's Reign* (London, 1899), p. 179.

14.   *Westminster Review*, LXXXVI (October 1866), quoted in Norman Page (ed.), *Wilkie Collins: The Critical Heritage* (London, 1974), p. 158.

15.   John Goode, 'Minor Nineteenth-Century Fiction', *Victorian Studies*, XI (June 1968), p. 538.

16.   Simon Nowell-Smith (ed.), *Letters to Macmillan* (London, 1967), p. 56.

17.   Henri Peyre, *Writers and their Critics* (Ithaca, New York, 1944), p. 185. See also Leslie Fiedler, 'The Death and Rebirth of the Novel', in John Halperin (ed.), *The Theory of the Novel* (New York, 1974), p. 191.

18.   'The Lighter Reading of the Eighteen-Sixties', p. xv.

19.   'Sensation Novels: Miss Braddon', *North British Review*, XLIII (September 1865), p. 104 (American edition).

20.   *London Quarterly Review*, XXVII (October 1866), p. 157.

21.   The Reverend Francis Paget, *Lucretia, or the Heroine of the Nineteenth Century* (London, 1868), p. 303. Paget, a Tractarian activist and novelist, was particularly scandalized by the fact that the most passionate novelists were unmarried women.

22.   See Page (ed.), *Wilkie Collins: The Critical Heritage*, pp. 19, 134, 156.

23.   Dee Garrison, 'Immoral Fiction in the Late Victorian Library', *American Quarterly* (Spring, 1976), p. 77.

24.   Braddon, *Aurora Floyd*, I, chap. 3.

25.   Lydia Gwilt in *Armadale*; she also has red hair and 'full, rich, sensual' lips.

26.   'Novels', *Blackwood's*, CII (1867), p. 259.

27.   September 1867: 'Devoted Disciple: The Letters of Mary Elizabeth Braddon to Sir Edward Bulwer-Lytton, 1862–1873', Robert Lee Wolff (ed.), *Harvard Library Bulletin*, XII (April 1974), p. 143.

28.   *Cometh Up as a Flower* (London, 1899), p. 158.

29.   'Miss Braddon', *Notes and Reviews* (Cambridge, Mass., 1921), pp. 115-116.

30.   'Cassandra', in Ray Strachey, *The Cause* (New York, 1969), p. 397. 'Cassandra', an essay dealing with the position of women in the family, was privately circulated and unpublished until the twentieth century.

31.   Isa Jane Blagden, *Agnes Tremorne*, 1861, p. 163; quoted in Brightfield, *Victorian England in Its Novels*, IV, p. 357.

32.   See Margaret Maison, 'Adulteresses in Agony', *The Listener*, 19 January 1961, pp. 133-34.

33.   Quoted in Wayne Burns, *Charles Reade: A Study in Victorian Authorship* (New York, 1961), p. 231.

34.   'Adulteresses in Agony', p. 133.

35.   'Sensation Novels', *Quarterly Review*, CXIII (1863), p. 489.

36.   Quoted in Page (ed.), *Wilkie Collins: The Critical Heritage*, p. 158.

37.   *Saturday Review*, 9 September 1871; quoted in J.A. and Olive Banks,

Feminism and Family Planning (New York, 1964), p. 54.

38.   For some examples, see Jeanne Rosenmayer Fahnestock, 'Geraldine Jewsbury: The Power of the Publisher's Reader', *Nineteenth-Century Fiction*, XXVIII (1973), pp. 253-72.

39.   See Banks, *Feminism and Family Planning*, p. 55.

40.   *Mrs Henry Wood: A Memoir*, 3rd ed (London, 1895), p. 228.

41.   W.B. Maxwell, *Time Gathered* (New York, 1938), p. 281.

42.   'A Lady to the End: The Case of Isabel Vane', *Victorian Studies*, XIX (March 1976), p. 337.

43.   *East Lynne*, Part II, chap. IV.

44.   Ibid., Part II, chap. X.

45.   Elizabeth Hardwick, *Seduction and Betrayal* (New York, 1974), pp. 206-7.

46.   *Lady Audley's Secret* (New York, 1974), p. 4.

47.   Ibid., p. 146.

48.   'Sensation Novels: Miss Braddon', *North British Review*, XLIII (September 1865), p. 96 (American edition).

49.   *Lady Audley's Secret*, p. 9.

50.   Ibid., pp. 248-9.

51.   Ibid., p. 2.

52.   Paget, *Lucretia*, p. 303.

53.   Elizabeth Longford, *Queen Victoria: Born to Succeed* (New York, 1964), p. 373.

54.   Fiedler, 'Death and Rebirth of the Novel', p. 193.

PART TWO KINSHIP AND COMMUNITY

7 VICTORIAN REFORM AS A FAMILY BUSINESS: THE HILL FAMILY*

Deborah Gorham

This essay might best be described as a variation upon a theme that is common enough in nineteenth-century British social history — the story of a family's achievement of a rise in social status through the success of a family business. In this case, however, the business involved was not primarily a money-making enterprise, but rather the marketing of reform ideas. Through a study of the inner dynamics and achievements of this one family I hope to contribute to our understanding of the milieu of those administrators and reformers who helped to create the large and powerful agencies of institutionalised Victorian reform. The family in question, the Hills, may be taken as representative of those members of the bourgeoisie who helped form the administrative and public service institutions of the Victorian state. In the course of three generations the Hills produced a remarkable number of administrators and reformers. By analyzing the interrelationship between the private development of this family and the growth of their ideological position, I hope to illuminate the interdependence between experience within the family and the creation of public ideologies stemming from it. The history of the Hills also illustrates the fact that the new activities of professional administrator and reformer could be supported by a carefully-constructed familial network of a kind usually associated with families involved in landholding, industry, commerce, or politics.

The story begins with Thomas Wright Hill and Sarah Lea who were married in the late 1790s. They settled in Birmingham and established the family group that is the starting point for this study. Their sons, the male members of the mid-Victorian generation that was active from the mid-1820s to the 1880s, form the central focus of this essay. Of the five brothers who survived to adulthood, three achieved major reputations (if not eminence) in the mid-Victorian period. Matthew Davenport, the eldest, was elected MP for Hull in 1833 and a few years later became the first Recorder of Birmingham.[1]

* I should like to thank David Roberts, who originally suggested this topic to me, and also W.R. Carr, Christopher Levenson and Anthony Wohl, who all read and commented on various drafts of the paper.

Frederic was one of the first inspectors of prisons, and later had a civil-service career in the Post Office. Rowland, the most widely known member of the family in his own time, is of course primarily remembered as a postal reformer and father of the Penny Post, although before this period in his life he was involved in a variety of other activities. The two other surviving brothers also had successful if more obscure careers, Edwin working for thirty years as Comptroller of the Stamp Department at Somerset House and Arthur remaining for all his working life as a schoolmaster in the school that was the original family enterprise.

All the brothers shared interests in an overlapping group of social concerns. At an early period in their careers Matthew Davenport, Rowland and Frederic were all interested in the development of popular education and they were all active in the Society for the Diffusion of Useful Knowledge, as was their brother Edwin. Matthew and Frederic both took a lifelong interest in penal reform, Matthew being especially influential in the movement to reform the treatment of juvenile delinquents. All the brothers were active in the temperance movement, and all participated in the development of the National Association for the Promotion of Social Science.

Throughout the lives of the brothers a commitment to a shared set of values underlay all these concerns. However, the way in which they thought these values could be best implemented changed radically over the years. In the early 1820s, the Hill brothers, inspired by constant discussions in the home, perceived themselves as radical reformers standing outside of a society whose fundamental structure they criticized. But by middle life they had all become supporters rather than critics of the prevailing economic, social and political structure of society. In this later period of their lives, although they did discern grave social ills, they defined them as anomalies in a basically successful system, as 'problems' amenable to reform or to rationalization and reorganization.

This growing faith in their society mirrors the progress of their own careers and the upward mobility of the entire family. By middle life, all the brothers had active London-based careers and had contacts with a wide variety of influential people including Jeremy Bentham, Charles Knight, De Quincy, Lord Brougham, Edwin Chadwick and Mary Carpenter, to name only a few of the friends and associates. From the late 1830s to the end of their lives the three most successful brothers moved with considerable assurance in what might be called the circle of the reforming 'establishment'. None acquired large personal fortunes but all had enough money to live comfortable middle-class lives and to provide their children with an upper middle-class education.

The children of the five mid-Victorian brothers and of their surviving sister (the third generation) were for the most part successful upper middle-class late Victorians. Although some of them pursued literary careers, a significant number became, like the preceding generation, administrators and active reformers. In ideological commitment and in the practice of their various professions this third generation of Hills exhibits a remarkable degree of fidelity to the patterns developed by the mid-Victorian generation. There were important differences between the mid- and late-Victorian generations however. In the late-Victorian generation, for the first time, some of the women had active public careers. Another important contrast between the mid- and late-Victorian generations resulted from the worldly success of the mid-Victorian Hills which ensured that members of the third generation began life feeling that they belonged in the world of the successful and powerful. This gave them a natural assurance that the mid-Victorian Hills lacked, in spite of their outward success.

The successes achieved by the second and third generations of the Hill family are in sharp contrast to the character of the original Birmingham family which was obscure, provincial, lower middle-class and beset by money problems. The first task of this essay will be to analyze the way in which the mid-Victorian generation managed to achieve its initial status and influence. One of my chief hypotheses is that the Hill brothers combined an interest in reform with an enlightened self-interest in their own advancement, and that as a cohesive family unit they were able to use the personal contacts of individual members of the family to benefit the careers of other family members.

As a family group, the Hills are best known as the proprietors of an experimental school, known successively as Hilltop, Hazelwood and finally Bruce Castle School. The Hills became known as educational theorists in the 1820s, and their educational work has been discussed in literature on eighteenth- and nineteenth-century educational reform.[2] Their 'experimental' philosophy is fairly well known — it involves self-government and a system of monetary rewards and punishments. What is less well known is the role the school played in both the family's developing social philosophy and in its upward mobility. The school was the family business in the conventional sense (in the sense of being central to the family's income) up to and throughout the 1820s. But after the school's success in the '20s, it became primarily a vehicle for valuable contacts and provided all but one member of the family with an alternative to schoolmastering.

To begin with the provincial beginnings: the early nineteenth-century family of origin is characterized in all the family memoirs and biographies[3] as close-knit, hard-working and goal-oriented; all the sources attest to the great importance of the mother as well as of the father in creating the family's distinctive character.

Thomas Wright Hill, the father, was born in Kidderminster in 1763. His father was a baker; his parents' household was Calvinist in tone and rigid in religious observance. T.W. Hill went to school until he was fourteen and although he wanted to be a lawyer his parents apprenticed him to an uncle in Birmingham who was a brass founder. As a young man in Birmingham, Thomas became a member of the congregation of Joseph Priestley, Birmingham's radical Unitarian minister and scientist. Priestley's influence helped to encourage the intellectual interests that were to stay with him throughout his life and were to play such an important part in the intellectual development of his sons: these were radical political beliefs, an interest in mechanics and a turning away from the strict Calvinism of his youth towards Unitarianism.

In political outlook, Thomas was an eighteenth-century radical in the tradition of Tom Paine. Up until the political era that opened with the Reform Bill of 1832, he was fundamentally hostile to the whole British political system, regarding it as the instrument of the aristocracy. Like many eighteenth-century radicals, he was an enthusiastic supporter of *laissez-faire* economics who believed that all problems in society were political in nature, and he ignored the inevitable economic conflict of interest between the middle and working classes. In addition to his interest in politics, Hill was an amateur astronomer, physicist and inventor with a wide range of interests, but with limited experiences.[4] His were the achievements of an untrained enthusiast working in provincial isolation, an isolation which would become less and less possible with the development of nineteenth-century advances in communication.

In his personal relationships, Thomas Wright Hill was a warm-hearted, kindly man, always willing to talk to his children. He was never a frightening, distant patriarch. As M.D. Hill recollected 'from infancy, he would reason with us. Arguments were taken at their just weight. The sword of authority was not thrown into the scale.' But for all his good nature and enthusiasm, he never accomplished anything that would cause him to be remembered if it had not been for the reputation of his sons. His children and grandchildren, while praising his good qualities, acknowledge at the same time his 'want of method', his lack of ambition, and his inability to manage money. Apparently, until his sons took over the management of the school, the family was never out of debt.[5]

Thomas Wright was almost thirty when he married a woman two years his junior. Sarah Lea Hill, who in her youth had been a 'nursery governess', as one son describes it, provided her family with just those Smilesian qualities that her husband lacked – perseverance, organization, thrift and ambition. She had little formal education but she was proud of her family background, for although her father had been a working man, her mother had been a gentleman's daughter.[6]

Thomas Wright and Sarah married in 1791; and over the next sixteen years proceeded to have eight children, two of whom died in young adulthood.[7] Although the Victorian family memoirs are discreet about most aspects of the private relationship of this late eighteenth-century couple, they say enough for us to glimpse an unselfconscious acceptance of prescribed roles and functions. Although Sarah Hill's sphere of activity was confined to the household, she was no mid-Victorian Angel in the House. She was rather the manager, decision-maker and backbone of the family. Nor did she defer to her husband. One grandchild recalls an incident from the couple's old age. In the course of a discussion, Sarah called her husband 'an old fool', whereupon Thomas Wright went off up the stairs, muttering to himself, 'she called me an old fool – an old fool; but a lucky dog I was to get her, tho!'[8] And all the accounts seem to agree with his assessment. The mother and father were both loved by the children, who acknowledge the influence of both parents and none seems to have felt that their mother's strength of character was 'unfeminine' in any way, although they all agree it was unusual.

Sarah Hill's household functions must have been visibly and obviously essential to the family's well-being, especially since in the management of a small school no sharp distinction would have been made between household functions and business-related functions. Because both the man and woman concerned accepted a social order in which women's and men's *functions* differed, one can surmise that they felt no need to develop a conscious ideology of masculinity and femininity in which male and female *natures* would be defined as fundamentally different.

The Hill's behaviour towards their daughter Caroline would seem to bear out this interpretation. Since Hilltop was a boy's school, Caroline did not attend it, nor does she appear to have received any other formal education. Here the Hills were following a well-recognized pattern in which lower middle-class female children received less education than their brothers. However, there is no indication that anyone thought she would benefit less from education from an intellectual point of view and within the household it appears that she was encouraged to participate in the family discussions on an equal footing with her brothers. She was 'as thorough a reformer as any of them — yet a woman too',[9] as her late-Victorian nephew, Birkbeck Hill remarks.

For many years — at least until 1810 — the family was not well-off financially. However, theirs was not a struggle for bare existence but rather a struggle to maintain their social status. Sarah Hill, especially, was determined that the family should not sink below the standard of lower middle-class respectability to which she considered them entitled, and she devoted her energies to practising frugality. Matthew recalls 'I know she lay in wakefullness, passing much of the night in little plans for ensuring food and clothing to her children by the exercise of the strictest parsimony. [I do not know how she achieved it] but we never lacked for food or raiment and were always looked on by the poor of the neighbourhood as gentlefolk.'[10]

Although Matthew remembers that they never 'lacked for food', at times their diet was scanty. In the family butcher's bills[11] for 1800–1803 the depressing item 'skin and bones' occurs frequently. It seems likely that Mrs Hill skimped on food because this saving could be concealed within the household and would thus entail less of a loss of status than saving on other items such as clothing.

The Hill household did employ servants, but never more than two,[12] and all the children had to help with the household tasks, the boys as well as their sister Caroline participating in cleaning and other housework. All the Hills recall the very hard work and long hours required of them as children, but without resentment. Rowland, indeed, regarded the experience as a good testing ground and talks of the feeling of responsibility he thus acquired at an early age.[13]

It was Mrs Hill who made the crucial decision in 1802 that her husband should take over a small proprietory Birmingham boys' school:[14] she desired this because she felt that schoolmastering would suit him better than trade and because she saw in it the only way, given their circumstances, that their own sons could be provided with a proper education.

After the family takeover of Hilltop school all the boys began attending it, and they all (with the possible exception of Edwin) began to teach in the school at the age of twelve or thirteen. Their own formal education thus came to an end very early. Yet all the brothers were well enough educated as adults to function as professional administrators at high levels. This level of competence was achieved not by means of formal education, but by self-education. T.W. Hill's inter- action with his children has already been mentioned; conversation, taking the form of argumentative discussion, was the foundation of their relationships to one another. As one brother remarked: 'Our family was a little political economy club.'[15]

In addition to the informal education received from their father, the Hill sons' desire for self-improvement was so great that the brothers in adolescence formed themselves into a 'literary improvement society'.[16] There were two 'outside' (i.e. non-family) members of this society, and these were among the very few intimate friends the brothers appear to have had at that time. The Hill family thus served the function of mutual self-help. The brothers were well aware of the deficiencies of this self-education and of its advantages. Rowland, quite late in his twenties, still wished to go to university and tried to plan for it with Matthew's help, but it was always too expensive. However, he remarked when older that the education they received 'was more favourable to originality than if [they] had made great achievements.'[17]

Thus as a family, the Hills shared experiences together to a remarkable extent. The immediate family formed an isolated, self- sufficient group, in which the virtues of mutual love, mutual improvement, unremitting effort and self-discipline were inculcated. 'I enjoy so much the society we have at home that I do not feel the want of a very extreme circle of friends' Rowland confided to his diary in 1815.[18] Their isolation from others outside the family circle was reinforced by their relative poverty, because an extensive social life would have over-taxed the family effort to keep up appearances. Like the family of Richard Edgeworth, the Anglo-Irish educational reformer whose daughter Maria the Hills greatly admired,[19] the Hills made a virtue of the necessity dictated by limited means and laid great stress on the moral superiority that comes from isolating onself and one's children from the corrupting influence of outsiders, including servants. But although it was enclosed and limited, the Hill household was not inward-looking: the purpose of the undertaking was always achievement in the outer world. The imagery of refuge-and-shelter which becomes such a common motif of the family later in the nineteenth century does not characterize this family group. It was, rather, a springboard for social advancement.

However, if it had not been for Matthew and Rowland, the family would not have advanced beyond the moderate success achieved in the second decade of the century. Both of them had ambitions that went beyond lower middle-class Birmingham. Matthew himself broke away separately, taking the decision, which his daughters describe as 'rash',[20] to read for the Bar. By 1818 he had moved to London and had it not been for Rowland, who transformed the school, Matthew alone might have made the escape from provincial obscurity.

Rowland began to take over the school around 1818 when he was in his early twenties. It was he and not his father who developed the Hazelwood System and decided to build a new school at Edgebaston. He even began to take over the school accounts. How did this shift in responsibility affect the family dynamics? Thomas was not an authoritarian patriarch, and apparently he did not resent it when his twenty-year-old son became the real power in the family enterprise; he responded by making Rowland his partner. Unlike his wife and children, Thomas Hill was not ambitious, and his reaction to the school's expansion was twofold: he was always urging caution and asking his children to be satisfied with what had been achieved (the sons report their 'despair' at their father's lack of interest in the school's development) and he constantly expressed solicitous concern about Rowland's health, which was always precarious during these years, because of overwork.[21]

In 1822, the fortunes of both the school and of the family were transformed, not by the school's reputation, but by a book the Hill brothers wrote about the school, which was first published in 1822.[22] The book was well reviewed, and to the Hills' great good fortune, Jeremy Bentham read it and liked it. Bentham asked Matthew to dinner and this friendship with Bentham was probably the single most important event in the family's transition from Birmingham obscurity to London success.

Overnight, Hazelwood was transformed from a small provincial lower middle-class school to a school with a wide reputation and a middle and upper middle-class clientele. Two nephews of George Grote's were removed from Eton and placed at Hazelwood and Bentham and other well-known reformers sent children there. Hilltop and the early Hazelwood had been extensions of the immediate Hill family, but after the publication of *Public Education* Hazelwood

exposed the family to that wider world that Sarah Hill and her sons
had always intended to enter. This new access to a wider community
brought with it pressures and tensions as well as new opportunities.
It brought to Rowland, for instance, a sharp and painful realization
that his own education had been narrow and limited: 'What was my
disappointment,' he writes, 'when the increasing character of the
school opened my way into a class of society among whom I found it
was taken for granted that a man should be acquainted with Latin,
Greek and French — languages of which I was profoundly ignorant,
and the knowledge of which I foolishly thought was confined to a
few.'[23]

These deficiencies were reflected in the school itself, which was
neither as good nor as experimental as the Hazelwood of *Public
Education*. The Hills had some trouble with complaints from parents.
For instance Francis Place sent two sons there and became most
dissatisfied with the school — probably unjustly. The way in which
the Hill family responded demonstrates that the transition from the
limited, enclosed early years to the challenges of new opportunities had
not damaged the strong family solidarity. Because of Place's
association with Bentham, the Hills were anxious to present Bentham
with their side of the story and Matthew, Rowland and Thomas Hill
all acted together to accomplish this result.[24]

When seen in the light of their future careers, the real significance
of the school's success was to bring to the Hill family new and
valuable contacts that served the individual future careers of the
brothers. This end was further served when the Hills changed their
locus of operation from Birmingham to London, with the establishment
of Bruce Castle School in the London suburb of Tottenham in 1827
and the closing down of Hazelwood a few years later.[25]

The founding of Bruce Castle School and the move to London mark
the final stages in the history of the family of origin. The Hill children
now entered the period where they established their adult career
patterns and their own families. The wider significance of the dynamics
of these second-generation families is apparent only when it is
understood in context: first in the context of the development of the
Hill brothers' own ideological position during the period 1820–1840
and then in a still wider context in which one can perceive the ways
in which these individual patterns formed part of more general social
and ideological tendencies. The most remarkable fact about the direction the Hills' ideological development took was the way in which the
progress of their own careers paralleled the more general success not

only of individuals like themselves but also of an ideology. The story of the Hill brothers' ideological development is in many ways a paradigmatic example of movement from the position of radical outsider to that of conservative insider.

As young men, the Hill brothers subscribed to the Tom Paine radicalism they learned from their father. Rowland, Edwin and Matthew demonstrated their active commitment to anti-aristocratic politics after the Napoleonic Wars, when they were all involved in post-war Birmingham radicalism.[26] The brothers' intellectual commitment to an eighteenth-century radical view of human nature is fully enunciated in the outline of the Hazelwood system, *Public Education*. The book is important because it reflects the brothers' intellectual heritage and at the same time foreshadows the development their thought would undergo in the years that followed.

The Hills, like other radical educational theorists of the period, believed that a rational system of education would almost invariably produce a desirable sort of adult. 'We endeavour to teach our pupils the arts of *self government* and *self education*'[27] the young authors say, thus stressing the value of those qualities of their own family life, which, by the early 1820s, they were beginning to regard as having more than the limited virtue of necessity. The description of the Hazelwood system that the brothers outlined in *Public Education* involved a programme of self-government (modelled on current radical ideas about representative government) and a system of rewards and punishments that was based on a mock currency. (Good conduct increased a boy's capital; bad conduct had to be paid for by fines.) In a number of significant ways, the Hazelwood plan resembled a plan for an ideal community governed by the values of representative government and of *laissez-faire* capitalism. The system was explicitly impersonal: the Hills were opposed to the use of fear as a method of discipline, but they were also opposed to excessive direct personal contact with the child. Under the Hazelwood system, the child's relationship to authority depended on a supposedly objective measure of his achievements rather than on the personal emotions of his teachers.

If the ideology behind the Hills' system of education comes from abstract political and economic theory, the immediate model for the Hazelwood plan was the Hill family itself. Many of the specific practices advocated in *Public Education* were part of the family tradition. Like the family, the school allowed ample opportunity to exercise independent judgement, to develop the moral and the reasoning powers

and to practise order, thrift and economy. The Hill brothers' faith in
the virtues of their own family, which they valued both as a training-
ground for professional life and as a model of family affection, formed
the foundation from which their subsequent views about society
developed. Hazelwood was a model republic based on the Hill family
itself. As the brothers went on in life to become administrators and
reformers their reform ideology continued to be shaped by a desire
to transfer the virtues of the Hill family to the public sphere. Thus,
for example, when M.D. Hill became involved in prison reform, he
always stressed the need for surrogate homes in the treatment of
juvenile offenders, and the surrogate homes were always designed to
inculcate the domestic and social values the Hill family had found so
useful in life.[28] And when Frederic Hill, as an old and respected
administrator, corresponded with Edwin Chadwick about the needs of
society it was the order and decency of his early life that he wished to
impose on those he perceived as less fortunate members of society.[29]

What the Hill brothers lost over the years was the optimism of their
father's libertarianism to which they themselves subscribed in early
life. In their working lives the brothers dealt with individuals who
could not be led in a non-coercive way to adopt the virtues they
exemplified and admired. This was especially true of Matthew and
Frederic who were involved as voluntary reformers and as professionals
with the problem of crime. As we shall see later, Matthew and
Frederic both came to support systems of criminal law and of prison
administration that were more coercive and offered less protection for
individual rights than the systems they sought to reform. Although it
was especially evident in relation to their criminal reform views, the
same regulatory spirit characterized other aspects of the social thought
of Matthew and Frederic and of Rowland as well. Thus, the Hill
brothers came to epitomize the type of Victorian administrator and
reformer who saw the working classes or certain distinct segments of
it in terms of a series of social 'problems'. The problems were to be
solved by legislation and by voluntary reform techniques whose
ultimate aim was to control and enforce conformity on the groups in
question.

The Hill brothers' ideas underwent this transformation from belief
in libertarianism to acceptance of regulation over a period that began
in the 1820s and was largely completed by the early 1840s. In order
to illuminate the way in which this ideological transition was related
to the transformation in their own personal lives it must be examined
concurrently with their personal rise in status.

It is with Matthew, the eldest brother, that we must begin in this context, because it was Matthew who first established an independent career and because it was Matthew's contacts which provided the basis both for the initial stages of his brothers' careers and also for the fortunes of the family school. By 1818 when he settled permanently in London, he had begun to make a name for himself as a young man of radical views and by the time he was called to the Bar (in November 1819) several leading figures connected with reform causes had begun to take an interest in him. By 1819 he had won the confidence of Major Cartwright and by 1821 (or perhaps even earlier) he had met Henry Brougham.[30] Among his more intimate friends at this period he counted Charles Knight (with whom he was to work in the Society for the Diffusion of Useful Knowledge) and de Quincy whose favourable review of *Public Education* in the *London Magazine* did much to ensure the book's success. And it was at the time of the publication of *Public Education* that he first made his acquaintance with Jeremy Bentham; this acquaintance quickly flowered, and Matthew and the whole Hill family appear to have become *protégés* of Bentham in the later years of his life.

The success of *Public Education* was the first point at which Matthew's own personal achievements began to affect the family: first, because it transformed the original Birmingham Hazelwood into an experimental school and second, because the founding of Bruce Castle in the London suburb of Tottenham came about through the agency of Matthew's new acquaintances. However, in this case it was not because the Hills received encouragement from their powerful supporters, but because early in 1825 it appeared that Bentham, James Mill, Brougham and some of their associates were themselves going to establish in London an experimental school based on a combination of the principles outlined in *Public Education* and those worked out by Bentham himself in *Chrestomathia*.

The way in which the Hills moved to forestall this plan reveals once again the strength of the family tie and illustrates the way in which individual family members were willing to put their own interests aside in favour of the family's general well-being.[31] Matthew might have chosen to ignore the hints that Brougham threw out about his plans. Instead he quickly informed his brothers and father. Without hesitation Rowland also acted against his own personal inclination. Although he had contemplated establishing a London school, the move was forced on him earlier than he would have wished by the threat of competition from such a powerful source. Now, after a family consultation, Rowland hurriedly departed for London to look for a suitable home for a London branch of Hazelwood and was richly rewarded in finding Bruce Castle, a beautiful sixteenth-century building set in attractive grounds in what was then virtually a rural area. In 1827 Rowland removed to Bruce Castle, and with the closing of Hazelwood in 1833 the rest of the family moved to London, the old couple settling at Tottenham, which until 1876 was to house several different groups and generations among the extended family.

The first London-based organization in which the Hill brothers all participated was the Society for the Diffusion of Useful Knowledge first organized in 1826 with a number of powerful backers, the most important of whom was Henry Brougham. Brougham's interest in Matthew (like himself a member of Lincoln's Inn) probably arose initially from their mutual concern for the education of the working classes. Brougham in the years 1818 to 1820 had distinguished himself as a vigorous advocate of state support for the education of working-class children. M.D. Hill, too, was convinced of the need to extend the benefits of education to the working class, both to children and to adults. He saw education as a universal right, but also he believed (as he was to do all his life) that an educated working class would be of benefit to the whole of society.

In this early stage in his career, support for the dissemination of education especially to adult working men arose directly from the experience of his own family. He both sympathized and empathized with the aspirations of intelligent working men and identified their problems with the struggles both he and all his brothers had experienced in their efforts to educate themselves. Later, when he became concerned with the problem of reforming juvenile and adult criminals, his support for education was grounded much more on a fear of an uneducated and therefore uncontrollable outcast class than it was on an empathy springing from a democratic commitment.[32] But in the late 1820s, when his democratic commitment was still strong, he was convinced that the educational ideas that the family had developed at Hazelwood could be extended to a wider field. There is ample evidence that Rowland and Frederic also believed in education as a force for reform during this period,[33] and it can be assumed (from their participation in the SDUK) that Arthur and Edwin shared these views as well.

The SDUK began with the sort of optimistic faith in education that I have suggested was characteristic of the Hill brothers during the late 1820s. As Frederic said of the organization years later, 'The aim of the society in its fullest scope was to promote a love of freedom and of peace by educating the people and elevating their tastes.' Although it very quickly dwindled into a publishing company run by M.D. Hill's close friend, Charles Knight, its original aims were more ambitious. The Hill brothers all gave extensive time to the society and sat on many of its committees throughout the 1830s and even into the 1840s.[34] By then, however, both they and the SDUK had changed profoundly.

Although I have said that the transformation that took place in the ideology of the Hill family occurred over a fifteen or twenty year period, there was one series of events that in later years became etched in the family's memory as a symbolic landmark in their lives. This was the crisis over the Great Reform Bill. For while the Hill family was transplanting itself from Birmingham to London, Britain was trans- forming its political structure. The Hills experienced the crisis over the Great Reform Bill as having immediate and direct significance for their own lives and characteristically, they approached the event as a family matter. Frederic Hill tells us in his autobiography that the family held a council and '. . . all agreed that one member should be spared from the work of the school and set at liberty to take an active part in the coming struggle'.[35] That was in 1831 when part of the family was still in Birmingham and it was Frederic himself who was selected to assume an active role.

The Hills had been active in 1817–1819 when the impetus for reform had come from obscure men like themselves. That radical agitation had failed. Now, in 1831–1832, the revival of agitation was connected to powerful middle-class interests to whom they found themselves allied. No wonder that the Reform Bill of 1832 figures as both a personal and as an ideological victory for the Hills. They had been fighting for a long time for moderate political reform and at last they were on the winning side.

For Matthew Davenport Hill, the personal transformation in his own life began immediately after the passage of the Reform Bill in 1832, and was a direct result of the bill. Matthew sat for the Borough of Hull in the first reformed parliament as one of a number of new reforming MPs.[36] He was defeated in the election of 1834 and therefore had only a brief parliamentary career; however, the fact that he had been an MP contributed to his success in his law practice, and in the 1830s, for the first time, he began to make a considerable income as a barrister. Although the most important part of his life work began only after 1839 with his appointment as the first Recorder of

Birmingham he had found a secure place for himself from 1832.

Matthew's career was flourishing by 1832, but such immediate success was not the experience of his two brothers, Rowland and Frederic. Rowland's nephew George Birkbeck Norman Hill, who wrote the standard Victorian biography of his uncle, said of the family and the Great Reform Bill: 'with the passing of the Great Reform Bill all bitterness passed away from him and his brothers.'[37] Birkbeck Hill, of course, was writing as a member of the late Victorian intellectual establishment and his purpose throughout his biography was to soften and in some cases suppress evidence of the early radicalism of his uncle and the other members of the family.[38] Throughout, he interprets their mature views as truly representative and regards their youthful radicalism as an aberration caused by the limited circumstances open to them in the period before the 1830s. As a general interpretation, Birkbeck Hill's assessment is correct: it does appear to have been individual, personal success, in the case of Matthew, Rowland and Frederic, that finally caused each of them to abandon the open and libertarian politics and social attitudes of their youth for the more authoritarian and regulationist ideology of their middle and later years. But Birkbeck Hill was incorrect when he asserted that Rowland and Frederic immediately abandoned their stance as radical outsiders in the early 1830s. The 1830s were in fact an interesting and suggestive period in the lives of the brothers, for it appears that under Rowland's leadership the family (with the notable exception of Matthew) might have developed in a very different way from the path of Victorian respectability that all the members eventually did take.

In the early 1830s, Rowland was still saddled with the responsibility of managing Bruce Castle school. However he was not really interested in making a career of schoolmastering and from the mid-twenties he was in search of alternative ways to use his talents. But his loyalty to the family would not allow him to relinquish his work at the school until 1833 when Hazelwood was closed down and the whole family removed to the neighbourhood of London. Rowland could then hand over the management of Bruce Castle to his brother Arthur. Arthur, who was the only one of the brothers who genuinely liked teaching, successfully and happily retained control of the school from the early 1830s until his retirement in the 1860s.[39]

But even before Arthur assumed responsibility for the school, Rowland had been contemplating alternative plans, and some of these plans had extraordinarily radical implications when one considers the pattern of his later life. It appears that during the late 1820s Rowland became interested in communitarianism and that he and two of his brothers seriously contemplated setting up a communitarian experiment using their own family as a nucleus.

The basis for Rowland's interest in communitarianism came from a combination of his interest in Owenism and a belief in the value of his own extended family. Rowland had visited New Lanark in 1822 and was impressed by it. He continued to maintain contact with Owen and his family during the 1820s, and when he heard favourable reports of New Harmony (Owen's communitarian experiment in America), Rowland wrote enthusiastically to one of his brothers saying 'What think you of selling Bruce Castle again and going off?'[40]

Rowland did not act on this impulsive enthusiasm for Owenite communitarianism. However in the early 1830s he did develop a characteristically down-to-earth plan for a private farming community that bears much more resemblance to the plan later adopted at Brook Farm in Massachusetts than it does to Owenism. The plan called for a community whose original membership would be the Hill extended family. Under 'advantages' the proposal suggested that such a community would provide 'Release from many unpleasant restrictions as to the free expression of opinion, to dress, to absurd customs' and allow for 'mitigation of the evils consequent upon the employment of servants.'[41] The proposal does not have the characteristics of an experiment with wide social implications, but is rather an immediate and private plan designed for a specific group of people.

It appears that Rowland had the interest and backing of Frederic for these plans and possibly also of Edwin and Arthur. Matthew, however, disapproved and so did Sarah Lea Hill, and the disapproval in both cases is in character. Matthew, although not unsympathetic to certain aspects of Owenism,[42] was already well launched on a successful career and could no longer see the point of such experimentation. Mrs Hill, from what we know of her, would have seen as a defeat any scheme which involved a suggestion of withdrawal from the struggle for success within the established framework of society. Thomas Wright Hill was not favourably disposed towards the scheme either, but his reservations were expressed in a gentle tone that corresponds well with his character: 'My dear son Rowland', he wrote, 'You and your brothers are the last men to make monks of.'[43]

As it turned out, the proposed community never developed beyond the planning stages and in the early 1830s Rowland was already directing his interest in communitarianism elsewhere. In 1832, he contributed a pamphlet to the growing debate on Poor Law Reform, which he addressed to Lord Brougham. The pamphlet was entitled *Home Colonies*[44] and in it Rowland advocated the establishment of agricultural communities of paupers in Britain. The pamphlet is helpful for an understanding of the development of Rowland's ideological position. It reflects both a sympathy with the condition of poverty and a fear of the evil influences of pauperism. 'Great poverty is always accompanied by ignorance, degradation and recklessness,' he declares. Thus, a major reason for alleviating pauperism is that it is dangerous to society. *Home Colonies* represents one of the first clear statements of regulationist views by a member of the family, although Frederic's book *National Education,*[45] written only a few years after *Home Colonies* reflects the same combination of fear and benevolence applied, in *National Education*, to the education of the poor rather than to pauperism.

In a private autobiographical sketch, Rowland frankly explained that he drew up this plan for home colonies and addressed it to Lord Brougham in the hope that Brougham would help him obtain a government post as investigator of the Dutch system of home colonies.[46] Although Matthew used what influence he could bring to bear on Brougham his efforts were not successful. However, very soon after the publication of *Home Colonies* Rowland made the acquaintance of Gibbon Wakefield, the originator of the South Australian colonization project. Rowland's involvement with the South Australia project led to the first genuinely satisfying employment of his paid career. Rowland helped to negotiate the passage of the South Australia Act through Parliament. Matthew, who was still MP for Hull at the time, provided valuable assistance and when the Act was passed in 1834 Rowland was appointed Secretary to the South Australia Commissioners.

Rowland did an efficient job for the commissioners for more than four years, but during the time he held this post he was already turning his attention to postal reform, the subject that was to be the great work of his life. It was apparently during the years from 1835 until his resignation in 1839 that he worked out his plan for the introduction of the penny post. Although it has not received as much attention from historians of Victorian administrative reform as Poor Law or Prison reform, the reforms instituted in the postal system over the years 1840–1864, for which Rowland had a major responsibility, are an excellent example of the same sort of administrative reorganization. The details of Rowland's reforms of the Post Office need not concern us here. What is important for our purposes is that, once the government accepted his plan in principle, Rowland began the central work of his life.

Rowland's career in the Post Office was not tranquil. He made many enemies and there seems little doubt that he was a difficult person to work with, especially during the early years of his postal career. But he did have a vision of efficiency and organization and by the 1850s his achievements were widely acknowledged. He had a number of powerful supporters in politics on the Whig-Liberal side, among them Gladstone, and by the late 1850s he was well on his way to becoming an Eminent Victorian. He received a knighthood in 1860, an honourary degree from Oxford, and when he died he was buried in the Abbey. His career is enshrined in a five-page entry in the *Dictionary of National Biography.* Sir Rowland was admired not merely as a model of efficiency, but also a social benefactor; cheap postage, by allowing the poor to communicate with one another, helped to preserve working-class family ties.[47]

Rowland Hill's life is interesting not so much because his was a typical Victorian success story, but rather because this style of success was by no means inevitable for him. The youthful iconoclast of the 1820s need not have been transformed into the embalmed figure that emerges from Birkbeck Hill's 'official' life. If one reflects on that crucial period in the 1830s when he was interested in communitarianism, one sees that he could have chosen a very different life pattern. Had the Post Office not provided him with a career, it is possible that Rowland might have developed into a mature radical critic of society, rather than the eminently successful administrator he in fact became.

'When I was a young man, there were very few careers open', Rowland Hill says in his autobiography. 'I never even dreamed of the possibility of getting into the Civil Service.' In sharp contrast, Rowland's brother Frederic apparently decided to be a professional administrator very early in life: 'Even in early boyhood I had conceived a strong wish to obtain someday a useful and important post under Government', he tells us in his autobiography.[48] In 1835 Frederic achieved his boyhood ambition at the relatively early age of thirty-two, when he was appointed Inspector of Prisons for Scotland. Frederic was eight years younger than Rowland and eleven years younger than Matthew. His birthdate and his position in the family had a significant influence on the development of his professional career. Frederic was young enough to benefit early in life from the widening of opportunities for professional administrators that characterised the 1830s. Moreover, Frederic, as Matthew Davenport Hill's younger brother, was able to benefit from Matthew's influence and experience which were by this time considerable.

It was on Matthew's advice that he decided to become a barrister, not so that he might practise law but 'so as to facilitate my entrance into the Civil Service'.[49] It seems to have been a matter of course that he should be entered at Lincoln's Inn where his brother's influence and connections would be open to him. Matthew obtained for Frederic his first post as Parliamentary Secretary to Sergeant Wilde (later Lord Truro), who was one of Matthew's Lincoln's Inn associates. In 1835 when the Whig government passed a prison reform act which established the Inspectorate of Prisons, it was through the influence and contacts of Matthew that Frederic obtained his post as Inspector of Prisons for Scotland. Frederic served as a prison inspector until 1851. In that year, he joined his brother Rowland at the Post Office, becoming Assistant Secretary and serving as his brother's aid and support from then until his retirement.

For both Matthew and for Frederic Hill, the criminal reform movement represented the most important part of their life work. For us, their position on criminal reform is important because it represents the point at which the ideology of the mid-Victorian Hills moved most sharply away from liberal individualism and towards regulation. The brothers were closely associated with prison reform during a period when the subject generated intense popular interest, and they were both part of that large group of Victorian prison reformers who believed that the reformation of the criminal was the moral duty of society and was at least as important a goal as was deterrence.

This moral concern was the driving force behind nineteenth-century criminal reform. Like many other reformers of this period, both Hill brothers believed that crime was a moral disease that could be eradicated only by effecting in the criminal a moral conversion. The prison itself was meant to be a place of reformation rather than a place of punishment: Matthew, accordingly, often referred to the ideal prison as a 'moral hospital'.[50] In the ideally constituted prison or juvenile reformatory, the prisoner's transformation was to be brought about by forcing him to recognize his inner spiritual corruption. The chief technique employed to achieve this inner spiritual self-realization was to separate the prisoner from corrupting influences and force him to look inward. This was the rationale behind the 'separate system' which was such an important influence in nineteenth-century penology and which both Matthew and Frederic vociferously supported.[51]

The Puritan origins of these methods are evident as are the

similarities between Puritan views about child-rearing and much
nineteenth-century penology. In the context that concerns us here, it is
significant that the moral suasion to be applied to the adult or juvenile
criminal was in some ways like the early child-rearing practices of
Sarah and Thomas Hill. Thomas Hill had been a Unitarian who had
come from a strict Calvinist background. The Hills, like so many other
nineteenth-century descendants of the Calvinist tradition, did not
abandon their belief in the need to develop a strong conscience when
they abandoned a belief in the necessity for a conversion experience.
Thomas and Sarah Hill had not, of course, isolated their children from
all human contact, but they had isolated their family group and they
had done this for the explicitly stated reason that it lessened the
danger of moral corruption. The practice of removing criminals from
corruption thus shared some of the characteristics of the early Hill
household: first, there was a shared imagery in which moral
corruption was seen as a contagious disease; second, the motives in both
cases were similar: in both household and prison, isolation was
intended to produce an individual capable of self-reliance and valid
self-judgement. An analysis of the development of the ideology of other
criminal reformers of this period might well reveal that, as in the case
of the Hills, a strong element of Calvinism in the family background
could result in support for the sorts of techniques that were meant to
bring about a 'cure' for crime by encouraging soul-searching.

A second important therapeutic technique advocated by nineteenth-
century prison reformers was work, which was regarded not merely
or even primarily as a training for future life, but as an activity that in
itself would lead to spiritual regeneration. Both Matthew and Frederic
vigorously supported work programmes in prisons and juvenile
reformatories: the links to their own family background in relation to
the character-building properties of work will by now be obvious to
the reader.

Although they both acknowledged that social and economic
inequities bore a part in the creation of crime, by the 1840s both
Matthew and Frederic had become so convinced that crime was
primarily a moral disease that they were led to support indefinite
sentencing and preventive detention. Indefinite sentencing involved
relating the criminal's sentence to his 'cure' rather than to the crime he
had been convicted of committing; preventive detention involved
imprisoning people of a 'criminal type' before they had even been
convicted of a crime. In a speech of 1845, Matthew asserted that the
prisoner must be made to cooperate with his reformers 'heart and soul'

and that only those blinded by 'false humanity' would oppose indefinite sentencing: 'The greater the kindness felt towards him, the stronger will the motive become to leave him under the operation of good training.'[52]

Indefinite sentencing and preventive detention would have involved the abandonment of the traditional protections afforded the individual under English law. Matthew's and Frederic's support for such measures indicates how far they had travelled from the liberal individualism of their youth. If we can define their original heritage as containing two essential elements — liberal individualism and Puritan rectitude — we see that in this instance they abandoned individualism in order better to support those Puritan values that here emerge clearly as the dominant element in their heritage.

Having examined the synthesis of the two major elements that made up the early experiences of the Hill brothers and having traced the development of the ideology of their years of success and power, it is now time to examine the internal structure of the extended family and of its various branches during this mid-Victorian period. In 1842 (the year of Sarah Hill's death), Thomas Wright Hill wrote a letter to his son Frederic in which he said: 'The union of my children has proved their strength.'[53] In 1851 when Thomas died, an obituary writer remarked on the unusual unity between his sons: 'All the brothers . . . by a sort of confederacy of talent, accordance of opinion and unity of sentiment, strengthen each other in their several departments.'[54]

This strong bond between the brothers does appear to have genuinely existed and to have affected both the public and the personal lives of the male family members. In the course of our examination of the development of their careers we have seen glimpses of a strong sense of loyalty and mutual commitment between the brothers. The bond continued throughout their lives. The family group that earlier had been a 'mutual improvement society' became in later years a society for the mutual advancement of its members. Initially, it was Matthew who used his influence with the contacts he made in the 1830s to aid his brothers. In the 1840s, when Rowland was embroiled with his many enemies over his position in the Post Office, the whole family rallied to his support. When Rowland and Frederic had become successful, they in their turn frequently used their influence to further the interests of family members. If this letter to Matthew from Rowland is typical (it was written in the 1820s in response to a request for assistance at an awkward moment) a strong degree of trust seems to have existed between them: 'If the probable advantage to yourself, and through you to other members of the family will, in your opinion, outweigh the probable inconveniences which we may sustain pray say so without the slightest reserve . . .'[55]

One can surmise that one reason that this long-lasting multiple relationship functioned so well was that all the brothers were talented and hardworking and none of them apparently ever desired a post unsuited to his talents. Were there then no strains and tensions in the mutual support network that these brothers developed? Although the authors of the family memoirs do their best to gloss over any difficulties and stress the harmony and spirit of cooperation that existed, there is some indication that Matthew (who was by no means a flexible person himself) was at some periods hard-pressed by the difficulties both Rowland and Frederic created for themselves through the uncompromising nature of their characters. But these were minor irritations and the overriding impression is that the advancement of any member of the group was genuinely seen as a matter that concerned the group as a whole.

The mutual support that the brothers gave to each other in their public careers extended to their private lives and even to their financial arrangements. For almost twenty-five years, the brothers maintained a mutual investment fund: 'The necessary expenditure of each branch of the family was assessed and half the remaining, surplus income in each case, was handed over annually to the "Family Fund" '. The fund was dissolved only when the 'improved circumstances' of each of the brothers made it no longer necessary.[56]

The brothers, then, maintained mutual contacts that benefited them professionally and helped to maintain them financially. Were these instrumental ties combined with personal closeness? Geographically, of course, some of them were separated from others for considerable periods. Frederic lived in Scotland from 1836 until the late 1840s and Matthew moved to a country house near Bristol in 1853. Rowland, however, lived in Hampstead for most of his middle and later years and Matthew and Frederic also lived there when they were in London. Frederic in fact moved to Hampstead in 1851 to be near his brothers and to be within 'easy reach of Tottenham, where my aged father lives'.[57] Frederic's choice of a house is but one indication among many that the various branches of the family saw each other frequently, spent holidays together and travelled together. In fact there is some evidence that some of the third-generation Hills may have found the closeness of the extended family somewhat trying on occasions. As a grand-daughter of Arthur Hill wrote:

The advantages of privacy and intimacy in their intercourse with
their children were . . . in some measure inevitably sacrificed to
advantages of mutual help and support which in the eyes of the
older generation, amply compensated for a scarcely felt loss. With
the younger generation, whose blood-tie was only that of cousinship,
this could not naturally be the case to the same extent.[58]

Great physical closeness existed between the families of Edwin and
Arthur Hill, who lived together 'in patriarchal fashion . . . in a joint
family household' at Bruce Castle.[59] In this joint household, personal
relations and economic functions were integrated: Arthur's wife died
in 1839 and it was Edwin's wife, Ann, who took over the management
of the housekeeping side of Bruce Castle School, thus performing an
obviously indispensable function. She continued to do so for more
than thirty years, until her brother-in-law retired as headmaster in the
1860s.

Ann Hill's participation in the operation of Bruce Castle School
raises questions about the female members of the family which one
wishes it were possible to answer. Throughout most of this paper we
have been observing the functioning of family institutions as they
related to the male members of the family because there is little
question that in the case of the Hills of the mid-Victorian generation it
was the male bonds that were of primary importance. Not very much
is known about the women who married into the family or about the
surviving sister, Caroline. Caroline had married Francis Clark, a close
friend of the Hill family.[60] Francis and Caroline settled near
Birmingham, where they remained until they emigrated to Australia
in the 1850s. Although the brothers maintained their connections with
their sister, the relationship was not as close as the relationship between
the brothers themselves, simply because throughout all their lives
all the men devoted such a large part of their energies to their careers.
Moreover, in contrast to their father, all of the brothers (except
Arthur) were involved in careers that not only involved a sharp
separation between the private world of the home and the public world,
but also, in the case of Rowland, Matthew and Frederic, involved
frequent absences from the home.

We have seen that in numerous ways the Hill men exemplify many
crucial social and ideological changes that occurred in the course of the
early and mid-nineteenth century. Do their private family lives reflect
the changes that occurred in the definition of sex roles? It is now
generally accepted that sex divisions increased among middle-class

people in the mid-Victorian period. As a family-centred economy
became less and less common, the wife's role became more restricted
to the purely domestic one of manager of consumption, her
economic function was de-emphasized and increasing emphasis was
placed on the moral and spiritual qualities of women which were
defined as being distinctively different from those of men.

Although the marriages made by the Hill brothers do not form a
uniform pattern, one can discern at least a tendency towards
conformity to this new mid-Victorian pattern in some of the branches
of the family. This tendency was probably least apparent in the
relationship of Edwin to his wife: Ann Hill, as we have seen,
performed a function very similar to that of her mother-in-law Sarah.
The tendency was probably most apparent in the relationship between
Matthew Hill and his wife Margaret.

Matthew, it seems, did want Margaret to be an 'Angel in the House',
a woman whose intellectual and emotional character was to be
determined by her function as his wife. Their courtship correspondence
is full of political talk on both sides, and it is clear that Matthew
appreciated his future wife's intelligence. However, her interest in
public affairs was to go as far as *he* not *she* wanted. He writes to her
in 1819, ' . . . I can get nothing from you which might not appear in the
newspapers. Instead of a young lady going to be married, you seem to
me like a young candidate for a seat in the House.' In another letter,
he told her that he was sure she would strike the right balance between
submission and independence, acting with him out of 'similarity of
taste and conviction of propriety, not out of blind and slavish
obedience'. But it is clear that *he* will determine the taste. His
daughters, who were early suffragists, but who accepted the
conventional mid-Victorian view of woman's role, say that her
education and enthusiasm were important for her husband, because
for him 'sympathy was a necessity of life'.[61]

As many writers have pointed out, religious observance played a
major part in the outward ritual of the ideal mid-Victorian family. Here,
too, it appears that some of the mid-Victorian Hills conformed to the
ideal pattern. They all appear to have become members of the Church
of England as they became successful and Rowland Hill appears to have
been particularly pious, even instituting family prayers in his household.
This religious conformity represents a sharp break with their early
upbringing. In the household of Thomas and Sarah, religious observance
was ignored and there is direct evidence that Rowland too, when young
was a non-believer: he annotated his adolescent diary in his old age and

cut out three pages, making the note that the pages removed contained some 'immature thoughts about religion'.[62] (Birkbeck Hill does not mention this in his biography.) But it should be noted that at least one member of the third generation reverted to the practices of her grand-parents: after her parents' death, Rosamund Davenport Hill became a Unitarian.[63]

Several of the third and fourth generation Hills were successful and even eminent. Matthew's children, who were active social reformers, provide the clearest example of the continuation of the tradition of a regulationist ideology into the third generation. Matthew's daughters Rosamund and Florence were, like their father, concerned with the problem of juvenile delinquency. They took a special interest in the problem of wayward women and girls and they both had a strong belief in the efficacy of a home-like environment in preventing and curing female delinquency. Although both of them were early supporters of female suffrage, they were neither democratic nor did they challenge conventional sex-role stereotyping. Rosamund Hill, who served for many years on the London School Board, was best known as a board member for her vigorous support for special domestic science classes for girls.[64] Rosamund's and Florence's brother Matthew Berkeley, who was a successful physician, was also active in relation to social issues. His regulationist proclivities were manifest in his vociferous support for the Contagious Diseases Acts, those acts that sought to control venereal disease by the enforced monitoring of the health of prostitutes.[65]

Berkeley Hill had a son who was named after his paternal grand-father.[66] The life history of this fourth-generation Matthew Davenport offers a number of poignant contrasts to the history of the earlier generations of the family and is a good place at which to end this family biography. In his reminiscences, M.D. Hill recalls a childhood complete with town and country houses and a faithful nanny who stayed with the family for thirty years. He attended Eton and Oxford and then returned to Eton as a master, where he remained for most of his life. The intense interest in reform that had characterized his grandfather, great uncles and great-grandfather is quite absent from his reminiscences. This Matthew Davenport Hill was a conventional upper middle-class gentleman, who accepted the class structure of his society and who, in his account of the family history, did his best to improve in the telling the social status of his paternal great-grandparents. One wonders what the proprietor of Hilltop and his wife would have made of their great-grandson, the master at Eton.

Notes

1.   A Recorder was the legal officer who presided over the Court of Quarter Sessions in a city or borough having its own Quarter Sessions.

2.   There is a full treatment of the development of Hazelwood in W.A.C. Stewart and W.P. McCann, *The Educational Innovators* (London, 1967). See also J.L. Dobson, 'The Hill Family and Educational Change in the Early Nineteenth Century', *Durham Research Review*, Vol. II, 10 (1959), pp. 261-71.

3.   The Hill family memoirs include: For T.W. Hill, *Remains of the Late Thomas Wright Hill, Esq., F.R.A.S. (Together with Notices of His Life, Etc.)* (London, privately printed, 1859). For Rowland Hill, George Birkbeck Norman Hill, *The Life of Sir Rowland Hill and the History of Penny Postage*, 2 vols. (London, 1880) and *Sir Rowland Hill, the Story of a Great Reform, Told by His Daughter Eleanor C. (Hill) Smyth* (London, 1907). For Matthew Davenport Hill, Rosamund and Florence Davenport Hill, *A Memoir of Matthew Davenport Hill* (London, 1878). For Frederic Hill, *An Autobiography of Fifty Years in Times of Reform (Edited with Additions by his Daughter Constance Hill)* (London, 1894). Although there are no memoirs of Edwin, Arthur or Caroline Hill, information about them is to be found in both the memoirs of their brothers and in the memoirs of the third generation members of the family. These third generation memoirs include the following: Ethel Metcalfe, *Memoir of Rosamund Davenport-Hill* (London, 1904); *Letters of George Birkbeck Hill, Arranged by His Daughter Lucy Crump* (London, 1906). Matthew Davenport Hill, *Eton and Elsewhere* (London, 1928), is a fourth generation autobiography. In addition to these printed sources there are some family papers, housed at the Bruce Castle Museum, Tottenham, London. These include Rowland Hill's diary, which he kept from 1813 until the 1820s. The diary is in five volumes.

4.   Thomas Wright Hill's work included a system of shorthand and a plan for proportional representation. He was an active member of the Birmingham Philosophical Society (a scientific society whose membership was wider than the more elite Lunar Society of Birmingham) and frequently gave papers and performed experiments at meetings of the Society. So did Rowland. For Hill's work see: Thomas Wright Hill, *Selections from the Papers of the Late Thomas Wright Hill* (London, 1860).

5.   For the sons' assessment of their father's character see: *Remains of T.W. Hill, (passim)* and G.B.N. Hill, I, pp. 18, 31.

6.   On Sarah Lea: G.B.N. Hill, I, p. 6 and Frederic Hill, *Autobiography*, pp. 14-15.

7.   The children of Thomas Wright Hill (1763–1851) and Sarah Lea Hill (1765–1842) were: Matthew Davenport (1792–1872); Edwin (1793–1876); Rowland (1795–1879); Arthur (1798–1885); Caroline (1800–1877); Frederic (1803–1896); William Howard (1805–1830); Sarah (1807–1840).

8.   G.B.N. Hill, I, p. 32.

9.   Ibid., I, p. 195.

10.   *Remains of T.W. Hill*, p. 121.

11.   These bills are in some papers relating to household accounts in the Hill family papers at Bruce Castle.

12.   In the *Remains of T.W. Hill*, two are mentioned (see p. 121). In his diary Rowland mentions visiting a servant who had worked for them for fourteen years, from 1795 until her father died. (See *Diary*, Vol. I,

p. 119 (1814).)

13. G.B.N. Hill, I, pp. 54 ff.

14. See ibid., p. 47 and Frederic Hill, *Autobiography*, p. 19.

15. G.B.N. Hill, I, p. 23.

16. Rowland Hill's *Diary*, I, p. 215 (for May 1816).

17. G.B.N. Hill, I, p. 66.

18. *Diary*, I, p. 198. Frederic in his *Autobiography* (p. 33) says he had three friends.

19. See Frederic Hill, *Autobiography*, pp. 26-7 for example. Maria Edgeworth is best known for her children's stories, but it is in *Practical Education* (1798), written with her father, that one sees parallels with the family style and educational practices of the Hills.

20. Rosamund and Florence Davenport Hill, *Memoir*, p. 16.

21. G.B.N. Hill, I, pp. 105-6.

22. When first published it had the title *Plan for the Government and Liberal Instruction of Boys in Large Numbers* (London, 1822). The more widely known second edition had the title *Public Education: Plan for the Government and Liberal Instruction of Boys in Large Numbers* (London, 1825). The authorship was anonymous. It has been attributed variously to Rowland, Matthew and Arthur, but was probably written in collaboration by Rowland and Matthew.

23. See G.B.N. Hill, I, p. 66 for this statement.

24. Place felt that his boys were not learning enough. The Hills felt that they were unruly, lazy children. The trouble occurred in 1824. Letters concerning the matter are in the Bentham MSS, University College, London.

25. From a prospectus advertising the new school dated March, 1827, it appears the school opened in 'Midsummer, 1827', Bentham MSS, item 18/182. The fees ranged from £60 to £80 a year. When Thomas Hill had opened Hilltop in 1802 he had charged £25 per annum for boarders, £4 for day boys, an indication of the fact that Bruce Castle served a more affluent clientele than the original Hill enterprise.

26. See Rosamund and Florence Davenport Hill, *Memoir*, pp. 49-50, and Frances D. Cartwright, *The Life and Correspondence of Major Cartwright*, 2 vols. (London, 1826), II, p. 212.

27. *Public Education*, p. xx.

28. Hill was one of the major English supporters of the Frenchman Demetz who ran the reformatory, Mettray. As he says in his book *Our Exemplars* (a collection of biographical sketches of people who have 'benefited their fellow creatures') Demetz defined the 'true reformatory element' as the ' "family system". It consists in restoring, as far as artificial means will permit, the feeling of home to the poor child, who for lack of its beneficient influences, has gone astray.': Matthew Davenport Hill, *Our Exemplars, Poor and Rich* (London, 1861), p. 262.

29. Frederic Hill's correspondence with Edwin Chadwick began in 1835 and continued until the 1890s. The correspondence is in the Chadwick Papers at University College, London.

30. In the Brougham Papers at University College, London, there is a very extensive collection of letters from Matthew Hill to Brougham extending from the 1830s until the 1860s.

31. For references to this correspondence: G.B.N. Hill, I, pp. 180-1.

32. See for example his letter to Brougham, July 30 1859 in the Brougham MSS.

33. *Hansard*, Third Series (1833), XV, 206. Frederic did his first important piece of writing on the issue: Frederic Hill, *National Education Its Present*

State and Prospects (London, 1836).

34.   The SDUK minute books and correspondence reveal that all five Hill brothers were continuously (if not closely) involved with the society. SDUK papers are at University College, London.

35.   Frederic Hill, *Autobiography*, p. 77.

36.   For his campaign see Rosamund and Florence Davenport Hill, *Memoir*, pp. 113-19. Rowland acted as his brother's campaign manager.

37.   G.B.N. Hill, I, p. 200.

38.   Although Birkbeck Hill used his uncle's diary, he suppressed parts of it, omitting for example the references to Rowland's youthful Deism.

39.   Arthur wrote one book on educational theory: Arthur Hill, *Hints on the Discipline Appropriate to Schools* (London, 1855).

40.   G.B.N. Hill, I, p. 206.

41.   Ibid., I, p. 208.

42.   Matthew admired New Lanark, but felt that Owen's socialism was a mistake: '. . . it was coincident with Owen's decline.' Rosamund and Florence Davenport Hill, *Memoir*, p. 371. Matthew was, however, an enthusiastic supporter of the co-operative movement. The Rochdale Pioneers figure in M.D. Hill, *Our Exemplars*.

43.   G.B.N. Hill, I, p. 213.

44.   Rowland Hill, *Home Colonies: Sketches of a Plan for the Gradual Extinction of Pauperism and for the Diminution of Crime* (London, 1832).

45.   In *National Education*, Frederic also stresses the need to educate to prevent 'Drunkenness, idleness and crime . . .' (p. 18).

46.   G.B.N. Hill, I, p. 202.

47.   See Gladstone's assessment of the 'social and moral benefits' of Rowland's reforms. British Museum Additional MSS 44753, f. 44-7.

48.   Frederic Hill, *Autobiography*, p. 113.

49.   Ibid., p. 114.

50.   E.g. in a speech given at the cornerstone laying ceremony for the new Birmingham Gaol, 29 October 1845. See Matthew Davenport Hill, *Suggestions for the Repression of Crime, Contained in Charges Delivered to the Grand Juries of Birmingham* (London, 1857), p. 103.

51.   For Matthew, idem. For Frederic, see his first report as prison inspector, *First Reports of the Inspector of Prisons*, XXXV (1836), p. 4 and *passim*.

52.   M.D. Hill, Birmingham Gaol Speech, 1845, in *Repression of Crime*, p. 105. For preventive detention see his 'Charge' in ibid., pp. 186-7.

53.   F. Hill, *Autobiography*, p. 334.

54.   *Spectator* obituary, 21 June 1851, quoted in ibid.

55.   G.B.N. Hill, I, p. 186.

56.   F. Hill, *Autobiography*, p. 110.

57.   Ibid., p. 291.

58.   *Letters of George Birkbeck Hill, Arranged by His Daughter Lucy Crump*, p. 9.

59.   Ibid.

60.   He was the son of Thomas Clark from whom Thomas Hill had originally bought the school that became Hilltop.

61.   On Hill and his wife, see Rosamund and Florence Davenport Hill, *Memoirs*, pp. 22 ff.

62.   The pages removed are in Vol. III, pp. 6-13.

63.   Ethel Metcalfe, *A Memoir of Rosamund Davenport-Hill*.

64.   Ibid., p. 52. Rosamund and Florence visited their Australian cousins after their father's death. For their suffrage involvement, see several letters in

the Autograph Collection, Vols. I, II and VIII at the Fawcett Society Library, London. For Florence's anti-democratic views, see a letter from Florence to M.G. Fawcett, 20 December 1906: she opposes 'adult suffrage' and wants a suffrage limited to propertied men and women.

65. For Berkeley Hill's support of the C.D. Acts, see for example papers read and accounts of meetings of the National Association for the Promotion of Social Science, where the issue was discussed: for example, *Paper read at the Health Department Meeting of the NAPSS*, 30 March 1868.

66. For Berkeley Hill's son see M.D. Hill, *Eton and Elsewhere* (London, 1928).

8 FAMILY DISINTEGRATION AND CREATIVE REINTEGRATION: THE CASE OF CHARLOTTE BRONTË AND *JANE EYRE*

Maurianne Adams

Jane Eyre, the novel, read in the context of Charlotte Brontë's biography is not only a 'family' novel, but can be seen as a reintegration in the form of imagination of a disintegrating family structure. The immediate context involved the collapse of the two men of the family — Branwell, the brother on whom the Brontë family had pinned its hopes, was a physical and moral wreck, and Patrick, the father on whose church incumbency the Haworth household depended, was growing frail and blind. Thus *Jane Eyre* was written after novels by Emily and Anne Brontë in a desperate collaborative effort toward financial stability and maintenance of the family as a social and personal unit. No wonder that *Jane Eyre* should suggest parallel and coexistent romantic and realistic solutions to the dilemmas threatening their sustenance and security as a family.

Jane Eyre in its form and context is thus deeply rooted in Charlotte's family experience, but at the same time it transforms and transcends the recurrent family traumas of illness, death, and separation experienced by Charlotte Brontë both as a child within her family of origin and as a governess and student-teacher on the peripheries of various families by employment. Both for Charlotte the creator and Jane her creature, family life came to represent a microcosm of a society, which like her own family, was threatened by economic instability and fluctuations of fortune. In the family as seen through the biography and as imaged in the novel, we are shown an internal structure which is a source of psychological support, a world unto itself, while its economic instability within the larger world kept its members separated from each other and perched on the edges of other family's households.

There is no need here to go into the details of the Brontë family history, which is amply covered in numerous biographies — the early work of Elizabeth Gaskell which still retains its primacy despite the more recent and more complete accounts in Ratchford, Gérin, Moglen and Peters.[1] But a few biographical points are worth isolating, in support of the two major arguments of this essay. The one is the ability of the sisters collectively to salvage a disintegrating family structure through the activity of writing and of Charlotte to imagine the family's reintegration in *Jane Eyre*; the second is the increasing importance to Charlotte of her sisters in replacement of the earlier primacy of both her brother and father.

The biographical factors I would lean on include the ambitions and the upward mobility of the father, who made his way through the Church of England via Cambridge University out of a poor, Irish, peasant background. These ambitions, which included intense pleasure and considerable accomplishment in writing,[2] were transferred to his only son, but ultimately carried out by Charlotte, Emily and Anne. It is also important to note that the children were extremely close in age: the two elder sisters who died early, Maria and Elizabeth, were born in 1814 and 1815. Charlotte followed in 1816, Branwell in 1817, Emily in 1818, and Anne in 1820. The mother, also named Maria, died a year later, after a lingering cancer which she tried to hide from the children, who apparently developed their private and secret system of mutual sustenance and support to replace her. Another fact which gains importance in the retrospective light of *Jane Eyre* is the birth- place of the younger four children at Thornton, a placename which emerges in the 'Thorncliffe' of the childhood writings of Branwell and Charlotte, and subsequently in Thornfield Manor of *Jane Eyre*, a place Jane calls 'my home, my only home'. Haworth, the incumbency to which the Brontës moved in February 1820 and with which they are usually identified, was the deathplace of their mother the following September. It was also the deathplace of Maria and Elizabeth, both of whom had gone to Cowan Bridge Clergy Daughters' School in 1824, to be followed by Charlotte several months later.

It is impossible to over-emphasize the importance of the activity of writing for these children as a means both of amusement and of consolidation despite physical separation. When Charlotte left for Cowan Bridge she gave Anne a tiny, carefully illustrated booklet ('There was a little girl and her name was Ane') and after the deaths of the two elder sisters, writing became for those who remained and emerged into adolescence a means also of emotional sustenance, of avoiding and of transcending the agony of separation and tragedy that continued to haunt this small family, now not so much a 'family' as a sister-brotherhood, with a withdrawn and absentee father, a severe maiden aunt and an elderly servant.

It is also a matter of some significance that Charlotte, sent off to join her elder sisters at Cowan Bridge at the age of eight was the same

age as Jane Eyre when we first meet her, alone and excluded from her
adoptive family, essentially homeless, bitterly lonely and on the verge
of rebellion. Much of the Cowan Bridge tragedy finds its way into
Jane Eyre — the anger and helplessness with which Charlotte watched
Maria's and then Elizabeth's rapid and unattended tubercular decline,
as well as the typhoid epidemic which claimed the lives of many of
her schoolmates. Maria died at home in May 1825; Charlotte
returned to Haworth in time to observe Elizabeth's death a fortnight
later. The sufferings of her sisters at school, and the humiliations that
attended their illnesses, are both lovingly and angrily registered in the
death of Helen Burns in *Jane Eyre*, insofar as the 'Lowood' of the
novel is a virtual carbon-copy of Cowan Bridge.[3] The six children who
had clung together and walked the moors while their mother slowly
died, had by now become only four. Charlotte, at the mere age of nine,
with the sudden and unexpected deaths of her older sisters in an
already motherless family, was thrust into a mother's role for the three
younger children behind her before she had even approached
adolescence. The record, from Gaskell on, suggests a tightly-knit
sibling network, the father Patrick by now a virtually invisible figure
secluded in his study and the maiden aunt, Elizabeth Branwell, an
outsider to this 'family' of children. The kindly servant girls from the
old Thornton home, Nancy and Sarah Garrs, were eventually replaced
by Tabitha Aykroyd ('Tabby') whose stories are integrated into
Bessie's fairy tales in *Jane Eyre* as well as into the portrait of the
servant Hannah of the last third of the novel.

The fictions shared and planned by the children were recorded
in the 'histories' of successive imaginary kingdoms, first Glasstown,
on which all four worked collaboratively, then Gondal, from which
Emily and Anne seceded, leaving Branwell and Charlotte to march
armies, plan coups and countercoups and develop the major characters
of Angria. These parallel fantasy kingdoms constituted a joint
creative activity recorded in tiny newspapers and novelettes and kept
a jealously guarded secret even from their closest friends — more
accurately, from Charlotte's friends, for Charlotte alone made friends
outside the family, friends whom she called 'sisters' but who knew
little of the inner workings of family life and nothing whatever of
shared family fantasy.[4] Whenever Charlotte was separated from
Branwell, letters from home and news from home meant news of
Angria. Nothing was more real, more gratifying, than this shared,
secret world of fantasy, whether among the three sisters and brother,
or the paired sets of Emily and Anne, Branwell and Charlotte. Thus a

family of children described by outsiders as clinging, peering out from behind each other when strangers came into the room, was strong within itself, bonded by a sort of family therapy into which the father consciously, and I suspect wisely, never intruded. There is one sense in which the 'real' life of this young family, at least the life that they themselves saw as most real and missed most keenly when separated, was a life of orphans. By an odd twist of fate the young Brontës actualized the sort of parentless childhood fantasies recorded in so many later Victorian and Edwardian children's books.

The pairing off started early, recorded as early as 1827 (Charlotte aged eleven, Branwell ten) in editorials written for *Branwell's Blackwood's Magazine* signed U.T. ('Us Two') or W.T. ('We Two'). Charlotte used male pseudonyms, many of them connected with Branwell's characters in their magazine stories and the chronicles which unfolded the fictional history of their imaginary kingdom, Angria, many of her male characters having Branwellian traits as well. The continuity of this collaboration in writing between brother and sister, extending until Charlotte picked up the thread of formal education in 1831, leaving home, brother and Angria, was a life-line between the two, which physical separation could not sever. The family biography suggests that brother and sister used the creation of their imaginary kingdom in the world of their writing to bridge separa- tion and transcend whatever privation daily life had to offer; the evidence suggests the total absence of any recognizable distinction between reality and imagination in their closed family system.

Gérin has remarked convincingly on the 'fusion of minds' connect- ing Charlotte with Branwell, suggesting that Charlotte's male characters in the Angrian sagas were as like her brother 'as two peas',[5] while Moglen finds their relationship symbiotic, in its way 'as incestuous as was Byron's with Augusta Leigh', although 'not an incest of body but of mind: an incest of the imagination. In the intense privacy of shared fantasy, their identities were fused.'[6] The Branwell-Charlotte sagas, therefore, show more of the inter- relation of brother and sister than of the later support network among the three sisters; Emily and Anne at this time were busily engaged on their own writings and Emily, evidently, on her own poetry. Not surprisingly, then, the first major 'separation' after Cowan Bridge, caused by Charlotte's departure for Miss Wooler's school at Roe Head in 1831, was overcome by the continued communication with Branwell as he and Charlotte wrote to each other in a self-perpetuating cycle of plot and characterization in the continuing Angrian saga.

But more was happening to Branwell than happy collaboration over imaginary kingdoms. Pushed forward by the family as a potentially great painter, the single boy-child, who was expected ultimately to sustain the family, went to London in 1835, shortly after Charlotte had accepted a post as assistant teacher at Roe Head where Emily joined her for a few months as a 'free' student. Thus, three of the four children (now in adolescence) were away from Haworth at the same time.

Branwell failed miserably – he used none of his letters of recommendation, drank away the small financial allotment the family could spare, and returned home in despair. The course from there was downhill: failure as a portraitist in Bradford by 1839, a brief stint as tutor in the family of the Postlethwaites from January to June 1840, a railway clerk on the Manchester -Leeds Line from October 1840 until March 1842 and, finally, the loss of his post as tutor to the Robinson family (where Anne was governess) after two-and-a-half years, in June 1845. He had been dismissed from the Postlethwaite position; he had faulted in his accounts on the railway position and fallen into wretched living conditions and worse company ('he was so shattered by "the cold debauchery of his life" as he himself spoke of it later, as to shrink from facing the loving glances of those at home');[7] he was expelled from the Robinson household in disgrace, his adulterous affair with Lydia Robinson, the wife, discovered finally by the husband although apparently already known to the children. From bad Branwell went to worse: alcoholism, opium addiction. Setting fire to his own bed (an episode recounted in *Jane Eyre*), he was taken into his father's bedroom where he was patiently nursed, despite rantings and threats on his father's life.

Charlotte's experience at Roe Head from 1835 on was altogether different from her first experience in 1831, when she had been supported by news from home and Angria. Branwell's decline was gradual, recognizable, and irreversible. His occasional letters still were imaginatively sustaining: of his letters, with new twists in the fate of their Angrian world, she wrote in her secret journal, 'I lived on [their] contents for days', worrying whether he had really killed one of her favourite characters and reliving in her mind's eye the Duchess, buried alone 'in the cold early on this dreary night . . . in a vault closed up.'[8] The preoccupation with death recalls an early fictionalized account of Maria's death by Branwell which Charlotte had cast in her own voice, under the female pseudonym of *Jane* Moore.

By now, however, alone as a teacher at Roe Head, with letters few and far between, Charlotte was overwhelmed by hallucinatory, uncontrolled, and terrifying fantasies of the imaginary kingdom, terrifying precisely because of their imaginative intrusion in the midst of everyday life at Roe Head. The hallucinations continued to bond her to Angria, and to home.

> That wind pouring in impetuous current through the air . . . that wind I know is heard at this moment far away on the moors of Haworth. Branwell and Emily hear it . . . they think perhaps of me and Anne — Glorious! Childe Harold! Flodden Field! the burial of Moore! why cannot the blood rouse the heart the heart wake the head the head prompt the hand? to do things like these?
>
> Then came on me rushing impetuously all the mighty phantasm that we had conjured from nothing to a system strong as some religious creed. I felt as if I could have written glorious — I longed to write . . . But then a Dolt came up with a lesson. I thought I should have vomited.[9]

Charlotte clearly abhorred teaching, but her depression appears to have been symptomatic of extreme homesickness, a homesickness of which her involuntary visions were the reverse side of the coin. She abhorred teaching because school was not home, her students were not her family, she was a dependent among aliens, losing hours from her precious and life-sustaining imaginary realm. Branwell was briefly in London, then ignominiously at home; Emily had gone home after homesickness led to serious physical decline; and Anne, a new student in another section of the school, was scarcely accessible to the busy and conflict-torn teacher Charlotte.

Only during school vacations could Charlotte write important and more sustained writings in the mode of Angria but written on her own: 'Passing Events' (Easter 1836), 'Julia' (June 1837), 'Mina Laury' (Christmas 1837-8). The desperation of the intervening years of family separation had led the sisters and brother to compile an inventory of their collective work, comprising stories by Charlotte and Branwell, Gondal verses by Emily and Jane. Their collective output had been formidable. Charlotte's surviving manuscripts for 1834 alone comprise 141,000 words of prose narrative and 400 lines of verse.[10] Briefly considering they might become writers, Branwell wrote to *Blackwood's* and to Wordsworth for encouragement, but his efforts were spurned; Charlotte inquired of Southey whether a woman might become a writer rather than a school-mistress or governess, but Southey

advised not. In a second letter, Charlotte told of her father's limited
and precarious income, her responsibilities to her family as the eldest
of the children, the family investment in her education, and the
promptings of duty to become a governess, despite the force of
her involuntary imagination — 'but I try to deny myself'. Southey
had advised that 'Literature cannot be the business of a woman's life
and ought not to be', and on her twenty-first birthday in April 1837,
back at Roe Head, Charlotte endorsed his advice with the sad note,
'Southey's advice to be kept for ever.'[11]

If family circumstances had not been straitened, if Branwell had
fulfilled his family's expectations, if the father's eyesight and
consequently his livelihood had not been threatened, this is perhaps
the last we might have heard of Charlotte Brontë, if one had even
known to look for her childhood writings and private journals. Continue
to write she did, but in the secrecy of the Angrian chronicles. Although
the vacation writings, written while at home from Roe Head and then
from her brief first stint as a governess at Stonegappe, are of a piece
with the earlier sagas of Angria, an objectivity towards writing and
towards Branwell emerges in the novelette, 'Captain Henry Hastings',
written in the interval between Roe Head (May 1838) and Stonegappe.
The novelette connects sister with brother in Charlotte's use of the same
pseudonym Branwell had used while she was at Roe Head. Branwell was
now painting in nearby Bradford on weekdays and often home on
weekends; we know of one occasion on which Charlotte visited his
lodgings at Bradford and she must have known he was drinking heavily.
The Byronism that pervades the male characters of Angria, and the
character of Branwell as well, emerges in 'Henry Hastings' with a clear
even though ambivalent attitude taken towards it. 'Henry Hastings' is
an explicit sister/brother story, the first of Charlotte's writings to deal
not with sadistic Byronic heroes and masochistic, dependent heroines,
but with a sister of independent mind whose publicly dishonoured
brother is not privately degraded, who gives up all for him, yet with
an implication both of Charlotte's obsession with Branwell's
deterioration, and her ambivalence towards it.

> It was very odd that his sister did not think a pin the worse of him for
> all his dishonour: it is private moments not public infamy that de-
> grade a man in the opinion of his relations. Miss Hastings had heard
> him cursed by every mouth . . . Yet after all she knew he was an un-
> redeemed villain — human nature is full of inconsistencies — natural
> affection is a thing never rooted out where it has once existed.[12]

The romantic heroines of the earlier vacation writings had been obsessed by their hero, by Zamorna:

> She had but one idea — Zamorna, Zamorna — ! It had grown up with her — become part of her nature — absence — coldness — total neglect — for long periods together — went for nothing — she could no more feel alienation from him than she could from herself.[13]

But 'Elizabeth' (the very name recalls the second Brontë sister whose death Charlotte observed upon her return from Cowan Bridge), Henry's sister, is 'plain and undersized', like the later Jane Eyre and like Charlotte herself, with many of the Jane/Charlotte traits: shy but proud, repressed but capable of passion, hopeful for some 'single individual equal to herself in mind . . . she was always burning for warmer, closer attachment.'[14] Nonetheless, she attaches her fidelity, indeed her love, to the brother in whose support she leaves home to become a successful teacher and schoolmistress (again anticipating Jane/Charlotte), where her experience echoes what we have already heard from Charlotte at Roe Head:

> She spent her mornings in her drawing-room surrounded by her class and not wearily toiling to impart the dry rudiments of knowledge to yawning, obstinate children . . . Sometimes, when she was alone of an evening . . . she would think of home, till she cried passionately at the conviction that she would see it no more.[15]

In 'Henry Hastings' — unlike, as I shall argue, *Jane Eyre* — the brother/sister motif is split off from the love motif and Elizabeth faces up to and spurns the offers of an illicit relationship with Sir William Percy, a rejection that anticipates in all its trappings of wealth, position and passion Jane Eyre's simultaneous attraction to and rejection of the wealthy and proud Edward Rochester. Elizabeth, like Jane Eyre and like Charlotte Brontë, feels 'with an intensity of romantic feeling that very few people in this world can form the remotest conception of',[16] while caring for her own integrity enough to choose financial independence and her brother.

Whereas the romantic elements of Branwell's Byronism are projected upon the spurned Sir William Percy, the self-destructiveness implicit in his day-to-day Byronism is separated out and focused upon the explicit brother-figure, Henry Hastings. Here we can indeed find evidence of Charlotte's working out of a painful and perplexing

emotional interdependency and intensity of feeling for a brother she
could no longer respect. The links between art and life are not difficult
to identify. Henry Hastings, 'a wild wanderer' like the later Rochester,
recalls Branwell's self-pitying poem about himself, first titled 'The
Wanderer' and later retitled 'Sir Henry Tunstall', a poem with close
affinities to Rochester's presentation of himself to Jane Eyre as an
outlaw, an alien and a homeless wanderer. Branwell's poem had been
written after his London failure and copied out by Charlotte. It records
in exaggerated, grandiose terms his inability to face up to the
disappointments of his family's aspirations:

> . . . I have seen her too
> The first I loved on earth — the first I knew —
> She who was wont above that very bed
> To bend with blessing o'er my helpless head,
> I have seen my sister — I have seen them all —
> All but myself. They have lost me past recall,
> As I have them. And vainly have I come
> Three thousand leagues — my Home is not my Home.[17]

I think we can see in Elizabeth Hastings's repudiation of Lord Percy and
her fidelity to her brother something more than a fictional gesture of
proud independence with a hint of the sibling intensity of incest. What
it indicates in Charlotte Brontë, as in her fictional counterparts
Elizabeth Hastings and Jane Eyre, is a refusal to sacrifice independence
to passion, compounded by the refusal to surrender either. (Recall that
both Jane Eyre and Elizabeth Hastings have important links with the
childhood writings that surmounted family disaster. It was Jane Moore
who recounted the fictionalization of Maria's and Elizabeth's deaths.)
      The coexistence of independence and passion in Charlotte's character
emerges clearly in her polite but scathing refusal of marriage to Henry
Nussey in 1838, the year of 'Henry Hastings', for reasons that point
up an integrity and self-knowledge that belong to the family and not
to outsiders. She explains to Henry, '*you do not know me*; I am not
the serious, grave, cool-headed individual you suppose; you would
think me romantic and eccentric.'[18] And to Henry's sister, her close
friend Ellen, Charlotte repeats, 'I was aware that Henry knew so little
of me . . . it would startle him to see me *in my natural home character*;
he would think I was a wild, romantic enthusiast indeed' (emphasis
mine).[19] Charlotte knows who she is; her family knows who she is.
But marriage, which would start a new family cycle, is out of the

question to this closely interwoven network of siblings. Being 'known' depends upon being inside the family of origin and marriage is at odds with the intimacy and self-enclosure of a family knit together by the experience of death and separation, and bonded by imaginative escape and transcendence. The Brontë children and the 'worlds' of Angria and Gondal kept the world at arm's length. Little wonder that Jane Eyre should insist on a psychic 'knowing' between her and her asexual lover, Rochester, and that the family theme and terminology of kinship dominate the plot, characterization, inter-relationships and language of the novel.

Thus, the transitional role of 'Henry Hastings' is important not only as a reflection of the progressive deterioration of Branwell but as a step toward a new role for fiction in Charlotte's assimilation of reality — the use of fiction to transform pain, insecurity and dis-illusionment into their opposites. Within this context, we can understand the emergence in *Jane Eyre* of three new themes — sisterhood as an alternative to romance, fiction as a therapeutic assimilation of alienated girlhood into integrated womanhood and redemption and diminution for the destructive and larger-than-lifesize Byronic male. These themes are clear responses to pressures upon the Brontë family solidarity and responses made in the mode of fiction which increasingly for Charlotte created a substitute world in which she could work through and transform trauma.

The shocks to the family solidarity were many and included Branwell's successive failures and physical self-destruction, precipitated by his humiliating (and to Charlotte inexcusable) adulterous attachment to Lydia Robinson; Patrick Brontë's deteriorating eyesight finally diagnosed as cataracts which constituted a clear and present danger to the Brontës economic survival as a family unit; Charlotte's gradual withdrawal from Branwell (implicit in her 'Farewell to Angria' of 1839) and her reciprocal and growing reliance upon her sisters; and Charlotte's experiences in Brussels, her secret and agonized adoration for her 'master', Constantin Heger, and her denial of a gnawing love which cannot but have exacerbated her antipathy to Branwell's opposite behaviour. By now, sisters and brother had become opposites, scarcely knowing each other, Branwell an invalid bent on his own self-destruction, cared for in the father's bedroom, and the sisters left to find some way of salvaging themselves, creating their future while witnessing the daily horror of Branwell's suicidal alcoholism and opium addiction.

The importance of Charlotte's years in Brussels to the themes I am exploring here emerges again in her isolation and loneliness on the edges of a family unit, which would have reawakened her sense of isolation and dependence as in the similar situation at Roe Head, but now with no Branwell to write to for support and no Angria to comfort her imagination. In her imprecise role on the outskirts of a family not her own (for the Pensionnat Heger was a family-run institution) and although invited to spend evenings with the Hegers, Charlotte (perhaps suspicious of her motives and uncomfortable because of them) felt once again an interloper and an intruder, the more bitterly so for her increasing separation from family rootedness.[20]

Once we have recognized the importance of family life to Charlotte's emotional survival, it is clear that the Brussels situation combined for her the worst elements of Cowan Bridge, Roe Head and Stonegappe. As at Cowan Bridge she experienced again the loss of a sibling, this time through the inaccessibility of a beloved brother who could no longer write to her, being no longer capable of any sustained effort or hope whatsoever. As at Roe Head she once again lost the company of Emily, who was rapidly failing from homesickness and who stayed to tend house while Charlotte returned to Brussels, as she had on an earlier occasion returned to Roe Head, a teacher among students with whom she could not identify, and who could not 'know' her. And as at Stonegappe she experienced family life from the outside, a situation which could not but exacerbate her need to belong to the very family which inadvertently but inevitably excluded her.

Necessarily, the language of life and fiction interact. Charlotte's complaints at Stonegappe, that Mrs Sidgwick 'did not intend to know me', recall the language of mutual acknowledgement in *Jane Eyre*, as does the single happy memory of that period, a walk taken outdoors with Mr Sidgwick and his magnificent Newfoundland dog, prototype of the landscape recaptured in Jane Eyre's outdoors encounter with Rochester and dog, here the employer of a governess who would in fiction acknowledge and know her. The pain of the Pensionnat Heger came out of an intensification of a situation by now paradigmatic for Charlotte and symbolic for her fictional creation. For in Heger, she found mentorship, mutual recognition of personal quality, an intimacy or fusion of minds (or so it seemed to Charlotte) reminiscent in kind if not degree of what she had experienced in the good old days with Branwell and her father and acknowledgement as an intellectual equal. But this was in a situation where she remained alienated and without status on the outskirts of family life, and in a fixed, demeaning and unsustaining role in the Heger educational institution. Family life, sustenance, and mutual education had once been of a piece for Charlotte. That cohesion could now be recalled and recreated only in a fiction.

But Charlotte, ever since the self-denial recorded on her twenty-first birthday in 1839, was no longer writing. That winter of 1839, all were at home, Charlotte after only six months at her first stint of governessing, Anne dismissed from her governess position with the Ingham family (whose name, exploitations and petty cruelties towards Anne recur in the Ingram family of *Jane Eyre*), and Branwell a failed portraitist, home from Bradford. Despite the Christmas reunion of the family, there was no joyful continuation of family collaboration, no writing. The early 1840s are the years during which Anne and Branwell were at Thorp Green with the Robinson family, Emily ventured to and departed from Brussels, and Charlotte — with her 'wish for wings' and her compulsive duty to prepare herself to teach or to run a school — was ultimately alone and lonely with the Hegers.

Upon Charlotte's return from Brussels in 1844 there is no record of writing except for her desperate letters to Heger and a scattering of poems recording her unbalanced state of mind. It is significant that Charlotte did not know of Emily's poems, nor the family, apparently, of Charlotte's. Instead the sisters began thinking how to keep the family together, their hopes for a jointly-run school having been dashed by midsummer 1845 when the conditions under which Branwell was dismissed made him hellbent upon self-destruction, home with him a hell on earth and a school at home a clear impossibility.

It was by accident that Charlotte discovered Emily's poems and insisted that the sisters combine their poems into a single published volume. Writing, long an emotional survival tactic, was now their last economic hope as well. The poems were published but failed, yet the sisterhood persevered, sending round to publishers a prospectus for 'three distinct and unconnected tales' which they were now writing and which grew to full-scale novelistic proportions: *Wuthering Heights, Agnes Grey*, and *The Professor*. The publishers accepted the first two, but turned down Charlotte's contribution.

By mid-summer 1846, Patrick Bronte was nearly blind, his cataracts requiring immediate medical attention. The experimental successes of a surgeon in Manchester were considered well worth the risk. With her two sisters making their arrangements with their publishers and while she continued to mail around her rejected manuscript, Charlotte took her father to Manchester (August/September 1846), where *Jane Eyre* was begun and nearly completed in darkened seclusion, the writer also tending a blinded, dependent father who relied solely on her. Charlotte wrote for three weeks without stopping in the old manner of what she used to call 'making up', her term for the hallucinatory hold upon her imagination of her Angrian characters during the days of isolation at Roe Head. But now she was *writing*, and for an economic purpose as well as for emotional release.[21]

It is no accident that economic survival, independence and family reunification should emerge as clear themes in *Jane Eyre*. Nor is it surprising that in a darkened room in Manchester, Charlotte should return to romance while retaining her hard-earned hold of reality.[22] The romances that forced their way into reality in the days when she involuntarily *saw* Angrian figures with her eyes closed at Roe Head could now be held in balance with realistic characterization, based upon independent experience. The Rochester-romance might well imaginatively redeem the doomed Branwell and heal the blinded Patrick, but the supportive sisterhood upon which Charlotte had come to depend and within which she was beginning to develop a fluid mother/sister role emerges in Jane's developing solidarity with important surrogate and blood-related family networks of mothers and sisters in the novel. Although the romance might 'tie' Charlotte with the fictional stand-in for a renewed, albeit diminished, Branwell in the old ways in which chronicles of Angria had linked a homesick Charlotte with life at home in Haworth, the compelling issues of economics, integrity, rebellion against her apparent unmarriageability, the isolation and humiliation experienced by teachers and governesses who aspired to something more worthy of themselves and of a wished-for integration in a family of equals who would recognize and acknowledge her personal and moral qualities — these are the issues that complicate the romantic resolution while running parallel to it and even suggesting alternative endings to the novel. For if the 'romance' of *Jane Eyre* is a Cinderella story, although with a chastened and repentant Prince, the 'anti-romance' of *Jane Eyre* raises a sociological dilemma basic to the Victorian family and the institution of marriage seen from the underside of class and of gender: how can an unlovely, unloved, orphan girl, without money, relations, connections or status, achieve an independent adulthood in a society in which female adulthood is virtually synonymous with marriage, marriage with upward mobility, and upward mobility with beauty, pliability, and the springboard of gentility substantiated by status, money, or connections?

Jane Eyre opens with a nine-year-old girl withdrawn into a windowseat, cut off by a heavy curtain and her book from her adoptive family, the Reeds, who are clustered around the symbolic family hearth. Curtain and book are barriers which protect Jane from the bullying she gets from her cousins and which symbolize her isolation on the edges of a family to which she only half belongs.

The opening scene is important for at least three reasons. It places Jane in a situation that recurs throughout the novel, 'in' but not 'of' the family with whom she resides as dependent or student or governess, in effect as a non-person. It is a recurrent scene, repeated in Thornfield where a similarly symbolic windowseat, barrier-curtain and bookish withdrawal both protect and isolate Jane from her beloved employer and master, Edward Rochester, and from his bullying guests, the Ingrams and Eshtons, 'family groups' of mothers-with-daughters who at that moment are complaining loudly about governesses. It is also important because it focuses our immediate attention upon the domestic contexts which make up the household interiors within which Jane moves and which are in turn identified with a larger social context which she feels she must reject if she is to retain her integrity. The fusion of family life with social life from Jane Eyre's perspective enables the reader to view the Victorian family from outside and from underneath. It is precisely Jane's isolation on the peripheries of family life and her awareness of her isolation as a consequence of her lack of place, caste and social status, that enable family life in this novel to be seen as a microcosm of genteel Victorian society. A romantic plot, a bit of luck, clear personal ambivalence as to her need both for family and for upward mobility through marriage, along with Jane's personal development in an appropriate family setting, enable Jane Eyre both to remake the family and to create an acceptable social context in her own image.

Just as the plot takes Jane, the 'poor orphan child' of Bessie's lullaby, from home to home like so many look-alike fake and real pearls on a chain (Gateshead, Lowood, Thornfield, Moor House, Marsh End, and finally Ferndean), so within each household we see complete family units which exclude Jane or incomplete family units which assimilate her. This bifurcation also follows the lines of class and caste: the wealthy and spoiled Reeds of Gateshead, the curled and dimpled Brocklehurst women of Lowood, the beautiful sleek Ingrams and Eshtons visiting Thornfield, all participate in the humiliation and rejection of our plain Jane along the lines of the Cinderella story. Complete triads of mother with two favoured daughters, fortune's darlings, allow Jane no seat but at the cinders, or away from the hearth, hidden in the cold windowseat. At the same time, an alternative pattern emerges: at Lowood Jane finds Maria Temple and Helen Burns; at Thornfield Mrs Fairfax and the young Adèle; at Marsh End Diana and Mary Rivers. In these cases, the family structures are incomplete, the roles fluid and indefinite, and there is 'space' for Jane alternatively as surrogate sister, mother or child, as well as 'place' among women who, like Jane, must work for their bread as teachers and governesses. The role of the male figure in positive as well as negative family groupings is one to which I shall return, for it differentiates a family constituted out of marriage, from a blood-related and psychically-bonded family of sisters.

Jane moves from one family grouping to the next precisely because she is an orphan, just as her orphan status draws the reader's attention to the developmental and social dilemmas of family solidarity posed by the novel. As a penniless and unloved dependant in the midst of a rich family which rejects and despises her, the connection is made early in the novel between family life presented as 'typical' on the one hand, cushioned by money, 'good' marriages, and status, and on the other hand, the rejected and isolated dependency of the dispossessed who must survive on crumbs of bread and affection on the outer edges of family life. Jane's feeling of rejection and isolation — so aptly symbolized in the first scene of the novel — is confirmed by her Aunt Reed's deathbed confession that Jane was, indeed, unloved and unwanted, a burden, and a threat:

> Such a burden to be left on my hands — and so much annoyance as she caused me, daily and hourly, with her incomprehensible disposition, and her sudden starts of temper . . . no child ever spoke or looked as she did; I was glad to get her away from the house . . . I wish she had died![23]

Even Jane's 'very first recollection of existence included hints of the same kind. This reproach of my dependence had become a vague sing-song in my ear; very painful and crushing.'[24]

> And you ought not to think yourself on an equality with the Misses Reed and Master Reed, because Missis kindly allows you to be brought up with them. They will have a great deal of money, and you will have none; it is your place to be humble, and to try to make yourself agreeable to them.[25]

Jane's experienced childhood dependency, verified by her Aunt's semiconscious deathbed admission, the servants' taunts and the cousins' bullying, recurs time and again through a series of novelistic recapitulations suggestive of montage in film and compulsion in dreamwork. Her daily and daytime nightmares of childhood burdensomeness and continued adult experiences of unwelcome and unrelieved impoverishment − personal, familial, social and economic − haunt her dreamlife as well, most significantly at Thornfield on the eve of her marriage to Rochester, disturbing her slumbers as an early warning signal. For her conscious, although suppressed, anticipation of her situation as Rochester's wife inevitably reactivates an unconscious fear that the humiliations of childhood dependency on someone else for money and station could well be perpetuated through marriage into a dependent adult life.

The burdensome children who haunt Jane's nightmares before her intended nuptials come, with some awareness on her part as to their portent if not their literal relevance, as a warning from within herself; but the threat to their marriage is confirmed by Mrs Fairfax's warning, that 'Gentlemen in [Mr Rochester's] circumstances . . . [are] not accustomed to marry their governesses.' The revelation that another and an independently wealthy (although insane) Mrs Rochester already exists, does more than verify Jane's fears that as a dependent wife she would be little better than a mistress. This turn in the plot gives substance to her fears; she would *in fact* be Mr Rochester's mistress. This fact necessarily reactivates other and more deeply based fears, psychological as well as economic, that as a mistress/wife/dependant, she would become with time the tiresome successor of Celine, Giacinta, and Clara, of whom Rochester had admitted, 'Hiring a mistress is the next worse thing to buying a slave: both are by nature, and always by position, inferior: and to live familiarly with inferiors is degrading.'[26]

Foreseeing a dependent marriage as a perpetuation of her childhood dependency, Jane clearly needs status, money and family of her own. Even before the emergence of Bertha Mason Rochester confirms and verifies Jane's prescience that as Rochester's wife she would be a 'kept' woman without independent|status. Jane had already felt 'degraded' (her word) by Rochester's lavish and expensive gifts and had already written to a long-lost uncle in Madeira to track down Aunt Reed's hint that Jane might have some small inheritance of her own. For, 'if I had a prospect of one day bringing Mr Rochester an accession of fortune, I could better endure *to be kept* by him now' (italics mine),[27] Harriet Martineau, Charlotte Brontë's contemporary in time and in awareness, called such dependent marriages 'legal prostitution' and more recently, Françoise Basch, drawing upon such nineteenth-century feminists as Barbara Bodichon and Caroline Norton, has documented the extent to which, 'treated as a minor, [the wife] entirely lost her own legal existence, and with it, any legal recourse against her husband or anybody else.'[28] Little wonder that Jane should insist, married or unmarried, that she continue to earn £30 per annum as Adèle's teacher.

The economics of status and the psychology of place are integrally interrelated with family life in this novel, in which feminist outbursts are rare and inevitably punished by ostracism, incarceration and regret. Instead, the novel focuses upon the efforts of the emergent Jane Eyre to define her 'place' in a family without losing herself in the process. Seen in terms of literary history, *Jane Eyre* is in the tradition of the *Bildungsroman*, the developmental novel, in which development is as much a psychological process as it is intellectual and artistic. And development is not necessarily a forward process in lock-step. Thus Jane's dreams of a perpetual childhood burdensomeness propel her into flight from Thornfield and into an unanticipated development by which she is rewarded both with an inheritance and with 'growing up'.

Kenneth Keniston has commented on personal development in a way that is helpful in understanding the *Jane Eyre* plot and its resolution through fiction of loose threads in Charlotte Brontë's early life. His observation is that although psychological development is irreversible, the ongoing developmental process does not preclude 'regressions, recapitulations, re-enactments, and reversions to earlier stages'.[29] Rather, '*essential* irreversibility means that regression to a level is in some sense different from the first experience on that level' and that 'it is possible to "leap-frog" levels so as to resume development at the point from which one regressed.' Jane does exactly as Keniston describes. Unable to marry and assume an adult status because (psychologically) she has not completed her childhood nor grown by stages into an independent female status, Jane must re-enact a symbolic infancy and childhood in order to exorcize the terrors of unending dependency by a rapid replication of childhood under a more welcoming roof. Symbolically, Jane re-experiences the destitution of her infancy on the stony ground at Whitcross, which she thinks of as the breast of 'the universal mother', only to be taken in, like a cold and shivering child, by St John, Diana and Mary Rivers, among whom, symbolically, she grows up from surrogate younger sister to become ultimately the financial resource and 'mother' to a family of unmarried siblings and equals. This is leap-frogging indeed. For a child whose small size had been a perpetual reminder of her 'physical inferiority', it is a psychological necessity that she should regress to the cold breast of the universal mother, just as, on the eve of the wedding to Rochester, she had taken refuge in Adèle's crib.

Jane is in some ways an adult at nine and an infant at nineteen, a fictional parallel for the uncertainty of roles confronting Charlotte Brontë who at nine, with the deaths of Maria and Elizabeth, had to assume a responsible and mothering role formerly held by Maria and Elizabeth to her motherless younger brother and sisters. Despite Charlotte's rejection of marriage as an option for herself, so long as her sisters and brother lived, she permits Jane to marry only on grounds that she would herself have found acceptable. We need to recognize the amalgam of realism and romance in this novel, its rootedness in the romantic earlier fictions that Charlotte had shared with her beloved brother who alone knew her, to understand why Charlotte would resolve Jane Eyre's personal and economic dilemma in two plots simultaneously—realistically, through the discovery of a sustained sisterhood among whom she might 'grow up' and become interdependent (with the lucky break of an inheritance that tied her to the Rivers family financially while revealing to all their natural family ties), and romantically, through marriage to a redeemed and diminished Rochester. The Rivers sisters bear close physical resemblance to Emily and to Anne; they also share the same books, posture, and dogs; all are governesses; all seek a freedom from demeaning work in money and reunification of the family unit. At the same time, Rochester (not St John Rivers) is the male figure who bears closest resemblance to Branwell; he, too, is an adulterer, a wanderer, a romantic and self-destructive although potentially heroic figure. The writing of *Jane Eyre* at a time of major disillusionment and crisis for the Brontë family allowed Charlotte to resolve her personal role in that family and to indulge her wish for a stable home with her sisters as distinct from renewed intimacy with a recuperating brother. She does so by splitting them off: one home with Diana and Mary, another with Rochester. Branwell, as we know, was at the time of the composition of *Jane Eyre* already outside the tight network of sisters, as is St John Rivers of the novel.

Jane's narrative, like Charlotte's life, confronts personal, familial, social and economic issues simultaneously as different aspects of a single problem. Jane, like Charlotte, lives out much of her young life on the peripheries of other families. For the literary critic and close

reader of the novel, Jane's estrangement is imaged in her withdrawal
from household interiors and her affinity with external landscapes
where she searches out spiritual 'kinship' (a recurrent clue-word for
Jane) and where she first meets Helen Burns and later Edward
Rochester. Jane attends Rochester by the library hearth only when
they are alone and at one with each other. More typically, they share
sequestered orchards and gardens, where they meet as kin and equals
outside the big house and where Rochester can identify with Jane's
alienation from a social world which he too rejects, a wanderer on the
earth, victim of a loveless boyhood and a mercenary marriage. Jane
recognizes their spiritual affinity when, looking out from her windowseat retreat and watching him flirt with his social peers, the Ingrams
and the Eshtons, she tells herself,

> 'He is not to them what he is to me,' I thought: 'he is not of their
> *kind*. I believe he is of mine': — I am sure he is, — I feel *akin* to him
> . . . though rank and wealth sever us widely, I have something in
> my brain and heart, in my blood and nerves, that *assimilates me*
> *mentally to him* . . . Did I forbid myself to think of him in any
> other light than as a paymaster? Blasphemy against nature! . . .
> For when I say that *I am of his kind*, I do not mean that I have
> his force to influence and his spell to attract; I mean only that I have
> certain tastes and feelings in common with him. I must then
> repeat continually that we are forever sundered; — and yet, while
> I beathe and think I must love him.' [Emphasis mine.] [30]

It is in this scene (Chapter 18) that Rochester disguises himself as a
gypsy (an image for Jane as well) in order to speak out to Jane her
innermost and hidden feelings, in a voice familiar to Jane 'as my own
face in a glass — as the speech of my own tongue.'[31] 'Familiarity',
'kinship', 'akin', 'kind', — these terms define an affinity based on moral
and spiritual qualities as a counter to the impoverishment of marital
relationships based on status and money, and characteristic of a world
from which Jane is ostracized, and to which she does not, and cannot
belong.

Further, Jane's alienation suggests a withdrawal far more profound
and destructive of an integrated adult life than can be accounted for
by the terror of continued social and economic dependency with its
attendant helplessness and perpetual humiliations. The symbolic
language of Jane's personal narrative suggests a dissociation of spirit
from flesh revealed in numerous ways: plain Jane is identified with

air (her given name affords significant puns),[32] while the 'real' Mrs
Rochester (i.e. Bertha Mason) is associated with large, fleshly, dark,
even monstrous women.[33] One indication of Rochester's affinity and
'kinship' with Jane is his recognition of her ethereal quality, not only
in his terms of endearment (she is his 'elf', 'sprite', and 'changeling'),
but in his seeing her as 'a curious sort of bird' whose native element
is the Eyre: 'were it but free, it would soar cloud-high.'[34] Rochester
thus emerges as a spirit-being intimately associated with the
etherealization that attends Jane's psychic withdrawal. He is her
spirit-mate, a mutual acknowledgement of each by the other that
suggests a modality of love and marriage as fusion and prepares for
the romantic ending at Ferndean.

The etherealization of the child-Jane can be traced back to an
extreme of family ostracism, Jane's incarceration in the Red Room,
a solitary confinement which causes severe psychic withdrawal into
her sole remaining retreat, the inner, untouchable and non-corporeal
core of self. The terror haunting the Red Room is not the ghost of the
uncle who died there, but Jane's reflected image, etherealized and
ghostly in the darkened mirror:

> All looked colder and darker in the visionary hollow than in reality;
> and the strange little figure gazing at me, with a white face and
> arms specking the gloom, and glittering eyes of fear moving where
> all else was still, had the effect of a real spirit . . . All John Reed's
> violent tyrannies, all his sisters' proud indifference, all his
> mother's aversion, all the servants' partiality, turned up in my
> disturbed mind like a dark deposit in a turbid well. Why was I
> always suffering, always brow-beaten, always accused, for ever
> condemned? Why could I never please? Why was it useless to try
> to win any one's favour? I was in discord in Gateshead Hall; I was
> like nobody there; I had nothing in harmony . . . My habitual
> mood of humiliation, self-doubt, forlorn depression, fell damp
> on the embers of my decaying ire.[35]

These oscillations of depression and rage, Jane's indignant rejection of
the values by which she has in turn been rejected, and her conscious
choice of personal values and integrity, are related to the absence of
overt and explicit physical attraction and sexuality in her relation with
Rochester. Given her psychic withdrawal from an ostracized physical
and familial mode, Jane has pulled inward, away from a self occupying
physical space at Gateshead, and into a 'placeless' and spirit-free

identity by which her ego is reduced to an invulnerable inner core. The coexistence of an etherealized non-presence with a sense of spiritual and moral integrity, fair play and survival, prepares for Jane's angry response to Rochester's apparent intention to send her away from her 'only home' at Thornfield when in fact his intention is to draw her out. In her indignant response, Jane is in fact drawn 'out': 'I am not talking to you now through the medium of custom, conventionalities, nor even of mortal flesh — it is my spirit that addresses your spirit; just as if we had both passed through the grave, and we stood as God's feet, equal — as we are.'[36]

Jane's perception, at the early age of nine when locked into the Red Room, of her lowly status, of her anger, and of her abandonment, brings together themes which recur as she moves towards womanhood and achieves the threshold of marriage on three separate occasions (twice with Rochester, once with St John Rivers). These major themes I would call the 'wishes of romance' and the 'exigencies of reality'. The one involves marriage to a social superior and the social sanctioning of bonds of affinity and of love rather than of money and convenience. The other involves an effort on Jane's part to be somebody in her own right, loved or unloved, a woman of integrity with an outlet in the world for her passions and her energies. The second of these is tested out at Morton where Jane becomes an independent, successful and resourceful schoolmistress, but where she feels 'degraded' among social inferiors, a term reminiscent in the novel of Rochester's 'degradation' among his mistresses and of Jane's sense of degradation when heaped by Rochester with money, satins and jewels; these terms echo Charlotte Bronte's aversion to teaching 'dolts' at Roe Head. The first of these themes, the 'wishes of romance', dominates the novel, although the hemmed-in and darkened quality of Jane's reunion with Rochester at Ferndean suggests the price exacted by domestic romance in that it is ultimately impossible to reconcile Jane's need to be loved and to be useful with the issues of money and status that attend marriage as a social institution. The atmosphere of Ferndean inevitably recalls the primary scenes of withdrawal and retreat.

I have already suggested the multiple complications that surround the romantic theme and make marriage without a status of near equivalence (Jane/Rochester) or a marriage without passion (Jane/St John Rivers) equally untenable. These interlocking elements are worth enumerating: Jane's need to *be* loved (direct loving she experiences as 'being useful') competes with a fear of a burdensome life without love as that experience is substantiated by her childhood ostracism and lovelessness; Jane's understanding that her alienation and lovelessness are the result of her economic, social and personal deprivation and dependencies; Jane's fears that the domestic, social and marital family groupings of her early experience (Reeds, Brocklehursts, Ingrams) constitute the *only* marriageable possibilities and that she will continue to be an outsider because of her lack of beauty, money and 'real' family, made worse by her unfeminine eccentricities of integrity, mutiny, intelligence, independence, and capacity for rage; and finally the novel's plot explicitly differentiating between Jane's blood relations (Reeds are all she knows until her fortuitous discovery of the Rivers) and her spiritual kindred (first Helen Burns and Maria Temple, later Edward Rochester), a split which is resolved only by the Marsh End integration of blood and kinship ties in which a familial resolution among the Rivers family prepares for the marital resolution with Rochester, in which affinity, monetary inheritance, social status and mutual interdependence are of a piece.

Kenneth Keniston's comments about the role of regression in the ongoing developmental progress through various life 'stages' help us to understand the 'poor orphan child' motif as it emerges in Jane's compulsive dream-life and her preoccupation with burdensome children as she approaches the threshold of maturity and marriage. Thus the Thornfield nightmares that terrorize Jane on the eve of her wedding focus upon psychic as well as social obstacles to the imminent marriage by exposing her obsessive anxiety over her humiliating childhood and perpetual homelessness. These dreams account for Jane's procrastination, neither explicitly nor rationally confronted, by equating her rebirth as a married woman with a new identity and a new name — Jane Eyre becomes Mrs Rochester — a 'newborn agony — a deformed thing which I could not persuade myself to own and bear.'[37] Images of stillbirth into a feared new life reinforce the awareness implicit in Jane's dreamwork of burdensome children, expressing her anxiety that she is not yet a complete adult but rather an incomplete child whose rebirth would replicate her lack of wholeness. The psychic and social obstacles to marriage at this point in Jane's narrative blend into her nightmares: the consciousness of some barrier between Jane and her husband-to-be; the burdensome child; the fettered movements hindering her efforts to catch Rochester. Then dreams of Thornfield in ruins, the child in Jane's arms nearly strangling her while Rochester disappears down the road. The adult 'Jane Rochester' with the abandoned and clinging child 'Jane Eyre' are fused in the fearful prospect of herself as *'young* Mrs Rochester — Fairfax Rochester's *girl-bride'* (emphasis mine).

These nightmares pave the way for a waking horror, the apparition of Bertha Rochester, her garb reiterating the visual blending of wedding gown and shroud that had earlier symbolized Jane's inner fears when confronting her wedding gown, and her presence confirming Jane's anticipation of a still-born marriage. Bertha *is* in fact the 'Mrs Rochester' whose identity Jane had feared and pondered when imagining herself in that role, and Jane's hopes now in fact lie dead, *'cursed like the first-born* out of Egypt . . . my love: that feeling which was my master's . . . shivered in my heart, *like a suffering child in a cold cradle'* (emphasis mine).[38] Once again, psychic and social/economic issues overlap, imaged in the fusion of Jane's face with Bertha's in the mirror and in the gesture by which Bertha tries on and then destroys the extravagant wedding veil which, because it symbolized Rochester's inordinant wealth, Jane had reluctantly accepted in place of the humbler veil which she had sewn for herself. Not surprisingly, the entire episode ends in the regressive mode, Jane put safely to sleep in Adele's crib, a child 'so tranquil, so passionless, so innocent . . . She seemed the emblem of my past life; and he, I was now to array myself to meet, the dread, but adored type of my unknown future day.'[39]

Rather than a smooth developmental passage, we have a rupture, which draws our attention to interrelated issues: the question of identity (who, and what, is a 'Mrs Rochester'?), and of integrity (is there an imaginable mutuality which changes the master/subordinate economics of Jane's status as governess and as wife?). Jane's flight from Thornfield leaves 'Jane Eyre, who had been an ardent, expectant *woman* — almost a *bride* . . . a cold, solitary *girl* again' (emphasis mine).[40] The language connects the terms of personal affinities ('kinship', 'my kind') with the 'good' family surrogates among whom Jane is attempting to find her place. Rochester playfully comments upon Jane's 'fear in the presence of a man and a brother — or father, or master, or what you will',[41] but the family catalogue of asexual roles is taken more seriously in Jane's ripening awareness of love as a sort of psychic kinship in which Rochester is seen to be 'my *relation*, rather than my master . . . So happy, so gratified did I become . . . that I ceased to pine after *kindred'* (emphasis mine).[42] Jane finds at Thornfield 'at last [a] safe haven', taking almost literally the biblical phrasing by which Ruth spoke to Boaz: 'Wherever you are is my home — my only home.'[43]

The parental language is a key to Jane's integration into the

Thornfield foster-family unit which is the opposite side of the coin from Rochester's social life and presumptive marriage to Blanche Ingram. We are here given Jane's participation in the kind of family scene from which she had been excluded up to this point. She is seated at Mrs Fairfax's side with Adele nearby in a family structure which defines Jane as both daughter to Mrs Fairfax and mother to Adele, while Rochester is cast as the protective Victorian pater-familias upon whose good auspices and money the entire family depends:

> Mr. Rochester entered, unannounced, and looking at us, seemed to take pleasure in the spectacle of a group so amicable — when he said he supposed the old lady was all right now that she had got her adopted daughter back again, and added that he saw Adele was 'prete a coquer sa petite maman Anglaise' — and I half ventured to hope he would, even after his marriage [to Blanche], keep us together somewhere under the shelter of his protection, and not quite exiled from the sunshine of his presence.[44]

This integral and harmonious family scene, with a beneficent guardian/ god protecting Jane in her fluid mother/daughter capacities, had already been hinted at in her relations with Maria Temple and Helen Burns at Lowood. It also looked forward to the important developmental sequence which occurs after Jane's flight from her male protector to the nurture of Diana and Mary Rivers.[45] And it foreshadows Jane's reunion with Rochester at Ferndean, where she is both mother and wife to him in his diminished estate and dependent state. It could be argued that the absence of a protective male presence among the mutually-nurturing sisterhoods at Lowood and Marsh End. makes it possible for the protective role to be shared among a sisterhood of equals within which Jane can literally 'grow up' and, recalling Keniston, 'leap-frog' into marriage. The sharing of the usual male protective role omits, of course, any romance and it is the romance, taken down a peg or two, i.e. the romance, domesticated, to which Jane finally returns.

Much has been said here about Jane's experience at Whitcross, Marsh End and Morton in a segment of her narrative that is for our purposes critical to Jane's emergence as a marriageable Victorian woman who nonetheless retains her integrity and sense of personhood and self — a married woman, that is, who is neither psychically nor economically a child and who is thereby an atypical Victorian wife if we look at literary conventions rather than real life. The bare outlines of the plot give us as 'Cinderjane', an impoverished but clear-seeing orphan, who supplants bad foster-families with good and wins her Prince Charming in a somewhat humbled condition. Not the patient, passive, submissive and beautiful Cinderella of fable, our Cinderjane is unrelenting on the issues of paying her own way and values being loved for her moral and personal quality alone.

Charlotte Brontë's refurbishing of this old fable allows us to see the resolution of Cinderella's multiple dilemmas within the very family structure in which they initially occur. All of Jane's sufferings because of cruelty, ostracism, dispossession, and unmarriageability are exorcized at Marsh End where the wealthy and favoured 'cruel' stepsisters, with their long curls and plumed hats and fancy gowns, are replaced by self-supporting and intellectually gifted 'kind' step-sisters among whom Jane becomes *prima inter pares*. Prior to Jane's inheritance, all are, like her, impoverished governesses, unmarried, not expecting to marry and earning their keep while attempting to maintain their gentility, integrity and family solidarity.

The difficulties that attend Jane's transition from poor orphan to secure woman require, it would seem, not a Cinderella marriage to the proud Rochester of Thornfield Manor, but a positive re-enactment of infancy and childhood. By leaps and bounds, Jane is younger, then older, sister and finally an heiress, the cause of her family's unification, independence, status, activity and honourable marriages within the larger social world. The plot most clearly interconnects the economic and family bonds in the episode in which Jane learns of her inheritance and discovers that her family-by-kinship is indeed her natural family as well.

> 'And you,' I interrupted, 'cannot at all imagine the craving I have for fraternal and sisterly love. I never had a home, I never had brothers or sisters; I must and will have them now . . . I do not want a stranger – unsympathising, alien, different from me; *I want my kindred:* those with whom I have full fellow-feeling. Say again you will be my *brother*: when you uttered the words I was satisfied, happy; repeat them, if you can repeat them sincerely.' [Emphasis mine.] [46]

The parallel discovery of an inheritance that will hold a family together, and the discovery of a family to be consolidated, leads in the novel to the penultimate episode – the Christmas reunion of the entire Rivers family, joyfully shared among the sisters and cousin, the brother a cold outsider to their festivities of home-making. This home-making scene prepares for the next at Ferndean and with Rochester in which Jane literally stirs up the embers of his dying fire and transforms a house into a home. I have already commented upon the 'splitting off' of the Branwell-prototype from the brother of the novel (St John Rivers) on to Edward Rochester while recreating a sisterhood which retains in its essentials the triad of Charlotte, Emily and Anne. This novelistic sleight of hand can be read in two ways, the one romantic, the other realistic. Both have important bearings back to the life of the author.

In the romantic reading, Jane Eyre regains and reunites a family of origin (equivalent to Charlotte's sisters) prior to establishing a family by marriage (but modelled on Charlotte's relation with Branwell, recaptured and renewed). In the realistic reading, one can imagine an alternative conclusion to the novel which emerges out of the theme of family and kinship and which is the 'plotting' of Jane's development and the language of her interaction with Rochester. One could say, indeed, that the romantic conclusion is out of keeping with this theme and that *Jane Eyre* is at its heart anti-romantic and anti-marriage. According to this reading, one focuses upon the significance of the initial hindrances to marriage with Rochester and the importance of their resolution at Marsh End with Jane's discovery of a warmth and kinship concomitant with equal status, shared wealth, and interdependency. A novel concluding on this note would have had St John missionizing in India, but the sisters continuing unmarried, reunited and at Marsh End, Jane perhaps teaching at Morton, her isolation and degradation no longer at issue. Some Victorian women's lives pursued this course. Charlotte Brontë is herself an instance as was her friend Harriet Martineau. Even her biographer, Elizabeth Gaskell, although married, spent far more time with daughters and female friends than with her husband. Such a reading of this novel is at odds with the romantic and biblical, indeed the incestuous ideal of marriage enunciated by Jane Eyre Rochester at the conclusion of her narrative: 'I am my husband's life as fully as he is mine. No woman was ever nearer to her mate than I am; ever more absolutely bone of his bone and flesh of his flesh.'[47]

The issues of family, socialization, creativity, and clarity of vision are as intertwined in the case of Charlotte Brontë and of Jane Eyre as they are in that central post-Victorian document, Virginia Woolf's *A Room of One's Own,* which reminds us of the paucity of women writers, the impoverishment of their situation and the expectations and training that for centuries sabotaged the public recognition of creative giftedness in women. This perception leads one to ask, what if Branwell had been successful or if Patrick had not been incapacitated, dependent upon Charlotte while she scribbled away in that darkened room in Manchester? The importance of family economics to family survival is only emerging as we study the lives of those women who were propelled to go public and publish their private writings because of financial exigency – the Brontës stayed together so long as they wrote together, Elizabeth Gaskell financed extras for her daughters through her publications, Mrs Oliphant was a mainstay for a fatherless family.[48]

It is dangerous to generalize on limited data, but the emergence of the novel as a 'domestic' form in the nineteenth century, the emergence of women writers focusing their attention upon the family while writing to keep it together and the evidence of family disintegration in the Victorian period are grist for the speculative mill. Even Charlotte's two closest friends were survivors in disintegrating families. Mary Taylor emigrated with her younger brother to New Zealand, the whole Taylor family having dispersed following the death of the father. Joshua, the eldest, inherited the father's cloth manufacture and Mary, firmly deciding not to be ' "a governess, a teacher a milliner, a bonnet-maker nor a housemaid" '[49] and finding marriage impossible (she, too, had loved Branwell), prepared to emigrate and set up a shop. Ellen Nussey's family was also in disarray, although Ellen lacked Mary's resourcefulness or Charlotte's supporting sisterhood and was unable to take responsibility for her own life or that of her family. The Nusseys were almost a mirror by which Charlotte could see the Bronte fortunes reflected; although wealthier and more genteel in their origins, the father's death and the mother's lack of managerial abilities forced them to live in reduced circumstances. Further, in the very year of Branwell's humiliating return from Thorp Green and collapse, Ellen Nussey's youngest brother went mad and had to be placed in York Asylum. The role of the Nussey sisters was clear and Charlotte commented on it in one of her many letters to Ellen, ' "Ann and Mercy [two of the four Nussey daughters] must have a wearisome and burdensome life of it, in waiting upon their unhappy brother." '[50] Another Nussey brother, the successor to his father in managing their cloth-manufacturing firm, had led a dissipated life, brought ruin on his family and himself and died in 1846.

At the same time that it was becoming clear to her that if the Brontë family was to remain intact the sisters must take responsibility, Charlotte was also relying more heavily upon the advice of another woman with sisters. It is of interest that her first confidante in the planning of a school at Haworth in the halcyon days prior to Branwell's deterioration was Constantin Heger to whom she wrote constantly of the developments in her plans. But just as Charlotte necessarily had to shift her dependency from her father and brother to her sisters, similarly she turned increasingly away from Heger and back to her former teacher, Miss Wooler of Roe Head, for advice. The Roe Head School had been run by sisters, so that Charlotte could expect empathy from someone similarly situated: 'You my dear Miss Wooler know fully as well as I do the value of sisters' affection to each other; there is nothing like it in this world, I believe, when they are nearly equal in age and similar in education, tastes and sentiments.'[51]

This assertion of an interdependency among sisters is virtually light years away from her earlier belief, shared by her sisters, that Branwell was the hope for the family. The shock of disillusionment with Branwell, of whom Ellen Nussey had recalled 'Happy, indeed, she then was *in himself,* for she, with her own enthusiasm, looked forward to what her brother's great promise and talent might effect,'[52] had significant repercussions on Charlotte's feelings for family and for marriage. On the one hand, her sense of family intimacy and bonding, albeit now among sisters, was intensified and outsiders the more excluded; and on the other, outsiders came to include potential suitors and husbands. It is important to recall that Charlotte rejected suitors on the grounds that they did not know her as her family did; she married only after the deaths of her sisters and brother, when she was left virtually familyless, with an ageing, querulous father.

As a situation or 'case' the Brontës are of interest because they in their lives, and Charlotte in her first published work of fiction, polarize the family of origin from the household of domestic employment. Excluding marriage as an option to perpetuate the family unit, these young women were thrust out into a world of other families. The intimacy of family feeling led ironically to their becoming 'Cinderjane' governesses, school mistresses and dependants to the children of wealthier and more secure households. It would seem from this perspective that the family was the whole of society for these Victorian women, whether as a source of passionate intimacy or of passionless employment. This perception leads us back into *Jane Eyre* where the increasingly painful actuality of Bronte family reunions are made joyful in fiction because the social and economic conditions of family togetherness (a somewhat pejorative term in the twentieth century) are imagined as possible.

Charlotte, writing *Jane Eyre* in Manchester at the bedside of a father dependent upon her in every way, was indeed imagining her way into full adulthood where the family of origin and family by marriage are for symbolic purposes one and the same because their models are one and the same. The fiction accomplishes for the family what reality coul could not — money, reunion and legitimacy as head of household. That the reunion was short-lived, that brother and sisters died quickly and in short order, even in birth order (Branwell, Emily, then Anne), leads us to the hopelessness of *Villette* as distinct from the hopefulness of *Jane Eyre*. But that is another tale.

Notes

1.   The major biographical sources used for this essay are Elizabeth Gaskell, *The Life of Charlotte Bronte* (first published London, 1857); Winifred Gerin, *Charlotte Bronte: The Evolution of Genius* (Oxford, 1967); Helene Moglen, *Charlotte Bronte: The Self Conceived* (New York, 1976); and Margot Peters, *Unquiet Soul: A Biography of Charlotte Bronte* (New York 1975). Gérin and Moglen have useful bibliographies for those who wish to go further. I have also drawn upon Gérin, *The Brontës: I The Formative Years, II The Creative Work* (London, 1973, 1974). All references to Gérin in the text and footnotes are from *Charlotte Brontë*, except for the reference on p. 151, which is to her *The Brontës*.

2.   Patrick Brontë's literary endeavours were almost as numerous as, and interspersed with, the births of his children: 'Cottage Poem' (1811); 'The Rural Minstrel' (1813); 'The Cottage in the Wood' (1815); 'The Maid of Killarney' (1818).

3.   See Gérin, pp. 1-16.

4.   Fanny Ratchford edited the Brontë *juvenilia* and interwove it with an account of their early life together in *Legends of Angria* (New Haven, Connecticut, 1933) and *The Brontës' Web of Childhood* (New York 1941). Charlotte's more sustained writings appear in Winifred Gérin (ed.), *Five Novelettes* (London, 1971). Ratchford's work has been amplified by *The Miscellaneous and Unpublished Writings of Charlotte and Patrick Branwell Brontë*, 2 vols. (Oxford, 1934) and *The Poems of Charlotte and Patrick Branwell Brontë* (Oxford, 1934). Ellen Nussey and Mary Taylor, Charlotte's close and life-long friends from Roe Head on, whom she thought of as sisters, ' ew nothing of these secret writings. An article by Carroll Smith-Rosenberg on 'The Female World of Love and Ritual: Relations between Women in Nineteenth-Century America' in *Signs*, I (1975), pp. 1-29 provides important contemporary analogous data on the inter-dependency among young women and the fuzzy distinctions between friendships and blood-related sisterhoods.

5.   Gérin, *The Brontës*, I, p. 55.

6.   Moglen, *Charlotte Bronte: The Self Conceived*, p. 38.

7.   Gérin, p. 178.

8.   Ibid., p. 107.

9.   Ibid., pp. 103-4.

10.   Ibid., p. 87.

11.   Ibid., pp. 110-11.

12. 'Henry Hastings', quoted in Gérin, p. 137.
13. 'Mina Laury', quoted in Moglen, *Charlotte Brontë: The Self Conceived*, p. 54.
14. Gérin (ed.), *Five Novelettes*, p. 181.
15. Ibid., pp. 243-4.
16. Ibid., p. 244.
17. Quoted in Moglen, *Charlotte Bronte: The Self Conceived*, p. 37.
18. Gérin, p. 128.
19. Ibid., p. 127.
20. Because of my deliberate emphasis upon the Brontë family and the role of family in *Jane Eyre*, I have underemphasized the role of Constantin Heger in the depiction of Jane's 'master', Edward Rochester. His importance is even more pronounced in *The Professor* and *Villette*. Elizabeth Hardwick's observation of the parallel of Charlotte/Heger to Branwell/Lydia Robinson is of use in confirming the perspective in this essay, that 'At the Pensionnat Heger in Brussels, Charlotte Brontë – alone, proud, disturbed in mind – was thrown into the middle of an unbalancing family life. She could no more have resisted falling in love with the husband than Branwell could have denied the presence of Mrs. Robinson.' ('Working Girls: The Brontës', *New York Review*, VIII, 4 May 1972, p. 16.)
21. As a context for the economic problems encountered by the Brontës, the Nusseys, and the Taylors – by which I mean the women in those families particularly, see Wanda Neff, *Victorian Working Women: An Historical and Literary Study of Women in British Industries and Professions, 1832–1850* (New York, 1966) and Lee Holcombe, *Victorian Ladies at Work: Middle-Class Working Women in England and Wales 1850–1914* (London, 1973). Holcombe has two sections on 'Women and Education' and 'Women in the Classroom'; Neff has an excellent section on 'The Governess.' Neff gives us census figures for 1851: 24.86 per cent unmarried Englishwomen over the age of 30; 17.89 per cent at age 35; more surprisingly, 25.89 Englishmen out of every 100 were unmarried at age 30 and 18 at age 35. Marriage looms larger in fiction than in Victorian life, an observation brooded upon in Susan Gorsky, 'Old Maids and New Women: Alternatives to Marriage in Englishwomen's novels, 1847–1915', *Journal of Popular Culture*, VIII, 1973, pp. 68-86. Gorsky points out that between 1851 and 1871 the number of single Englishwomen over the age of 15 rose from 2,765,000 to 3,228,700, while their job opportunities remained limited essentially to domestic roles: governesses, lady's companions, or companions within their families of origin. See also M. Jeanne Peterson, 'The Victorian Governess: Status Incongruence in Family and Society', in M' Vicinus (ed.), *Suffer and Be Still* (Bloomington, Indiana, 1972).
22. The 'Author's Preface' to *The Professor* takes as its central figure the male who reverses the Cinderella twist of fortune. *The Professor* was written by late June 1846, and offered, with *Wuthering Heights* and *Agnes Grey* (another 'governess' novel), to six successive publishers before the novels of Emily and Anne were accepted in July 1847. *The Professor* was published posthumously in 1857.
23. I use the Norton Critical Edition of *Jane Eyre*, Richard J. Dunn (ed.) (New York, 1971); this initial reference is from p. 203. The Norton Critical Edition has a sampling of *Jane Eyre* criticism, with a useful, brief bibliography of further critical essays, which should be supplemented by the critical essays in Moglen's bibliography. Some of the points made glancingly in my second section here form the central arguments of my *'Jane Eyre:*

Woman's Estate,' in *The Authority of Experience: Essays in Feminist Criticism,* Arlyn Diamond and Lee R. Edwards (ed.) (Amherst, Mass Massachusetts 1977), pp. 137-59.

24.   *Jane Eyre*, ed. Dunn, p. 10.
25.   Ibid.
26.   Ibid., p. 274.
27.   Ibid., p. 236.
28.   In 'Society in America,' excerpt in Alice Rossi (ed.), *The Feminist Papers* (New York, 1973), p. 133. Françoise Basch, *Relative Creatures: Victorian Women in Society and the Novel* (New York, 1974), sections 2, 'The Legal Position' and 9, 'Revolt and Duty in the Brontës' especially.
29.   Kenneth Keniston, 'Psychological Development and Historical Change,' *Journal of Interdisciplinary History,* reprinted in Theodore Rabb and Robert Rotberg (eds.), *The Family in History: Interdisciplinary Essays* (New York, 1971), p. 145.
30.   *Jane Eyre,* ed. Dunn, p. 154.
31.   Ibid., p. 177.
32.   Naming in this novel, as in all of Charlotte Brontë's fiction (and pseudonyms) is of considerable symbolic importance: plain Jane is distinct from the fancy heroines Blanche, Georgiana, and Eliza, as 'Eyre' is more elemental than the Ingram/Eshton names so closely allied to the families for whom Anne worked as governess and the Miss Currer of Eshton Hall whom Charlotte had encountered as benefactress to Cowan Bridge and neighbour at Stonegappe. I explore the multiple puns revolving around *eyre* in note 2 of 'Jane Eyre: Woman's Estate' (notes p. 292). The integral symbolic relation of name to identity makes the crossing of the threshold from girlhood to married adulthood focus, in part, on the changing of names – Jane Eyre to Jane Rochester.
33.   Despite the translation of Blanche's French name, she is described in the novel as a large, dark woman; her mother 'reminded [Jane] of Mrs. Reed.' who was also large and dark; Blanche, described as 'dark as a Spaniard' (p. 151) is thus linked with the monstrous Bertha Mason. Jane's small, pale frailty thus polarizes her from these women, making them into opposite types, with sexual-etheralized implications. Even Rochester says he first saw in Bertha Mason 'a fine woman in the style of Blanche Ingram; tall, dark, and majestic' (p. 268).
34.   *Jane Eyre,* ed. Dunn, pp. 122 and 280.
35.   Ibid., pp. 11-13.
36.   Ibid., p. 222.
37.   Ibid., p. 214.
38.   Ibid., p. 250.
39.   Ibid., p. 252.
40.   Ibid., p. 260.
41.   Ibid., p. 122.
42.   Ibid., p. 129.
43.   Ibid., p. 216.
44.   Ibid.
45.   Brocklehurst, a religious hypocrite, 'a black pillar' (p. 26), is likened to St John Rivers, 'too often a cold, cumbrous column, gloomy and out of place' (p. 346), his missionizing zeal admittedly tainted by the 'human deformity' of 'a cold, hard, ambitious man' (p. 360). Both are aliens and intruders upon the female support networks at Lowood (Maria Temple and Helen Burns) and at Marsh End (Diana and Mary Rivers).
46.   *Jane Eyre,* ed. Dunn, p. 341.

47. Ibid., pp. 396-7.
48. Charlotte would also have had the examples before her of her maiden aunt, Elizabeth Branwell, who, unmarried and in command of her limited finance, could pay Charlotte's way to Brussels and leave a small inheritance; the Wooler sisters also paid their way as unmarried and self-supporting women. Margaret Oliphant's assessment of her condition upon the death of her husband with three dependent children speaks to the situation of women without male mainstays by terse understatement: 'A thousand pounds in debt. Two hundred pounds insurance money. Some furniture warehoused. My faculties, such as they are.' *'Dictionary of National Biography,* Supplement, vol. LXVI, 231). And Elizabeth Hardwick points out that if, for the Brontës, Haworth was a retreat, 'it was at least better to have the freedom and familiarity of the family than the oppression of the life society offered to penniless, intellectual girls.' ('Working Girls', p. 11).
49. Gérin, p. 174.
50. Ibid., p. 299.
51. Ibid., p. 304.
52. Ibid., p. 85.

9 THE FAMILY AND THE MILL: COTTON MILL WORK, FAMILY WORK PATTERNS, AND FERTILITY IN MID-VICTORIAN STOCKPORT

R. Burr Litchfield

The skill that historians have recently acquired with the computer to carry out detailed analysis of the household enumeration books of the nineteenth-century census has created an ability to see how changing patterns of industrial employment affected living conditions, family relationships and general population trends.[1] The changing environment of the industrial city had an impact on the family. By the 1850s in the cotton towns of the north the practice of employing parish apprentices had ended; small children appear to have been infrequently employed in the mills. Still, the number of older children, beginning at age twelve to fourteen remained high, and the number of women in their twenties and thirties seems particularly to have been increasing.[2] This is not to say that women and young adolescents had not worked in pre-industrial situations or that they did not continue to work in areas of non-industrial employment outside the mills. The family domestic work-group to which all contributed had been the typical group of production on farms and in artisan industry. It was the long hours women worked away from home in the regimented situation of the mills that made contemporaries fearful that the working-class family was breaking down. One remembers the despondent unemployed workman living off the earnings of his wife described by Engels at St Helens in the 1840s, and Lord Shaftesbury's fears of the social evils he thought would result from the continued employment of married women.[3]

Studies of family and household structure have found it difficult to substantiate the contemporary view that factory employment was dissolving family ties. Instead, as M.S. Anderson has shown for Preston in Lancashire, recent migration, poverty, inadequate housing and the nature and lack of public relief crowded families together, enlarged household size, and made a calculative dependence on kin a basic means of survival.[4] As N. Smelser earlier observed, technological change and the increasing specialization of factory work had an effect on the family as the increasing age and sex selectiveness of the labour market created differentials in opportunities for employment among family members, decreased the availability of domestic work in the home, and made parents less able to supervise children in the mills.[5] But family budgets and the low level of wages still required the employ- ment of more than one household member, and thus the family work- group persisted in a modified form through the secondary wage contribution of wives, children, and kin to family income.

The interaction between this changing pattern of industrial employ- ment and working-class family and household dynamics has attracted the attention of demographers attempting to explain nineteenth- century population trends and particularly the beginnings of the tendency to limit births, the new development of the later decades of the century. Changes in the economic roles of family members can be a factor affecting the birthrate: the likelihood that couples will have more or fewer children. Generally, in situations of high fertility, as in the nineteenth century, when costs of raising children were less than parents' perceptions of their ultimate contribution to family income and well being, it is argued that family and household size would tend to be large and even increase when it was possible through earlier marriage or a decrease in infant mortality to bring more children to maturity. But when costs of raising children tended to increase or children began to contribute more indirectly to income, parents may have become more likely to consider a large family to be an inconvenience, to send children away from the household at a younger age or to want to assure the benefits of more costly upbringing to a smaller number of children and begin to limit the number of conceptions and births.[6]

It has been noted in studies of industrializing regions in the eighteenth century that expansion of rural industry and early factory employment tended to lower marriage age thus increasing fertility and the number of children who could be employed in domestic industry or accompany their parents to the mills.[7] But what then happened to working-class families in the mid-to-late nineteenth century when industrial processes matured and changed, and small children were less likely to be employed in industry? This essay suggests some answers to these questions by focusing on Stockport, a cotton- mill town in northern Cheshire, where there was early marriage, moderately high fertility, and large family size in the 1840s to 1860s. It will be argued that changes in the age and sex composition of the factory work-force in cotton were beginning to decrease the contribution of children to family budgets at a critical stage of the family cycle and that this change may have contributed to the new tendency to limit births.

Stockport is about ten miles south-east of Manchester and in the 1850s was a cotton town fairly typical of the Lancashire-Cheshire region. In 1851, the population of the borough was just over 53,000, and 36 per cent above the age of twenty were employed in the cotton mills. The power loom had been successfully introduced at Stockport before 1820 and the city had grown rapidly in the following decades. Among other new factories the Orrell Mill, which opened in 1838, was one of the largest establishments of its time, a gigantic six-storey three-winged edifice equipped with 45,000 yarn spindles and 1,100 power looms. Its ruins are still an impressive sight when viewed from the brick railway viaduct of 1840 that spans the valley of the Mersey River where Stockport is located.[8] By 1841, handloom weaving in cotton had all but disappeared. Factory spinning and weaving, with the subsidiary industries of dying and calico printing, dominated the city and had largely supplanted its older artisan industries, chiefly silk spinning and weaving and the manufacture of felt hats, an old established trade in this region.

A sample of households drawn from the enumeration books of the censuses of 1841, 1851 and 1861 provides the basis for a close look at the pattern of family employment among cotton-mill workers.[9] The census registration districts do not correspond precisely to the municipal boundaries of Stockport, but the district sampled, the central part of the city south of the Mersey between Hillgate and Wellington Road, and the recently built streets of working-class houses to the west, contained more than half of the population. The changing age and sex composition of the factory work-force emerges very clearly from the occupations recorded by the census takers. Table 9.1 shows the age and sex distribution of differential occupational groups from the three censuses. Occupations have been classified along a scale to indicate gradations of work situations and wages: (1) the professional and managerial class; (2) shopkeepers; (3) artisans and workers in small-scale manufacturing; (4) higher- and (5) lower-paid factory workers in cotton; (6) common labourers including the small number of domestic servants; and (7) persons living as dependents or not reported in the census as employed. Cotton factory work comprises occupational groups four and five together.[10] One can see the changing balance of employment of men and women at successive periods of age. A typical configuration of employment in cotton appears in all three census years, that is, a predominance of the young among mill workers and a tendency for both men and women to leave factory work for other occupations as they grew older.

When one compares the three years, a third aspect of work in cotton becomes clear: mill workers at Stockport were becoming more predominantly younger women in the middle decades of the century. Women made up 44 per cent of cotton workers aged ten to sixty-nine in the sample in 1841, 49 per cent in 1851, and 55 per cent in 1861, while the proportion of women under thirty increased from 36 to 41 per cent and the proportion of women in their twenties increased from 14 to 20 per cent. One might expect unmarried women to increase in number as the proportion of young women workers increased, but in fact the opposite was taking place. The proportion of married women among female mill workers increased from 18 per cent in 1841 to 28 per cent in 1851 and to 33 per cent in 1861. Precision in the observation of this trend is marred by special circumstances in 1841, which was a year of depression and unemployment. Both men and women were later to enter and earlier to leave the work-force in this year and occupations seem generally to have been under-reported in comparison with the two later years; undoubtedly to a larger extent in the age-group ten to nineteen and among women. Persons doing out-work at home, as opposed to persons with definite employments outside of the home, may have been overlooked by the census takers particularly and this may help to account for the fact that the proportions of women and children engaged in non-factory work appear to have increased as much as those doing factory work between the censuses of 1841 and 1851. But under-reportage of women's employment in 1841 probably would not reverse the trend that appears in the later years, for there are other indications that new employment opportunities were becoming available for women. The proportion of women among migrants to the city was increasing. As this happened the sex-ratio of men to women in the migratory and child-bearing years of fifteen to forty-nine was decreasing. It was 88 in 1841, 83 in 1851, and 82 in 1861.

The change in composition of the work-force probably resulted from a development of managerial practice in the mills themselves. The legislation of the 1830s, which had restricted the employment of young children and the hours of children under thirteen, appears to have had approximately the effect that Smelser observed for the 1830s and 1840s, but the change at Stockport continued up through the 1860s. Smelser observed the exodus of young children from the Lancashire mills.[11] According to an inquiry of 1833, 21 per cent of

Table 9.1: Stockport Age-Distribution of Occupations, 1841–1861 (proportion of total population at age by occupational group)

Age:	10-14	15-19	20-29	30-39	40-49	50-59	60-69	Total
Professional and Managerial								
Males								
1841			1.2	1.5	2.1	1.7	2.0	1.2
1851	0.2	1.3	1.0	1.9	2.9	1.2	1.0	1.4
1861	1.2	1.1	1.7	0.9	2.0	2.0	4.0	1.6
Females								
1841			0.2		1.2	1.1	1.0	0.4
1851	0.2			0.5	0.3	0.6		0.1
1861		0.2				0.8		0.1
Shopkeeping								
Males								
1841			2.1	2.7	4.2	4.1	4.0	2.1
1851	0.5		1.8	5.9	2.3	4.8	6.3	2.6
1861	0.3	0.8	2.0	4.7	5.5	4.9	3.3	2.9
Females								
1841			0.4		0.4	1.7	3.0	0.4
1851		0.3		0.5		1.2	2.1	0.3
1861			1.4		2.0	2.8	0.6	0.8
Artisan and Small-Scale Manufacturing								
Males								
1841	1.8	8.5	**13.4**	**14.5**	**14.0**	**16.1**	**17.0**	**11.6**
1851	4.7	6.1	9.9	**10.7**	**14.4**	**14.5**	8.4	9.6
1861	4.7	**10.8**	**11.7**	9.7	**12.7**	**16.1**	**14.6**	**11.1**
Females								
1841	2.5	2.1	5.3	2.1	3.4	1.7	3.0	3.1
1851	5.0	6.4	5.4	3.3	5.5	4.8	1.0	4.9
1861	2.8	2.6	4.2	3.9	2.6	1.6	2.6	3.1
Higher Factory								
Males								
1841		1.4	**15.3**	**12.4**	**11.0**	**11.9**	9.0	9.2
1851	0.2	**10.2**	**16.2**	**13.3**	8.5	**10.3**	5.2	**10.0**
1861	1.2	7.9	**13.6**	**10.9**	7.5	9.0	9.3	9.1
Females								
1841			0.4	0.9	0.4			0.3
1851	0.5	2.0	1.4	1.4	0.6	0.6		1.1
1861		1.4	1.0	2.2	1.1	0.4	0.6	1.0
Lower Factory								
Males								
1841	**15.2**	**25.2**	8.9	7.8	5.5	6.5	3.0	**11.2**
1851	**19.8**	**19.4**	9.0	9.6	6.2	4.2	4.2	**11.4**
1861	**21.5**	**21.9**	9.7	5.7	4.3	4.1	2.6	**10.5**
Females								
1841	**19.6**	**35.2**	**20.9**	9.3	6.3	2.9	1.0	**16.3**
1851	**19.5**	**37.8**	**29.9**	**14.7**	6.2	6.0	5.2	**20.0**
1861	**21.2**	**42.8**	**35.6**	**19.2**	8.4	7.8	4.0	**23.0**
Common Labour								
Males								
1841	0.3	1.7	3.8	7.2	4.6	4.1	4.0	3.7
1851	0.8	3.7	6.7	7.0	**11.8**	**12.1**	4.2	6.4
1861	1.8	1.7	6.1	**10.9**	**11.9**	**10.3**	**12.0**	7.3
Females								
1841	0.7	1.4	2.5	3.3	1.7	2.3	4.0	2.2
1851	3.8	3.0	3.7	2.5	6.0	2.4	8.4	4.0
1861	2.2	2.6	4.2	4.2	9.0	7.8	8.6	5.0
Dependents								
Males								
1841	**30.9**	9.6	2.5		3.8	2.9	3.0	7.5
1851	**23.0**	3.7	0.6		0.6	1.2	6.3	5.0
1861	**18.0**	1.4	0.6		0.5	1.2	4.6	3.2
Females								
1841	**28.7**	**13.5**	**21.7**	**37.8**	**40.8**	**40.7**	**46.0**	**29.8**
1851	**21.0**	5.4	**13.7**	**28.0**	**32.5**	**35.7**	**47.3**	**22.4**
1861	**24.6**	4.1	9.0	**25.4**	**31.6**	**30.1**	**32.6**	**20.0**
Total (N)								
1841	275	281	465	330	235	165	100	1,851
1851	338	293	474	353	302	165	95	2,020
1861	316	341	586	401	344	242	150	2,375

Significance: **bold figs** = ten per cent or more of total population at age.

operatives in the cotton mills of Stockport were under fourteen.[12] The
reportage of employment of children in the censuses seems to have
improved in completeness between 1841 and 1861 and in this last
year when the most children were reported working the proportion of
mill workers under fourteen was only 8 per cent. The demand for
cotton operatives was chiefly for young people aged fourteen and
above and the new women operatives in their late teens to early
thirties were not merely replacing children in the relatively simple
operations of the card rooms and around the spinning frames.
Instead, as the cotton industry expanded, women were moving into
areas of more skilled work previously carried out largely by men.
The Ten Hours Act of 1847 and subsequent legislation appears not
to have stemmed this development. One area of women's work was
power loom weaving, which had long been mechanized. More than
half of the weavers in the sample (55 per cent) were women in 1841.
In 1851, 60 per cent were women and in 1861, 65 per cent. The
average age of male weavers remained about the same between 1841
and 1861, while as more married women now worked as weavers the
average age of women increased from twenty to twenty-four years.
Spinning remained more an occupation of men since the mules used
to a large extent required more strength than the operation of power
looms or throstle spinning-frames. Only 30 per cent of spinners in the
sample were women in 1841, but with the gradual introduction of
self-acting mules changes were also taking place in this area for in
1851 51 per cent of the spinners were women and in 1865 56 per
cent.[13] The age of male spinners was also affected, and fell from
thirty-three years in 1841 to thirty years in 1861.

The experience of cotton workers was, in fact, quite different from
that of other occupational groups in the city. In the 1850s Stockport
was what one would call a mill town, i.e. cotton predominated, but
there were nonetheless other sectors of employment: non-factory
industries, chief among them hatting, but also builders, bakers, shoe-
makers, a small number of shopkeepers and at the bottom of the
occupational ladder a large number of common labourers.

It is significant that the non-mill occupations tended to be more
predominantly male and to have occupied rather older men than
cotton. The hatters are a good example. Felt hatting was an old and
well-established trade in this region. It was carried out in small
workshops, partly through domestic out-working. A London firm,
Christy's, became an important outlet for the Stockport hatters in
the 1820s, and then was instrumental in the factory mechanization

of the hatting industry in the 1860s.[14] It is difficult to assess the total extent of domestic out-work in hat making, chiefly in hat trimming, and the extent of female employment at home. Still, hatting seems to have been a male-dominated and fairly sedentary trade. Between 60 and 80 per cent of the hatters were males throughout the period, and more than half were males over forty. The building trades and shoe-making were similarly male-dominated and although the average age was younger than with the hatters, still the majority of workers were over thirty. The proportion of males in the cotton mills was largest between the ages of fifteen and twenty-four and then decreased markedly, while the proportion of males in artisan industries like hatting began to increase between twenty and twenty-nine, and then continued to increase. The same was true of men listed in the census with occupations in the category of common labour. This is a com-posite category of jobs such as 'labourer', 'jobber outdoors', 'hawker', 'railway navvy', 'porter'. Such work was for the very poor and for persons who may have been displaced from other employments. It fell to the lot of an increasing proportion of Stockport males from their thirties until they reached their sixties when the proportion living at home with no stated occupation began to grow.

It seems clear that at Stockport cotton mill work was an episode of youth and young adulthood. One might think some trades were in decline and simply ageing in these years were it not that much the same age-distribution is repeated from census to census. The shape of the distributions is similar to the one found by Anderson at Preston, as is the drift of persons from occupation to occupation.[15] Age determined the employment of family members in a differential manner. Women left the cotton mills in their thirties in part because of their place in the family. Migration affected the age distribution of employment, for older migrants, and particularly the Irish, seem to have had difficulty in securing mill work and instead swelled the number of common labourers, while children in Irish families did not have this difficulty. A fairly large number of males probably remained in one job or another at the mills throughout their working lives and may have moved, as they grew older, from less skilled and lower paying jobs to more skilled and higher paying ones. But others took a different direction. In 1861, married male heads of households were more likely to be employed outside the mills than working males generally. If wives worked, two-thirds, by far the largest proportion, were employed in cotton. When one considers children between the ages of ten and nineteen, factory work had undermined traditional training in non-factory trades. A common occurrence was for both a parent and children to be employed in cotton, but sons of fathers working in non-factory trades were more likely to be working in the mills than in their fathers' occupations. At the lowest level, 80 per cent of the sons of common labourers were employed in the mills.

What effect did this changing pattern of work have on the family, the relationship between parents and children, and fertility? It is difficult to be more than approximate since we do not know in detail the pattern of work before 1841 and comparisons with other than cotton mill towns, which tended to be similar, would be necessary to put the pattern of family employment at Stockport into better perspective. To see the nature of secondary employment at different stages of the family's existence it is important to assess experience over time. The ten-year gap between censuses and volume of in- and out-migration make it difficult to trace individual families from census to census. Still, it is possible to distinguish the pattern of employment in households at successive stages of the developmental cycle of the family and thus to have a picture of family employment at successive stages of child-rearing. This method has the drawback of grouping together different generational experiences present in the same year and of assuming that younger families would necessarily reiterate the experience of older families in their later development. But generational change can be assessed to a certain extent by comparing the experience of age groups from one census to another.

Table 9.2 shows the pattern of employment in working-class households from the sample in 1861 at different stages of the family cycle. Since employment in cotton cut across the experience of families in all Stockport trades, married couples who were heads of households and the husbands were employed either in the non-factory trades, cotton, or as common labourers have been selected for particular attention. These three groups all tended to have secondary family members employed in the cotton mills. Broken households headed by widows or widowers involve special circumstances and have been excluded. The bars in the table are average numbers of kin working, kin not working, and paying lodgers at different stages of the family cycle. Husbands, wives, kin, and children under age five, in education, and working have been distinguished separately.

The relationship of the changing occupational structure to secondary employment in the family has to be understood in the context of marriage, the formation and composition of households, and the relationship of family budgets to the family cycle. Marriage

Table 9.2: Family Work Pattern of Stockport Working-Class
   Households, 1861

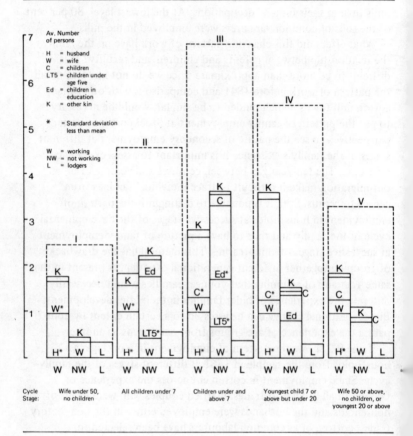

Cycle Stage:	I Wife under 50, no children	II All children under 7	III Children under and above 7	IV Youngest child 7 or above but under 20	V Wife 50 or above, no children, or youngest 20 or above

Av. Number of persons

H = husband
W = wife
C = children
LT5 = children under age five
Ed = children in education
K = other kin

* = Standard deviation less than mean

W = working
NW = not working
L = lodgers

was moderately early at Stockport in these decades, about ages
twenty-five to twenty-six for men and twenty-four to twenty-five
for women, and was nearly universal; only 4 to 8 per cent of the men
and 7 to 12 per cent of the women, remained unmarried in their
late forties, an indication that the over-balance of women was slightly
disadvantageous to their marrying. But marriage was not always
followed immediately by the establishment of an independent household, for the central section of the borough was becoming
increasingly crowded between the 1840s and 1860s with the effect

that families lived compacted together. Sharing quarters with kin or lodgers cramped living space, but permitted both a saving on rent for parents and married children, and a means for providing increments of income to the family of the household's head. The proportion of young couples in their twenties living with parents or as lodgers, increased from 28 to 38 per cent between 1841 and 1861 and in this last year nearly a third of all households were augmented by a secondary nuclear family unit, or by single lodgers or kin.

Both the dense occupancy of housing and the need for secondary household members to work were related to the low level of wages. Estimates made for Preston and Oldham in this period suggest that wage levels in the 1850s were not sufficient in the total earnings of the family group to prevent some 20 per cent of households from falling below a poverty line of bare subsistence, while some 30 per cent more were close to this level.[16] Information from contemporary surveys of wages for Stockport is available only for the textile industry, which makes it difficult to estimate a total of family earnings when family members were employed outside of the mills.[17] In 1861, however, when the single wages of household heads in cotton are compared with estimated minimum weekly living expenses of their primary families, husband, wife, and children, the earnings of half appear to have been less than the minimum necessary for family support. This deficiency was greatest at lower paying levels of mill work — card-room hands, piecers, and spinning room workers; higher paid workers — weavers, mule spinners, dyers, and printers — could be in better circumstances, but if the number of dependent unemployed household members too greatly increased, few mill workers at Stockport earned enough to be immune from falling below the poverty line.

Need was thus related to the stage of the family cycle of households at a particular moment.[18] The proportion of earning units to the number of household members tended to be highest shortly after marriage, when couples were in their mid-twenties and both husband and wife were working. With the arrival of children the margin of income fell until the point when children still living at home began working was reached, which in situations of high fertility could be an extended period. At this point the income of the family as a whole might rise to and exceed its initial level, only to fall again with old age and the departure of children from the home. The cycle of family income might be affected by the presence of working kin or paying lodgers, although where housing was cramped and in short supply as at Stockport, there was little room for additional household members when the number of children was greatest. When there were kin or lodgers at this point, such tolerance of crowding in cramped households already containing seven or more members, as among some of the Stockport Irish, may have been a sign of extreme need.

In Table 9.2 work units have been counted as the number of persons working rather than in terms of estimated wages, although the wage contribution and living expenses of working wives and children should be weighted at less than for older adult males. The cycle stages correspond to distinct stages of family life, and have been devised to cast light on the relationship between family budgets and child raising. The first stage is the early period of marriage without children and the second the early years of child-bearing. Stage three is an intermediate period when there are both young and older children in the home. At stage four all children were older, but the majority under the customary age of leaving the household. Stage five is a later stage of the family, viz. older childless couples or couples with the youngest child at home aged twenty or over. As one might expect from the long period of child-bearing at Stockport, the largest proportion of households, 30 per cent in 1861, were at cycle stage three. At this stage, the disproportion between the number of household members working and not working was most great.

The relationship between the changing age- and sex-pattern of employment in the cotton mills and the changing balance of secondary employment in the family at Stockport emerges from Table 9.2 fairly clearly. Husbands were employed at all stages of the cycle, although the age and sex selectiveness of mill work brought about their tendency to change employment which is evident as one moved from families at earlier to families at later cycle stages. Nearly h ʳ of the husbands in the sample were employed in the cotton ʲills iu families at stages one and two of the cycle, when they were in their late twenties or early thirties, but less than a third in families at stage four when these men were in their late forties and children were well established in employment. Low wages and the instability of work for men was compensated for by the employment of wives and children, although with uneven consequences as the family moved from earlier to later points of its development. There was, to be sure, a variability from household to household. Not all households contained kin or lodgers and it was more uncommon to find households with children in school at stage two or with wives working at stages four and five. Still, working

wives were the most important contributors of secondary income
shortly after marriage and when all children were small. Then children
working in the mills replaced wives as the chief supplement to
income in families at stages three, four and five. Two factors were
involved: the wage level of the head of the family and the number and
wages of its subsidiary members who were working. In households at
stages three and four of the cycle, with husbands employed in higher
paying factory jobs and in non-factory trades, a smaller proportion
of wives and children worked. In families with heads in lower paying
factory jobs, or in common labour, secondary employment was most
likely.

A remarkable feature in this pattern of secondary employment
was the cycle of women's work. The majority (62 per cent) of
women working in the Stockport mills in 1861 were single, but two-
thirds of these were women living as secondary family members,
children or kin. The remainder were heads of households, or most
likely, lodgers. But the most rapidly expanding group of working
women in the 1850s was married women and the employment of married
women is a revealing indicator of family relationships. One generally imag-
ines a pattern of women's work in which many single and young married
women worked, left the work-force when they had young children and
then returned to work when children reached a certain age. This pattern
assumes a child-centred family, but is, in fact, a low-fertility pattern, and a
relatively recent one.[19] At Stockport where single women and young married women worked, but older married women did not return to the work-
force, the situation was different. It is true that the increase in number of
married women working between 1851 and 1861 was chiefly that of women without small children in families at stages one, four and five of the
cycle. Still, it is surprising how many mothers of small children worked; at
cycle-stage two two-thirds of mothers with one child under five and nearly
half with two. More than half the mothers with children at home aged
under one year were listed as working in the census, a situation fraught
with strain for mothers and with peril of death for small children.[20] The
return from the mill to the family appears to have been an event
less related to the nurturing of small children than to the moment at
cycle-stage three when children were beginning to be old enough
to contribute independently to family support. Since children were
entering the work-force at a later age, mothers were likely to
continue working for a longer period. There was some tendency
among older married women, as among older men, for employment
to be outside of the cotton mills. But in families at cycle stages four

and five, while there were working children at home, married women
tended not to return to the mills.

This pattern of family employment would seem at first sight to fit
rather closely the high fertility strategy associated by demographic
historians with the first stages of industrialization. Children did
contribute to family income at Stockport, although with later entry
into the work-force this contribution was more likely to become
significant when children were older, at stage four of the family cycle,
rather than when they were younger, at stage three. Judging from the
long period of child-bearing and the age of parents when older
children began to work and when younger children were likely to
leave home, parents in their mid-to-late thirties began to experience
a period of about twenty years when children contributed to family
income. Indeed, even after marriage, working children tended to
live at home with their parents into their mid-to-late twenties, an
indication of a solidarity of family relationships that an established
pattern of contribution of secondary wage earners to family budgets
might create.

Nonetheless, the changing age- and sex-composition of the work-
force may also have been producing tensions in the family which made
a large family size seem disadvantageous. The crucial point would
seem to have been family composition, size and employment at cycle
stage three. This is an important point in the development of the
family for demographers since it is generally when parents reach their
thirties that they begin to decide to stop having children. The fact
that children were entering the work-force at a later age meant that
fewer family members were working at this stage of the family's
development, a fact that was likely to create a strain on family
resources.

Was this changing pattern of employment engendering second
thoughts about the utility of a large family? One wonders what older
children at home but not yet old enough for steady employment were
doing. Undoubtedly, older children took care of younger children
to a certain extent while parents worked and one notes that kin or
lodgers who might have helped to look after small children were
somewhat less likely to be present in the household at stage three of
the cycle than at earlier periods in the family's development. In 1861,
most children at home and not working were listed in the census as
'scholar' or 'attending school'. Historians of education have begun to
notice the expansion of schooling in England well before the
Education Act of 1870, although judging from the educational census

of 1851 Stockport had a relatively low proportion of children in regular day schools.[21] Schooling at Stockport in the 1850s was as yet not far advanced, although it was improving. Among working-class families from the census samples, 45 per cent of children aged five to fourteen in 1851 were reported to be in school, and 55 per cent in 1861. This proportion undoubtedly increased later in the century, a further rise in the cost of child raising for parents to the extent that children in school were not also employed part time in the cotton mills.

It is unfortunately difficult to assess the precise level of fertility in the 1850s from the enumeration books of the census, chiefly because of the very high rate of infant deaths. In 1851–1860, 45 per cent of all deaths at Stockport were of children under age five. In effect, 20 per cent of children died before reaching their first birthday and 32 per cent died before reaching their fifth.[22] This fact gives a certain unreality to the construction of child-woman ratios, that is, the average number of children under the age of five living with mothers aged fifteen to forty-nine in each five-year group of mothers. It is uncertain whether a decrease in the number of small children reported in the censuses really resulted from limitation of births or, rather, from a rising deathrate of children who died before they could be counted, a likely eventuality with a rising proportion of married women working. This might make family size seem to be decreasing when fertility was actually still high. The fertility ratio of the borough of Stockport as a whole was higher than that of working-class families in the first district and the number of surviving children of mill workers decreased slightly between 1841 and 1861; but the deathrate was also highest in this central part of the city nearest to the river and the mills.

In early industrial England child mortality was one of the chief delimiters of family size and it seems likely to have been as much child mortality as a systematic limitation of births that still helped to bridge the gap between household size, family budgets and the proportion of family members working at Stockport in the 1850s. The fertility ratio of the borough as a whole did not begin to fall significantly until the 1880s, three decades after the period considered here.[23] Given the present unavailability of schedules of the English census after 1871, one can only speculate about the precise nature of this ulterior development, but it seems likely that two changes in the period after 1861 further affected the situation that has been described here: first, a decrease in the rate of infant mortality by the end of the century which meant that more small children remained alive; and second, a further reduction in opportunities for regular employment of children living at home.

This is not to say that the need for secondary employment decreased, especially as Stockport began to suffer the effects of the cotton famine of the 1860s, and then further crises of the cotton industry up to and throughout the 1890s. But in the last quarter of the century family size began to diminish. One can derive some indication of this later development from the census of 1911, the first published English census that permits analysis of the age-distribution of employment for men and women at an individual town level and thus an indirect assessment of secondary employment in households. By 1911, the general fertility ratio for the Borough of Stockport was about three-fourths what it had been in 1861 and the general and infant deathrates had also fallen significantly. The occupational structure of Stockport was also changing in that by 1911 the city was less dependent on textiles and employment in the building trades, transport, dealing and public service had increased. Only 18 per cent of the population above age ten was employed in cotton, fewer married women were working than in 1861 and the proportion of young adolescents aged ten to fourteen reported as working had fallen from 42 per cent in 1861 to 23 per cent.[24] This indicates that there was a further decrease in opportunities for employment of secondary household members after the 1850s, a development that it would have been difficult to accommodate to family income, considering the importance of the contribution of children to family budgets in the 1850s, without there being a considerable rise in wages, or a reduction of family size through the limitation of births.

Notes

1.   This essay is based partly on material from the Comparative Cities Project which the author organized jointly with Professor H.P. Chaducoff of Brown University with support from the National Endowment for the Humanities in 1972–1974. This material is being developed into a study of occupational change, family patterns, and demography in four cities of the mid-to-late nineteenth century: Pisa (Italy), Amiens (France), Stockport (England) and Providence (Rhode Island, U.S.A.).

2.   On the general increase in the proportion of women working, see M. Hewitt, *Wives and Mothers in Victorian Industry* (London, 1958).

3.   F. Engels, *The Condition of the Working Class in England*, W.O. Henderson and W.H. Chaloner (trans. and eds.), (Stanford, California, 1958), pp. 162-4. Hewitt, *Wives and Mothers*, pp. 48-61.

4.   M.S. Anderson, *Family Structure in Nineteenth-century Lancashire* (Cambridge, 1971).

5.   N. Smelser, *Social Change in the Industrial Revolution* (Chicago, 1959).

6.   Gary S. Becker, 'An Economic Analysis of Fertility', in Universities National Bureau Committee for Economic Research, *Demographic and Economic Change in Developed Countries* (Princeton, New Jersey, 1960); 'A Theory of the Allocation of Time', in *Economic Journal*, 71, 229 (September 1965). There is a useful summary of this work by T. Paul Schultz, 'A Preliminary Survey of Economic Analysis of Fertility', in *American Economic Review*, 63, 2 (May 1973). For a good formulation of theory in consideration of historical dimensions of the demographic transition, R.A. Easterlin, 'An Economic Framework for Fertility Analysis', in *Studies in Family Planning*, 6, 3 (March 1975).

7.   J. Krause, 'Changes in English Fertility and Mortality, 1781–1850', in *Economic History Review*, 2nd ser., XI (1958–1959); J.D. Chambers, 'The Vale of Trent, 1670–1800: A Regional Study of Economic Change', in *Economic History Review Supplement*, III (1957); D. Levine, 'The Demographic Implications of Rural Industrialization: A Family Reconstitution Study of Shepshed, Leicestershire, 1600–1851', in *Social History*, II (1976).

8.   A. Ure, *The Cotton Manufacture of Great Britain* (London, 1836), I, pp. 297-304. On the general history of Stockport in this period, W. Astle (ed.), *The Stockport Advertiser Centenary History of Stockport* (Stockport, 1922); H. Heginbotham, *Stockport Ancient and Modern*, 2 vols. (London, 1882–1892).

9.   The samples used here are 1:10 house samples of individuals in the registration sub-district Stockport First, which encompassed the bulk of the city. These consist of 2,510 cases for 1841, 2,680 cases for 1851, and 3,073 cases for 1861, and correspond well with general characteristics of the population of the Borough as a whole. I wish to thank Mr Steven Hochstadt, and Mr John McArthur for coding and helping to prepare the census sample for 1861.

10.   For comparative purposes, occupational recoding from the census had been rearranged in general accordance with the procedure used by M.S. Anderson (*Family Structure*, pp. 22-9). Distinction between higher and lower paying levels of mill work requires assessment of wages, and in some cases adjustment of wage rates downward for women and persons under age eighteen. For the procedure used to estimate wage rates, see note 17 below.

11.   Smelser, *Social Change*, p. 202, *et passim*.

12.   Ure, *Cotton Manufacture*, II, p. 346.

13.   Stockport appears to have differed from the general pattern described by Smelser for Lancashire in the relationship of technology to the changing nature of the work-force, chiefly in the fact that power looms were used commonly at Stockport earlier than elsewhere. The greater prominence of male spinners may have been due to a relative slowness of utilizing self-acting mules, which facilitated employment of women. According to G.H. Wood, 'The change from hand-mule spinning to self-actor minding has taken place gradually, and commenced about 1836. In the districts using American cotton – Manchester (partly), Oldham, Preston, Ashton, etc. – the change was completed many years ago, hand mules being the exception and not the rule in the sixties and seventies. In the Egyptian cotton using districts – Bolton, Stockport and Manchester (partly) – the change came later.' (G.H. Wood, 'The Statistics of Wages in the

United Kingdom during the Nineteenth Century. (Part XVI): The Cotton Industry', in *Journal of the Royal Statistical Society*, 73 (1910), p. 134.)

14.   On the hatters, P.M. Giles, 'The Felt-Hatting Industry c. 1500–1800 with Special Reference to Lancashire and Cheshire', in *Transactions of the Lancashire and Cheshire Antiquarian Society*, 69 (1960).

15.   Anderson, *Family Structure*, pp. 22-32.

16.   Ibid., pp. 29-32; J. Foster, *Class Struggle in the Industrial Revolution: Early Industrial Capitalism in Three English Towns* (London, 1974), pp. 95-97.

17.   Wage rates in the cotton industry at Stockport, which distinguish higher from lower factory employment in Table 9.1 have been estimated for single occupational titles reported in the census samples from those recorded as current by D. Chadwick, 'On the Rate of Wages in Manchester, Salford, and the Manufacturing Districts of Lancashire, 1839–1859' (*Journal of the Royal Statistical Society*, 23 (1860)). G.H. Wood thought wages at Stockport were higher than the average for Lancashire-Cheshire in the 1830s, but that this relative advantage was lost in the following decades. (Wood, 'Statistics of Wages', p. 294.) From the time of B.S. Rowntree in the 1890s, social investigators have attempted to estimate minimal living expenses based on common costs of rent, heating, clothing and food for persons of different sexes and ages. When the weights adopted from Rowntree by J. Foster for Oldham, north of Stockport, (*Class Struggle in the Industrial Revolution*, pp. 255-9) are applied to the primary families of household heads employed in cotton at Stockport in 1861 and are compared with estimated weekly earnings of household heads at different levels of wages and with different family sizes, family size appears to have been the most systematic determinant of expenses exceeding the head's wage.

18.   For a discussion of determinants of income levels at successive stages of the family cycle, B.S. Rowntree, *Poverty: A Study of Town Life* (London, 1901), pp. 86-145.

19.   Note the discussion in M. Young and P. Willmott, *The Symmetrical Family* (London, 1973), pp. 1-33.

20.   A comparison between mothers working and the age and number of small children at home suggests that it was less the age than the number of children that affected women's leaving employment. Among working-class families, 54 per cent of mothers whose youngest child was less than a year old were reported in the census as working; 50 per cent with the youngest child between ages one and two; 45 per cent when the youngest child was between ages two and three; and 46 per cent when the youngest child was between ages three and four. While 76 per cent of mothers whose only child was under a year old were reported as working, mothers with both a young child and older children were less likely to be employed. On related problems of child care and mortality, M. Hewitt, *Wives and Mothers*, pp. 99-122, *et passim*.

21.   *Parliamentary Papers*, XC (1852–1853) (Educational Census, 1851), pp. 4-6, 167.

22.   Registrar-General, *Annual Reports of Births, Deaths, and Marriages in England, Supplement to the Twenty-Fifth Annual Report* (1863), p. 321.

23.   The ratios for Stockport as a whole (average of children under age five to married women aged fifteen to forty-four) were: (1861) 1.001; (1871) 1.036; (1881) 1.021; (1891) 0.928; (1911) 0.778. *Parliamentary Papers*, Censuses of 1861, 1871, 1881, 1891 and 1911.

24.   *Parliamentary Papers*, XXXIX (1913), pp. 56-58.

10 SEX AND THE SINGLE ROOM: INCEST AMONG THE VICTORIAN WORKING CLASSES

Anthony S. Wohl

In his seminal *Family Structure in Nineteenth-Century Lancashire* (1971), which is largely based on computer analysis of census data, Michael Anderson has rightly questioned the validity of many of the sources historians have traditionally relied upon to recapture family life among the Victorian working classes. 'Impressionistic work by middle-class persons,' works in the genre of Kay, Gaskell, Mayhew and Engels, he wrote, tend to 'emphasize the more remarkable features of family life . . . without any attempt to assess quantitatively either their frequency, or their distribution over the population as a whole.'[1] Anderson's criticism is well-taken, for generalizations abound concerning 'stern' Victorian parents and 'repressed' children, 'large' families, or 'numerous' servants, arrived at without any effort at quantification or sufficient caution about typicality. The new surge of interest in family history and awareness of the strictures of Anderson and other historical sociologists will, one hopes, lead to more precise and rigorous analysis. But, unfortunate as it may be, not all aspects of family life are subject to quantification and it would be a sad loss if social historians, intimidated by the new emphasis upon statistical analysis and paradigms, turned away from the study of such intangibles and immeasurables as love, happiness, respect, leisure, personal relationships or sexual practices and attitudes or many other aspects of family life that do not lend themselves readily to measurement.

Clearly there are many vital aspects of family life where the historian is forced to turn to precisely those 'impressionistic' qualitative materials disparaged by Anderson. He may run the risk of having his work dismissed as trivial or imprecise, but unless the social historian is prepared to interpret this material cautiously but confidently, using his general understanding of the period to read between the lines and to speculate or take up innuendoes, many of the intense and intimate relationships, which existed within the Victorian family, will remain unexplored. Like the psychologist, the historian of the family must often be prepared to pick his path among the delicate sub-structure of his subject and delve into a twilight region of uncertainties where evidence is more latent than overt. As a test-case for these observations I would like to consider one unexplored, but possibly widely-experienced, facet of family life in the Victorian slums – incest.

It may be asked, why bother to study incest? One could answer that all aspects of human behaviour, however deviant or rare, merit study, and, indeed that until they are studied one cannot use such words as 'deviant' with any authority or meaning. More to the point from the perspective of this book most sociologists and social anthropologists have argued that the incest taboo is essential for the continuance of the family. 'The prohibition of incest', writes Kingsley Davis, 'is absolutely indispensable to its [the family's] existence as a part of social organization.' 'No known human society could tolerate much incest without ruinous disruption', conclude the authors of *Sex Offenders*, published by the Institute of Sex Research. 'One feature of the human family is so universal and so essential to man's survival, that it would seem to qualify as one of the irreducibles', writes Leonard Benson in *The Family Bond*. 'This is the incest taboo. Without such a taboo, it is difficult to imagine a human family system at all.' 'Incest is behaviour that disrupts or destroys the social intimacy and sexual distance upon which family unity depends', writes S.K. Weinberg, in *Incest Behaviour*.[2]

These statements are misleading if taken out of context, for they are based upon an assumption of what might happen if incest were practised so widely as to supplement or replace exogamous sexual relationships. One could even argue that under certain conditions incest is psychologically beneficial or that it represents a symptom, not the cause, of a disrupted family.[3] As the *International Journal of Offender Therapy and Comparative Criminology* has recently had cause to deplore, there are not enough long-term studies of the psychological effects of incest upon members of the family to state with any degree of certainty how disruptive a practice it is.[4] Obviously there have been societies, both ancient and modern, and the family structure within them, that have survived despite the practice of incest.

Nevertheless, the confusion of role identity produced by incest (especially father-daughter, mother-son) invariably creates much tension within the family and alters the family's behaviour and attitudes towards society. Perhaps it is horror at violating the taboo (and consequent trauma of prosecution and seeing one's parents or siblings branded as criminals) rather than the actual act of incest itself which creates or heightens these tensions. But, whatever the reasons, modern clinical research does suggest that in our western

society wherever incest exists normal family relationships and roles
are often challenged and put under severe strain. Even R.E.L. Masters,
who has argued that the incest taboo is far from universal and that
incest between consenting adults should not be prohibited by law,
agrees that 'the always precarious harmony of the family unit could
not survive the tensions' of incest as a frequent or regular practice.[5]

However unclear the psychological and sociological impact upon the
family, incest still merits study by the historian of the Victorian family,
if for no other reason than that the incest taboo was as strongly held
in the nineteenth century as in most other centuries (one has only to
think of the treatment of Byron) and its violation suggested disease
at the heart of what Victorians regarded as essential to the moral,
religious and social harmony of their society: the virtuous Christian
family. Thus a study of their reactions to exposes of incest among the
masses might reveal much of value about their attitude towards the
family in general and to working-class sexuality in particular.

Given the nature of the incestuous act, inevitably little firsthand
information exists concerning its extent (or precise nature) in the
dwellings of the poor.[6] Lawrence Stone has written in another
context that if Freud is right, and it is the bedroom, the bathroom,
and the nursery, 'where the action is, there is not much the historian
can do about it'.[7] I must concede at the outset that it may well be
impossible to determine the consequences of incest upon the psychodynamics of the Victorian family. But there is much we can learn from
the upper- and middle-class responses to it. Throughout the nineteenth
century there were frequent references, both direct and oblique, to
the prevalence of incest among the poor, and these references demand
some response from the historian of the family. Did they represent,
for example, a defamatory but valuably emotive part of the social and
moral reformer's vocabulary, part of his armoury of reform rhetoric?
Or did they represent a willingness to believe the very worst of the
lower orders and their family lives? Did they perhaps indicate the
dread of sexual forces below the surface of restrictive respectability,
or did they represent some or all of these attitudes and also indicate
the *existence* of incest as part of the 'remissive culture of sexual
license', to use Professor Morse Peckham's telling phrase?[8] Was incest,
in fact, an integral part of a Victorian 'culture of poverty', modifying
or determining relationships within the family and demonstrating, in
the most dramatic way, the wide gulf between middle-class ideals and
working-class reality? Did these revelations of incest suggest to the
Victorians that the working-class family unit was a sexually exploitive

one, with women and children the probable sufferers? And if so, how did those who knew about it, or were told about it, respond?

There was, of course, in Victorian England a conspiracy of silence on most sexual matters – on incest the conspiracy reached Watergate proportions. Although the subject of incest formed part of the academic literature of Biblical exegesis and anthropological inquiry – incest and exogamy were discussed at length in such works as E. Tylor's *Primitive Culture* (1871) and Westermarck's *The History of Human Marriage* (1891) – there was no discussion of incest in the periodical press or among the public in general. This silence could be interpreted to mean that the Victorians considered that there was no incest worth talking about. No doubt many contemporaries did think this (Westermarck himself maintained that the incest taboo was so instinctive that it was observed universally) but the absence of detailed analysis or discussion was, I think, more the result of other attitudes of mind. Nor can we attribute the silence to a total indifference to incest, to 'a feeling', in the words of Robin Fox (*Kinship and Marriage*, 1967), 'that only half-wits would want to sleep with their sisters anyway . . . no one gets in a sweat about it'.[9] This statement is certainly debatable, to put it mildly, today; for the Victorian period it has almost no applicability. For although Engels considered that the 'sexual license' of the working classes marked them 'a race wholly apart from the English bourgeoisie', and argued that the bourgeoisie did not have the energy to impress its own moral code upon them, in fact the Victorians, acting through the agency of the law, equated sin with crime and made private sexual morality the business of the state.[10]

Sanguine belief in the upright morality of the working classes on the one hand, cool indifference on the other, do not offer adequate or convincing explanations for the failure of Victorian legislators to take up the question of incest even though it was presented to them, specifically and frequently, as a 'social question' on several separate occasions: it was brought up before the City Corporation, the Privy Council, Parliament, the 1882 House of Lords Select Committee on the Protection of Young Girls, the 1884-5 Royal Commission on the Housing of the Working Classes and the 1888 House of Lords Select Committee on the Sweating System. All these bodies, with the partial exception of the commission on housing, failed to respond with any detailed examination of witnesses or with a call for further investigation.

At the root of this lack of official response lay reticence, 'grisly horror',[11] idealism and a certain pragmatism. Even today there is still acute sensibility about public discussion of incest. There is a certain unspeakable horror surrounding it, and, as the *Sunday Times* wrote a year or two ago, 'even newspapers tend to be muted in reporting such events'.[12] Apparently incest was virtually the only subject left untouched in Dr Reuben's *Everything You Always Wanted to Know about Sex – But Were Afraid to Ask.*[13] The *Lancet* was typical in its Victorian reticence on the subject. In its pages there were several responses to correspondents seeking medical advice about the possibility of physical degeneracy resulting from marriage between first cousins (it pointed out that there was no scientific proof for the commonly expressed fear that incest could lead to 'sterility, idiocy, insanity, deafness, deformity, and scrofula'), but it quickly drew back from any discussion of incest when it stumbled across it during its social investigations. 'There are things "done in secret" ', it declared in 1885,'which "should not be so much as named" in family circles or in newspapers which have entrance into private houses.' It further justified itself by saying that publicity would achieve little good and that everyone knew that 'it is to the religious subjection of the body that we must look for the spread of personal purity and sexual innocence' – a revealing statement at that late stage, coming as it did from the leading medical journal, and one, moreover, which through its own special investigations was well acquainted with the depths of despair and poverty, of irreligion and overcrowding, in the slums.[14] Even when legislation prohibiting and punishing incest was introduced in 1903 and again in 1908, the tone of the debates, even among the eminent jurists in the Lords, was one of timidity and embarrassed awkwardness. Amid a welter of euphemisms the 1903 bill was introduced as this 'rather . . . unpleasant subject'.[15] Even social investigators like Gaskell and Chadwick, discovering incest, almost never used the word, preferring 'promiscuous herding', or 'unnatural outrage and vice', and other dramatic euphemisms. Thus incest, like most forms of sexual deviation, was too dreadful and scandalous to be aired in public.

Combining with reticence to draw a veil over the subject of incest was a basic conviction, amounting to a fervent idealism, that the Home was the rock on which civilization was founded. Unlike prostitution, which was a public vice, incest, after all, evoked the nightmare of exploitation and animal sexuality within the most sacred of institutions, the home and family. The passionate and widely held belief, the basis, one might say, of an entire social programme, in the family as a depository of virtue, a foundation for civic and social duties and responsibilities and a school for social discipline and moral rectitude, could hardly permit the most sordid and bestial *realities* at the lower depths to endanger the highest *ideals*.[16] The ideal, as Gaskell wrote in exposing its emptiness, was that the family constituted 'a little kingdom within itself . . . a domain shut out from the operation of those [immoral] influences' at work in society as a whole. That the family in fact did not exist *in vacuo*, but was rather, as Gaskell discovered, 'a microcosm' of the failings of society in matters of sobriety, tenderness and love, was a bitter enough pill for Victorians.[17] That it was actually the setting for the perversion of love and affection was too unpalatable and public and parliamentary discussion about it was too drastic a Morrison Pill to swallow. Some may see in this averting of the eye by Victorians an example of their hypocrisy, but perhaps it would be more compassionate and understanding to say that it was more a question of their determination to ground religious ideals in the domestic setting and to preserve those ideals from corrosion by base reality.

Besides what good could public discussion about incest possibly do? Mingled with reluctance to discuss sexual matters and to expose ideals was a seasoned pragmatism in matters deemed appropriate to social legislation. Operating was a kind of pleasure-pain utilitarianism and, surely, the alleged private vice of incest was not so widespread or so great a social threat as to warrant the far greater vice of government inspection of private homes? Even in matters affecting the public health, medical officers of health almost never conducted night-time inspections even though they possessed the authority. Legislating authority in the home was entirely different from legislating public morality and perhaps if the official policy was to let sleeping siblings lie it was because *laissez-faire* was preferable to state intervention. One is reminded of Lord Shaftesbury's response to a plea to sponsor legislation which would protect children from parental cruelty. 'The evils you state are enormous and indisputable', he conceded, 'but they are of so private, internal and domestic a character as to be beyond the reach of legislation, and the subject indeed would not, I think, be entertained in either House of Parliament.'[18]

For much of the nineteenth century the sexuality of the working classes, when it was discussed, was lumped together with other acts of immorality and condemned as the pathological conduct of a debased and degenerate mass. 'In a great city', wrote one medical officer of health, 'there must and always will be produced a number of degraded

forms deficient in intellect, relapses to the wild man, possessing all . . .
the moral obliquity . . . of savages.' It was necessary, wrote another,
'to rouse up all the strength of my previous reasonings and convictions,
in order to convince myself that they were really fellow-beings.'[19]
If medical men, innured to the sights and smells of the slums, felt that
way, one can sympathize with Rosa Dartle's sweet innocence in *David
Copperfield*: 'Are they really animals and clods and beings of another
order? I want to know *so* much.' 'Why there's a pretty wide separation
between them and us,' Steerforth answered, with indifference.[20]
Sexuality and animalism were often equated in the prescriptive
literature of the day: as Archbishop Ireland wrote, 'the strongest hold
which animalism has over the race lies in sexual passion. The triumph
over this passion, the reduction of it under the law of reason, is the
supreme act of Spiritual power in man.'[21] Perverted sexuality, rather
like sexual over-indulgence among the working classes, though, of
course, condemned, could also be dismissed as irrational, animalistic,
inhuman behaviour – a mental aberration, not a social disease.

At the close of the nineteenth century, however, investigators
emerged, somewhat dazed, from the slums to argue that if the poor
were compelled to herd like animals they would breed indiscriminately
like animals. In her autobiography Beatrice Webb confessed that
when writing of her sweat-shop experiences for the *Nineteenth
Century* the code of decency had obliged her to omit all references

> to the prevalence of incest in one-roomed tenements. The fact that
> some of my workmates – young girls, who were in no way
> mentally defective, who were, on the contrary, just as keen-witted
> and generous-hearted as my own circle of friends – could chaff
> each other about having babies by their fathers and brothers, was
> a gruesome example of the effect of debased social environment
> on personal character and family life . . . The violation of little
> children was another not infrequent result.

She concluded: '. . . to put it bluntly, sexual promiscuity, and even sexual
perversion, are almost unavoidable among men and women of average
character and intelligence crowded into the one-roomed tenements of
slum areas.'[22] Although her language was unusually explicit, her
association of one-roomed living with sexual immorality was a
commonplace of Victorian housing reform literature. To Shaftesbury
the link between overcrowding and sexual indecency was as 'clear,
simple, unmistakable as any proposition in Euclid', or, as one doctor

addressing the Church of England's Young Men's Society graphically put it, 'talk of morality amongst people who herd — men, women, and children — together, with no regard of age or sex, in one narrow, confined apartment! You might as well talk of cleanliness in a sty, or of limpid purity in the contents of a cesspool.'[23] One should add that modern sociological investigations indicate that these views are far more accurate than those held by other Victorians who maintained that familiarity, even in the most crowded conditions, bred a kind of natural contempt.[24]

Although reformers had for many years associated high-density living with sexual immorality, it was widely believed that overcrowding existed among the residuum, the 'outcast' only. It was not until the 1880s that the widespread nature of overcrowding and single-roomed living was generally grasped. By the end of the century it was incontestable that overcrowding was the norm for vast numbers of working-class families. London, which was by no means as overcrowded as some northern industrial towns, had in 1901 56,000 one-roomed and 55,000 two-roomed flats in which the occupants were overcrowded. A decade later over three-quarters of a million Londoners — more than the *entire* population of either Liverpool, Manchester, or Birmingham — were living in overcrowded dwellings, according to official census figures. In the 1901 census, 45.2 per cent of Finsbury's population lived in either one-roomed or two-roomed flats and over one-third were similarly housed in Stepney, Shoreditch, St Pancras, St Marylebone, and Holborn.[25] In a government survey, conducted in 1887, fifty per cent of all dock-workers and forty-six per cent of all costermongers were living with their families in only one room.[26] In most large industrial towns overcrowding was an ineluctable feature of working-class family life: in 1891 fifty-nine per cent of Glasgow's total (not just working-class) population, forty per cent of Gateshead's and thirty-five per cent of Newscastle's was overcrowded.[27]

I am not suggesting that overcrowding or the incest that resulted from it were uniquely urban phenomena. Indeed, there were several quite explicit references to incest in rural cottages.[28] But, as in so many other areas, the *concentration* and *magnification* of old conduct in a new urban setting eventually forced a more critical awareness. The statistics of overcrowding should be related to family size and kinship patterns. In 1851 over twenty-one per cent of Preston's families had over eight persons, and from our special perspective of possible causes of incest, it should be noted that boys and girls tended to remain at home, despite overcrowded conditions (and because of

high rents) until they were adults. In Preston, for example, eighty-
five per cent of the girls between ten and fourteen, and sixty-seven
per cent between fifteen and nineteen years of age were living at home,
and figures for boys are higher still.[29] These family patterns, together
with drunkenness, overcrowding, poor education and generally lax
standards of sexual morality formed the culture of poverty, and recent
sociological studies have indicated that where these conditions prevail
incest may well result.[30] Faced with the realities of family life in the
Victorian slums, and especially the coincidence of one-roomed living
with easy-going attitudes to pre-marital sex, we should not be at all
surprised that incest did exist in Victorian England. We may speculate
also that in an age of high maternal deaths in childbirth, where
grown-up daughters acted as surrogate mothers, the atmosphere and
relationships were no doubt even more conducive to incest. All this
is, of course, circumstantial evidence; but while it would be manifestly
wrong to insist that incest had to exist, I think we may safely suggest,
given other evidence, that it probably did exist. Before getting to
this other evidence, we should note that Stephen Marcus argues in his
The Other Victorians that pornographic literature, which often portrays real rather than ideal, or prescriptive behaviour, was full of
incest. 'Pornography exists in order to violate in fantasy that which
has been tabooed', he writes, 'and incest occurs in it with about the
same frequency as marriages occur at the end of the English novel',
and he comments that incest was usually portrayed as great fun,
'and therefore everyone available is enlisted in the goings on.'[31]

   Granted that the conditions which often produce it abounded;
but what hard evidence do we have that incest actually existed in
Victorian working-class families? Throughout the nineteenth century
there were veiled hints about it. Gaskell, for example, in his *The
Manufacturing Population of England* (1833) called the working classes
'children of nature' and drew attention to 'the promiscuous way in
which families herd together, a way that destroys all notions of sexual
decency and domestic chastity'. And in a more direct reference, he
commented that overcrowding resulted in the sexes 'mingling in wild
carouse, and crimes of all shades are perpetrated, blasphemy, fornica-
tion, adultery, incest, child-murder.'[32] Henry Mayhew, too, gave
several examples of adult siblings, parents, uncles and nieces sharing
the same room and concluded that 'in the illicit intercourse to which
such a position frequently gives rise, it is not always that the tie of
blood is respected. Certain it is that, when the relationship is even but
one degree removed from that of brother and sister, that tie is

frequently overlooked.'[33] Engels and Acton mention incest and many journalists hint darkly at it.[34] But it is to more reliable evidence that we should turn. Who knew most about family life in the slums? Sanitary inspectors, medical officers of health, poor law guardians, school inspectors (truant officers), slum clergymen, and the fact is that reliable representatives of all these groups were prepared, from their personal house-to-house visitations, to state before official bodies, confidently and matter-of-factly, that incest existed.

Take for example two men who devoted their lives to work among the poor and who were regarded as the greatest authorities on working-class domestic arrangements – Sir John Simon, the medical officer of health in turn to the City of London, the General Board of Health, the Privy Council and the Local Government Board, and Lord Shaftesbury, the great social reformer who was for so many years the leading parliamentary spokesman for housing reform. Simon lifted a 'curtain which propriety might gladly leave unraised' to reveal in his reports families 'styed together . . . in the promiscuous intimacy of cattle'. 'Of the poor', he sadly wrote, it was 'superfluous to observe that in all offices of nature they are gregarious and public; that every instinct of personal or sexual decency is stifled; that every nakedness of life is uncovered there', and that their acts were 'ruffianly and incestuous'. Fifteen years later Simon was still reiterating the same theme.[35] Other medical officers of health made similar findings, and at their Association meeting in 1868 it was stated that overcrowding had reached proportions where 'sex and consanguinity count for nothing'.[36]

A few years earlier, in the House of Lords, Shaftesbury presented evidence of families, seven or eight persons in all, living in single rooms no larger than eight feet by nine feet, and he stressed:

> It is impossible, my Lords, to exaggerate the physical and moral evils that result from this state of things . . . I would not for all the world mention all the details of what I have heard, or . . . seen, in these scenes of wretchedness. But there are to be found adults of both sexes, living and sleeping in the same room, every social and every domestic necessity being performed there; grown-up sons sleeping with their mothers, brothers, and sisters, sleeping very often, not in the same apartment only, but in the same bed. My Lords, I am stating that which I know to be the truth, and which is not to be gainsaid, when I state that incestuous crime is frightfully common in various parts of this Metropolis – common

to the greatest extent in the range of these courts [in and around the City].[37]

These revelations provoked no response nor did the evidence of John Horsley, Chaplain of the Clerkenwell prison, before the Select Committee on the Protection of Young Girls in 1882. Horsley, speaking from his official position, insisted that incest was 'common', but not 'very common'.[38] Incest was finally discussed at some length in an official government inquiry in 1884 when the Royal Commission on the Housing of the Working Classes questioned several witnesses on the subject. The Commission had been called partly in response to a widespread agitation created by a reform tract published by the London Congregational Church, *The Bitter Cry of Outcast London*. In it, the author, the Rev. Andrew Mearns, maintained that he had toned down the 'horrors and abominations' which 'no respectable printer would print and certainly no decent family would admit'. Yet he went on to state that as a result of overcrowding 'incest is common and no form of vice or sexuality causes surprise or attracts attention'.[39] Called before the mildly incredulous commission on housing, Mearns stood by his original statement. He cited examples of incest both between siblings and between parents and children, and then, prevaricating somewhat, stated, 'I should not like the impression to be that "common" meant very frequent. You do meet with it [incest] and frequently meet with it, but not very frequently.'[40] Most of the other witnesses questioned on the subject supported Mearns. One clergyman, A.T. Fryer, argued that incest between parent and child occurred only when the father was drunk, and, quite remarkably, he held that knowledge gained in the home could never be so harmful as knowledge learned outside it and that little harm could come to siblings who engaged in incestuous activity. This opinion directly contradicted Mayhew and Acton, both of whom thought incest was one of the forces precipitating young girls on the road to prostitution, and also Simon, who considered the family atmosphere of the poor a very 'baptism into infamy'.[41] Among the witnesses backing up Mearns were prison officers, sanitary officials, slum clergymen, and the Inspector for Schools of the London School Board. Was it this body of evidence, or some more general knowledge, that prompted Tennyson to write in his *Locksley Hall. Sixty Years After* (1886) of 'the crowded couch of incest in the warrens of the poor'?[42]

Unfortunately for the historian, the various committees and commissions failed to press for more, or more precise, information.

Lord Shaftesbury, who was the first witness to be called before the
Royal Commission on the Housing of the Working Classes, started to
give evidence of sexual immorality in overcrowded dwellings, but
Sir Charles Dilke, the Chairman of the Commission, and no model
of sexual probity himself, did not encourage him to develop the theme
and at a later point in the same commission the testimony of a witness
was cut short with the curt observation that there was no need to go
into the 'graver questions of morality', as these stood 'self-
condemned'.[43] When Dr David Davies, medical officer of health for
Bristol, gave evidence of 'girls sleeping with their grown-up brothers
and cousins, and . . . a great deal of immorality' resulting from this,
he was immediately asked, not about incest, but 'Is not a very low
state of health produced by rooms containing only 300 ft of air for
each person sleeping there?'[44] At one stage one of the commissioners
did wonder, in a rare substantive question on incest, if 'familiarity
begets a certain indifference or obtuseness to what might be otherwise
injurious'; this the witness stoutly denied.[45] The housing commission
devoted much space in its reports to the prevalence of the one-roomed
tenement, but it passed over incest as did the Select Committee on the
Sweating System (1888). This committee was informed by one of the
sanitary commissioners of the *Lancet*, a man with twelve years'
experience in social investigation behind him, that in industrial towns
young women of eighteen or twenty were sleeping with their
brothers of a similar age. This revelation immediately provoked a
question about the size of the windows! Similarly a Worcester
magistrate, giving evidence before the same committee of siblings
sleeping together, was cut short with the abrupt observation that this
was 'an evil which is common in various parts of the country'.[46]

This seeming acceptance, or indifference, or reluctance to interfere
in family relationships, however ungodly they were, was reflected in
the law. For, unlike Scotland, where incest was punishable by death
up to 1887, or several American states, England, remarkably, had no
civil law on incest although the Matrimonial Causes Act of 1857 did
include incestuous adultery as grounds for divorce. Cromwellian
England had imposed the death penalty for incest but that was swept
away, with much moral legislation, at the Restoration, and in the
Victorian period incest taboos were left, in Blackstone's correct and
memorable phrase, to the 'feeble coercion of the spiritual courts,
according to the rules of canon law'.[47] Under the English canon law the
guilty party convicted of incest had to do solemn penance at church or
in the market place, bare-legged, bare-headed, and wrapped in a white

sheet. The penance was to continue for two or three years, although mercifully this was interpreted to mean at Lent only.[48] The only cases I have been able to discover involved incestuous marriage rather than incestuous intercourse, usually marriages between uncles and nieces or with deceased wife's sister, and penance was generally waived after the accused paid full court costs.[49] To force the issue of incest into the glare of public debate at a time when the church courts were in such bad odour — they were virtually abolished in 1857 — would have been injudicious.

The absence of secular law might indicate a conviction that, as Westermarck and others argued, the incest taboo was too natural and universally observed to require the assistance of the law.[50] But rather, I think, it reflects, among other things, the general unconcern which prevailed in Parliament and among the public for so much of the nineteenth century over parental abuse of children. The National Vigilance Association from its establishment in 1885 drew attention to father-daughter incest, but it was not until the National Society for the Prevention of Cruelty to Children (NSPCC, founded in 1889) turned to the subject that something approaching a pressure group was established, and legislation introduced into Parliament.[51] The incest Bills presented during the first decade of this century were not so much examples of moral statute law aping or underscoring theological prescriptions as a quite explicit attempt primarily to protect children from victimization, which is, perhaps, the only really valid grounds for any law on incest.[52] During the debates on the 1908 bill, which was introduced in the Lords in response to 'the great frequency of incest', it was asserted that the Home Office was convinced that incest was on the increase.[53] This may have been so, but perhaps it was simply that the NSPCC was petitioning the Home Office and for the first time a national organization with child care as its sole concern was presenting in statistical form carefully gathered evidence. The NSPCC found a valuable ally in the National Vigilance Association, which presented to the government the results of an inquiry it had sent out to head constables and superintendents of police throughout England and which showed that the majority of these law enforcement officials were in favour of a statute prohibiting incest.[54] Certainly the work of the NSPCC and the National Vigilance Association indicated for the first time that the advantages of an incest law might well be greater than the disadvantages. Thus parliamentary resistance or indifference were overcome, and the question of incest publicized. As General Booth of the Salvation Army wrote in his *In Darkest England and the Way Out*

(1890), a 'fabulous number of fathers' were being prosecuted by the NSPCC for 'unnatural sins with their children', and 'incest is so familiar as hardly to call for remark'. Commenting on NSPCC statistics General Booth asked the inevitable question, 'If so many were brought to justice, how many were there of whom the world never heard in any shape or form?'[55]

Cases of incest which were prosecuted prior to the passage of the 1908 Incest Act had to be tried either as rape or under the Offences against Minors Act. The 1908 Incest Act (8 Edw 7 ch xlv) made incest punishable by imprisonment up to seven years and not less than three and the definition of an incestuous relationship included grandparents, parents and sibling, but not step-children. Interestingly, only males could be prosecuted under the Act; not until 1956 was the act extended to include women in a role other than as victim — an indication, surely, of the limits of the Victorian and Edwardian conception of female sexuality. Among the concerns expressed during the debates on the 1908 Bill was the quite legitimate fear that, since the poor were crowded together in single-room tenements or single bedrooms, they might always be under some suspicion and that (perhaps rather like the witchcraft legislation in Elizabethan and Jacobean England) the legislation would lead to a witch-hunt and the discovery of non-existent crimes.[56] Another concern was expressed over the material the new law might provide for irresponsible and sensational journalism. Under the Act all proceedings were, in fact, held *in camera* until the Criminal Law Amendment Act of 1922.

Although in the words of one witness before the Royal Commission on the Housing of the Working Classes incest between father and daughter was 'regarded by the people with horror' and provoked 'an outcry in the neighbourhood', neither it, nor incest between siblings, was frequently reported perhaps because, as Shaftesbury once observed, witnesses usually doubted if they would be believed.[57] In his evocative *The Classic Slum*, Robert Roberts relates how in the Edwardian Salford where he grew up one got to know as a teenager 'the damned houses where incestuous relationships' occurred, and he comments:

Here stood a hazard that faced all poor parents of large adolescent families sleeping together, perhaps with older relatives, in two small bedrooms. In their hearts they harboured a dread of what seemed to a respectable household the ultimate disgrace. Such sin, of course, had to be recognized in whispered tête à tête;

but I don't recall a single prosecution: strict public silence saved
the miscreants from the rigours of the law.[58]

Thus even after the 1908 Act only a fraction of the actual cases of
incest would ever probably be reported: for a variety of reasons the
wife, or, in the case of sibling incest, the parents, would be unlikely to
talk about the deed.[59]

The frequent attempts of various social workers, reformers, and
philanthropists acquainted with the slums to bring before official
investigating committees the seriousness of incest make it impossible
to say that the Victorian governing classes remained ignorant about its
existence. What is true, however, is that as a social and personal abuse
incest, unlike the overcrowding from which it issued, was never
presented in the nineteenth century in an irrefutable, statistical form.
Incest, for example, was never taken up in the pages of the *Journal
of the Statistical Society of London*, although sodomy, rape, bestiality,
and bigamy were included as 'moral statistics'. Generally speaking the
Victorians only responded to social abuses with social crusades when
these abuses were demonstrated in a clear, statistical and persuasive
form. Thus incest, far more hidden than prostitution, gambling,
drunkenness or even the white slave trade, was unlikely to become the
subject of a Victorian hue and cry. Its setting – the home – precluded
it; those exploited by it, mainly young girls, had no one to champion
their cause until the last decades of the century. That the state should
be called in to protect girls from the lust of brothers and fathers was
too unpalatable a notion for the mid-Victorian generation. Even after
the general acceptance in the 1880s of the environmentalist argument
that man was what his surroundings made him, it was not until specialist societies focused narrowly on the domestic plight of children that
incest called forth legislative action.[60]
    I have suggested that more than reticence in sexual matters or
legislative pragmatism delayed this legislation. Incest represented in
its most debased form the horror of the realities of family life in
overcrowded rooms: to admit its existence publicly when it was clear
that one-roomed living was widespread was to admit that the social
system itself was to blame for its existence. Indeed, it was to confess
that, despite all the talk of 'progress', the masses, not in some far-
flung corner of the Empire, but at its very heart, remained 'lesser
breeds without the law'. In short, to take up the problem of incest was
to cast doubt on the success of the Victorian programme to bring
'civilization' to the lower orders. As General Booth sadly concluded,

it was so-called progress which had produced a society in which 'it is the home that has been destroyed, and with the home the home-like virtues'.[61] Despite the many Victorian forays, in the genre of anthropological journalism, into the customs of the working man — a literary tradition well-established with Mayhew, and continuing through Hollingshead, Greenwood, Sims, Haw, Mrs Pember Reeves, Charles Booth, and a dozen others — there were so many forces operating that it was inevitable that a veil would be discreetly drawn over the subject of incest in the homes of the poor.[62]

I am not suggesting in this essay that incest was ever so widely practised that it threatened exogamous sexual relationships, or that it ever became an accepted relationship between parents and children or between siblings. Margaret Mead has concluded that 'widespread failure to observe incest regulations is an index of the disruption of a socio-cultural system that may be even more significant than the more usual indexes of crime, suicide, and homicide'.[63] Clearly no such threat to the family or society existed in nineteenth-century England. It may be assumed that incest among children and young adults was much more common than between drunken fathers and daughters and that incest was generally casual and temporary rather than long-term.[64] It probably did not, except in very rare cases, create any of the problems of physical degeneration associated with inbreeding or interfere with contacts outside the family, especially in the towns. The Inter-Departmental Committee on Physical Degeneration (1904), though it conducted its inquiry in an atmosphere bristling with Darwinian concerns, did not even consider incest as a possible cause of physical degeneration.

Nevertheless, in terms of the history of the Victorian family it is necessary to place in the balance, against the optimistic picture recently presented by Anderson and others, of family life in the industrial towns of Victorian England, the existence of incest as a potentially disruptive and probably exploitive result of one-roomed living. In his *Sybil* Disraeli reflected that 'incest and infanticide are as common among them [the working classes] as among the lower animals'. An exaggeration, certainly, but he was surely closer to the mark when he pointed up the great gulf between Victorian ideals and reality: 'The domestic principle wanes weaker and weaker every year in England, nor can we wonder at it when there is no comfort to cheer and no sentiment to hallow the Home.'[65] Demographic pressures resulted in various forms of urban social and moral pathology — infanticide, drunkenness, murder, theft — and to this we must add,

however tentatively, incest. Its existence, though limited, may have
created enormous individual strains and may cast light on the family
as an association, in Peter Cominos's phrase of 'dominance and
submissiveness'.[66] Certainly it is of sufficient interest to warrant
further research by historians of the family, and I hope that my
exploration, whatever its shortcomings, will persuade them that there
are insights to be gained about family life and Victorian attitudes
towards it even in the most fragile and unquantifiable evidence.
Indeed, I would suggest that no study of family life in the slums of
Victorian England is complete without some references to incest.

Notes

1. M. Anderson, *Family Structure in Nineteenth Century Lancashire*
   (Cambridge, 1971), p. 3. Anderson is referring to J.P. Kay, *The Moral
   and Physical Condition of the Working Classes* (London, 1832),
   P. Gaskell, *The Manufacturing Population of England* (London, 1833),
   H. Mayhew, *London Labour and the London Poor*, 4 vols. (London,
   1861), and F. Engels, *The Condition of the Working Class in England*
   (London, 1844). Mayhew's work first appeared in the *Morning Chronicle*
   as a series starting in 1849.
2. K. Davis, *Human Society* (New York, 1949), in N. Bell and E. Vogel (eds.),
   A Modern Introduction to the Family (New York, 1963), pp. 400-401;
   P. Gebhard, J. Gagnon, W. Pomeroy, and C. Christenson, *Sex Offenders*
   (New York, 1965), p. 208; L. Benson, *The Family Bond* (New York,
   1971), p. 362; S.K. Weinberg, *Incest Behaviour* (New York, 1955), in
   R.E.L. Masters (ed.), *Patterns of Incest. A Psycho-Social Study of Incest
   based on Clinical and Historical Data* (New York, 1963), quoted p. 3.
3. National Council for Civil Liberties, Report No. 13, Evidence to the
   Criminal Law Revision Committee, February 1976, *Sexual Offences*, p. 15.
   Dr Melitta Schmideberg, of the Association for the Psychiatric Treatment
   of Offenders, claims that it is the criminal charges, not the incest itself,
   which are most harmful. See the *Sunday Times*, 26 October 1975.
4. Quoted in ibid.
5. See note 2 above for some of the modern research on incest. Masters,
   Pattern of Incest, p. 60.
6. This still applies today, and sociologists and social welfare workers talk of
   reported cases as the tip of the iceberg.
7. L. Stone, 'Prosopography', *Daedelus*, 100 (1971), p. 33. See L. Demause,
   'The History of Childhood: the Basis of Psychohistory', *The History of
   Childhood Quarterly* (Summer 1973), Vol. I, 1, for an interesting rebuttal.
8. M. Peckham, 'Victorian Counterculture', *Victorian Studies*, XVIII, 3
   (March 1975), p. 259.
9. R. Fox, *Kinship and Marriage* (London, 1967), p. 72.
10. I am here using the language of the Wolfenden Report (*The Report of the
    Committee on Homosexual Offences and Prostitution*, 1957), quoted in
    Sexual Offences, p. 1.
11. The phrase is Margaret Mead's, used to describe the common reaction to
    violation of the incest taboo. See her article on 'Incest', in the

International Encyclopaedia of the Social Sciences, VII (1968), p. 115.

12.   *Sunday Times*, 26 October 1975.

13.   L.P. Santiago, *The Children of Oedipus* (New York, 1973), cover

14.   For physical degeneracy see *Lancet* 18 October 1862, p. 426; 13 March 1875, p. 378; 8 May 1875, p. 668; 22 May 1875, p. 145. For the statement quoted in my text see 22 August 1885, p. 350.

15.   *Hansard*, Fourth series, CXXV (1903), 820.

16.   For expressions of this idealism concerning the family see the introduction.

17.   Gaskell, *The Manufacturing Population of England*, pp. 51-52.

18.   Quoted in I. Pinchbeck and M. Hewitt, *Children in English Society*, 11 (1973), p. 622.

19.   A.W. Blyth, 'Tenement Dwellings', *Transactions of the Society of Medical Officers of Health*, 1882–1883, p. 82; quoted in M. Bruce, *The Coming of the Welfare State* (London, 1961), p. 53.

20.   Quoted in ibid.

21.   Quoted in P. Cominos, 'Late-Victorian Sexual Respectability and the Social System', *International Review of Social History*, VIII, Part I (1963), p. 310, note.

22.   B. Webb, *My Apprenticeship* (New York, 1926), p. 310, note.

23.   Lord Shaftesbury, 'Address on Public Health', *Transaction of the National Association for the Promotion of Social Science* (1858), p. 89, and G. Godwin, *Town Swamps and Social Bridges* (London, 1859), reprinted Leicester University Press, A.D. King (ed.) (Leicester, 1972), quoted p. 21.

24.   See for example evidence cited by Santiago, *The Children of Oedipus*, p. 171.

25.   London County Council, *London Statistics*, XII (1901–1902), table B, p. x and ibid., XXIV (1913–1914), p. 31; *Parliamentary Papers*, CVII (1908), 'Report of an Inquiry by the Board of Trade into Working-Class Rents, Housing and Retail Prices . . .', appendix B, p. 60.

26.   *Parliamentary Papers*, LXXXI (1887), 'Tabulations of Statements made by Men Living in Certain Selected Districts of London in March, 1887', p. 34.

27.   B.S. Rowntree, *Poverty. A Study of Town Life* (London, 1901), p. 171.

28.   See for example Dr H.J. Hunter's special report of his 'Inquiry on the State of the Dwellings of Rural Labourers' in *Parliamentary Papers*, XXVI (1865), *Seventh Annual Report of the Medical Officer of Health of the Privy Council, for 1864*, appendix 6, p. 146. In the hamlet of Southery, in the Norfolk fens, there were said to be only three surnames in the entire parish in 1876. See W.J. Reeder, *Life in Victorian England* (London, 1967), pp. 47-8. In the West Country it was reported that 'the consequences of the lack of proper accommodation for sleeping in the cottages are seen in the early licentiousness of the rural districts – licentiousness which has not always respected the family relationship.' *Parliamentary Papers*, XII (1843), 'Poor Law Commission on the Employment of Women and Children in Agriculture', p. 8, and see Document D, pp. 206-7.

29.   M. Anderson, 'Household Structure and the Industrial Revolution', P. Laslett and R. Wall (eds.), *Household and Family in Past Time* (Cambridge, 1972), p. 291, table 7.1.

30.   Contemporary sociologists stress broken homes, drunkenness, poverty, overcrowding, lack of moral training, feeblemindedness, drug addiction and promiscuity, while psychologists stress oedipal complexes, pedophilia, nymphomania, satyriasis, homosexuality, illness and trauma as causes of incest. D.W. Craig and R.E.L. Masters, *Violation of Taboo. Incest and the Great Literature of the Past and Present* (New York, 1963), p. 10. Masters draws attention to youthful exhibitionism and has also argued that when

the men in the family know the females are engaging in premarital sex there
is stronger tendency towards incest: Masters, *Patterns of Incest*, pp. 66, 81.

31.   S. Marcus, *The Other Victorians* (Corgi edition, London, 1971) p. 248.
There is very little father-daughter or sibling incest in Victorian
literature as far as I have been able to determine, although love and
marriage between first cousins did form the theme of several novels.
P. Keating in his *The Working Classes in Victorian Literature* (London,
1971) mentions William Barry's *The New Antigone* (London, 1887)
and its theme of incest, but otherwise he agrees with Walter Besant that
in these matters working-class literature tended to avoid 'useless realism',
pp. 44, 91. S. Kern, in his 'Explosive Intimacy: Psychodynamics of the
Victorian Family', *History of Childhood Quarterly*, I, 2 (Winter 1974),
p. 451, states that 'the themes of father-daughter incest and conflict were
the subject of numerous important literary works'.

32.   Gaskell, *The Manufacturing Population of England*, pp. 29, 137; see also
pp. 110, 133.

33.   Quoted in W. Acton, *Prostitution, Considered in its Moral, Social and
Psychological Aspects* . . . (London, 1857), reprinted by Praeger,
P. Fryer (ed.), (New York, 1969), p. 131.

34.   Engels, *The Condition of the Working Class in England*, pp. 149, 203;
Acton, *Prostitution*, pp. 130 ff. Typical of journalists drawing attention
to sexual immorality in the slums were George Sims and James Greenwood,
see note 62, below.

35.   Simon, *Second Annual Report to the City of London* (1850), pp. 118-119;
Parliamentary Papers, XXVIII (1866), 'Eighth Annual Report of the
Medical Officer of the Privy Council, for 1865', especially p. 207.

36.   *Lancet*, 22 February 1868, p. 265; 4 August 1883, p. 187.

37.   *Hansard*, Third series, CLXI (1861), 1070-1071. Shaftesbury's speech was
reproduced in J. Hollingshead, *Ragged London in 1861* (London, 1861),
p. 233.

38.   *Parliamentary Papers*, XIII (1882), 'Select Committee of the House of
Lords on the Law relating to the Protection of Young Girls', *Minutes of
Evidence*, p. 31.

39.   Reverend A. Mearns, *The Bitter Cry of Outcast London* (London, 1883).
This tract, together with others, has been reprinted by Leicester University
Press, A.S. Wohl (ed.), 1970.

40.   *Parliamentary Papers*, XXX (1884–1885), 'Royal Commission on the
Housing of the Working Classes', II, *Minutes of Evidence*, p. 177.

41.   Ibid., p. 79; Acton, *Prostitution*, p. 134; and Simon, 'Eighth Report to
the Privy Council', p. 207.

42.   For this evidence see *Parliamentary Papers*, XXX (1884–1885), 'Royal
Commission on the Housing of the Working Classes', II, *Minutes of
Evidence*, pp. 65, 79, 87, 89, 121, 164, 258.

43.   Ibid., p. 59.

44.   Ibid., p. 225.

45.   Ibid., p. 168.

46.   *Parliamentary Papers*, XX (1888), 'Select Committee on the Sweating
System', *Minutes of Evidence*, III, pp. 400, 413.

47.   B. Gavit (ed.), *Blackstone's Commentaries on the Law* (Washington,
1892), p. 778.

48.   R. Burn, *The Ecclesiastical Law* (London, 1842), III, p. 101.

49.   See W.C. Curteis, *Reports of Cases argued and determined in the
Ecclesiastical Courts of Doctors Commons* (1883–1884).

50.   Just as one hardly needed a law telling a man to pull his hand out of a fire.

That analogy was made by Sir James Frazer, who disagreed with Westermarck's thesis of universal, natural aversion to incest in his *Totemism and Exogamy* (London, 1901), p. 97.

51. National Vigilance Association, *Executive Committee Minutes*, 5 July 1887 and 29 April 1890. I am grateful to Professor Deborah Gorham for drawing my attention to the Association's papers in the Fawcett Library in London.

52. Masters, *Patterns of Incest*, pp. 4, 6.

53. *Hansard*, Fourth series, CXCVII (1908), 1408.

54. National Vigilance Association, *Executive Committee Minutes*, II, 28 February 1899, p. 79.

55. W. Booth, *In Darkest England and the Way Out* (London, 1890), pp. 65, 193. Booth may possibly have been influenced by his friend Mearns's *Bitter Cry of Outcast London*.

56. *Hansard*, Fourth series, CXCI (1908), 284.

57. *Parliamentary Papers*, XXX (1884–1885), 'Royal Commission on the Housing of the Working Classes', II, *Minutes of Evidence*, p. 191. Shaftesbury quoted one minister as saying, 'We do not dare say what we know' and he told the Commission, 'If I were to go into the details of the consequences of overcrowding, particularly in single rooms, very few people would believe what I said.', p. 2.

58. R. Roberts, *The Classic Slum* (London, 1973), pp. 43-4.

59. L. Radzinowicz gives the following figures in his *Sexual Offences* (London, 1957), p. 12. In 1947 there were 152 and in 1954, 252 indictable offences, and between 1937 and 1954 incest constituted only about two per cent of all heterosexual offences. For Home Office figures see the *Sunday Times*, 26 October 1975 and for cases brought to the attention of the authorities before the 1908 Act, see *Hansard*, CXCI (1908), 278 ff. Somewhat ironically the Incest Act was passed right after the 1907 Act legalizing (making non-incest) marriage with deceased wife's sister.

60. For a discussion of the importance of the 1880s in the development of environmentalist social theories see my book, *The Eternal Slum: Housing and Social Policy in Victorian London* (London, 1977).

61. Booth, *In Darkest England*, p. 68.

62. For these works of 'higher journalism' see my bibliography in *The Eternal Slum*. Typical of the drawing back of these sociological and anthropological works was R.W. Vanderkiste's *Notes and Narratives of a Six Years' Mission principally among the Dens of London* (London, 1854), in which the author explained 'details of gross vulgarity I have omitted, and a mantle has been thrown over much vice . . . had the work not been intended strictly as a family book, it would have included other [descriptions]', preface, pp. vi-vii.

63. M. Mead, 'Incest', p. 120.

64. See for example recent findings in Kinsey et al., *Sexual Behaviour in the Human Male* (London, 1948), in Masters, *Patterns of Incest*, quoted p. 64.

65. B. Disraeli, *Sybil*, Book III, chap. 5.

66. Cominos, *International Review of Social History*, VIII, Part I (1963), p. 250. I should mention that I have not explored in this essay another possible theme, and that is that the extremely close relationship that often existed in Victorian England between siblings may have made it even more difficult for them to discuss incest. For the line between extremely deep intimacy and incest in middle- and upper-class Victorian families, see the letter to the *Times Literary Supplement*, 9 August 1974, p. 859.

CONTRIBUTORS

Maurianne Adams is Lecturer in English and Coordinator of Academic
Affairs at the University of Massachusetts (Southwest Residential
College). Publications include *Samuel Taylor Coleridge: An
Annotated Bibliography of Criticism and Scholarship, Vol. I,
1793–1899*, edited with Richard and Josephine Haven (Boston,
1976) and an essay on *'Jane Eyre*: Woman's Estate', in A. Diamond
and L. Edwards (eds.), *The Authority of Experience: Essays in
Feminist Criticism* (Amherst, Massachusetts, 1977).

Michael Brooks is Professor of English at West Chester State College,
Pennsylvania. He has published articles on George Moore and Oscar
Wilde and is completing a manuscript on John Ruskin and
Victorian architecture.

Deborah Gorham is Assistant Professor of History at St Patrick's
College, Carleton University, Ottawa. Her publications include
articles on the Canadian suffragists in G. Matheson (ed.), *Women
in the Canadian Mosaic* (Toronto, 1976), and on English militancy
and its effect on the Canadian suffrage movement for *Atlantis:
A Women's Studies Journal*.

R. Burr Litchfield is Associate Professor of History at Brown University,
Rhode Island. He has published articles in *Annales: Economies
Sociétés Civilisations* and the *Journal of Economic History*. He is
preparing for publication a book on *The Offices of the Florentine
Patricians between Renaissance and Risorgimento, 1530–1790* and
is currently engaged in research on the changing patterns of work,
family, and demography in four nineteenth-century cities: Pisa,
Amiens, Stockport, and Providence.

Theresa McBride is Assistant Professor of History at Holy Cross College,
Massachusetts. Her publications include *The Domestic Revolution:
The Modernisation of Household Service in England and France,
1820–1920*, published by Croom Helm (London, 1976). She is
currently at work on a study of the social origins of service and
clerical workers in France in the Belle Epoque.

John Hawkins Miller teaches English at the Ellis School in Pittsburgh,
Pennsylvania. He is currently engaged in research for a book on
Victorian attitudes towards childbirth.

David Roberts is Professor of History at Dartmouth College, New

Hampshire. He is the author of *Victorian Origins of the British Welfare State* (New Haven, Connecticut, 1960) and of articles on Lord Palmerston, Jeremy Bentham, the Victorian Poor Law and Victorian newspaper editors. He has recently completed a manuscript on *Paternalism in Early Victorian England.*

Elaine Showalter is Associate Professor of English at Douglass College, Rutgers University, New Jersey. She is the author of *A Literature of Their Own: British Women Novelists from Brontë to Lessing* (Princeton, New Jersey, 1977); *Women's Liberation and Literature* (New York, 1971), and articles on Victorian women, women novelists, and feminist criticism.

Anthony S. Wohl is Professor of History at Vassar College, New York. He is the author of *The Eternal Slum: Housing and Social Policy in Victorian London* (London, 1977), and editor of *The Bitter Cry of Outcast London* (Leicester, 1970). He has written articles on housing reform for H.J. Dyos and M. Wolff (eds.), *The Victorian City* (London, 1973), *Journal of British Studies, International Review of Social History* and for S. Chapman (ed.), *The History of Working-Class Housing* (Newton Abbot, 1971). He is currently writing a book on public health in Victorian Britain.

INDEX